*Figuring Authorship
in Antebellum America*

Figuring Authorship
in Antebellum America

Michael Newbury

STANFORD UNIVERSITY PRESS

STANFORD, CALIFORNIA

1997

Stanford University Press
Stanford, California
© 1997 by the Board of Trustees of the
Leland Stanford Junior University

Printed in the United States of America

CIP data are at the end of the book

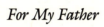

For My Father

Acknowledgments

I owe thanks to many people. Richard Brodhead generously read most of these chapters more than once and made helpful suggestions every time. Alan Trachtenberg, Bryan Wolf, and Michael Denning were encouraging and critical readers at steps along the way. Wai-chee Dimock, Dori Hale, Stephen Rachman, Elizabeth Abrams, Doug Levin, and Onno Oerlemans have read various parts of the project and given me the benefit of insightful comment. An anonymous reader, later revealed to me as Dale Bauer, twice read the entire manuscript and saved me from errors of excess, omission, and underdevelopment. Any fault remaining is my own.

The colleagues I see every day have been a reliable and valuable resource. Brett Millier had confidence and interest in the project all along the way. Tim Spears and John McWilliams read chapters on short notice, reaffirmed the work, and recommended useful revisions. I had many productive discussions with Nancy Schnog, especially about Susan Warner. At Stanford University Press, Helen Tartar took an active and supportive interest. Jan Spauschus Johnson eased the evolution from manuscript to book. Casey FitzSimons attended to my stylistic and other gaffes with meticulous attention.

My family at times might have wondered what I was doing. My mother, Rita, always asked questions. My father, Robert, and his wife, Diane, provided encouragement. My sisters, Karen, Jennifer, and Sandra, have always supported my intellectual efforts and eccentricities. Finally, Holly Allen listened to me ramble and interrupted those ramblings in the most educational ways.

Significantly different versions of two chapters have appeared elsewhere. A version of Chapter 2, "Eaten Alive: Slavery and Celebrity in Antebellum America," appeared in *ELH* (Spring 1994), copyright Johns Hopkins University Press. A version of Chapter 3 appeared in *American Quarterly* (December 1995), copyright Johns Hopkins University Press.

M.N.

Contents

Figuring Authorship
in Antebellum America

Introduction

Labor and Letters in Antebellum America

In a letter written to his mother on March 13, 1821, while he was still a student at Bowdoin College, we find Nathaniel Hawthorne's first known expression of a desire to write professionally:

I have not yet concluded what profession I shall have. The being a Minister is of course out of the Question. I should not think that even you could desire me to choose so dull a way of life. . . . As to Lawyers, there are so many of them already that one half of them (upon a moderate calculation) are in a state of actual starvation. A Physician, then, seems to be "Hobson's Choice," but yet I should not like to live by the diseases and Infirmities of fellow-Creatures. . . . Oh that I was rich enough to live without a profession. What do you think of my becoming an Author, and relying for support upon my pen? . . . How proud you would feel to see my works praised by reviewers, as equal to the proudest productions of the scribbling sons of John Bull.[1]

Writing to his mother, Hawthorne chooses authorship as a profession by eliminating other more likely possibilities and by recognizing a lack of independent wealth. By the paragraph's end, as he contemplates the possibility of good reviews, Hawthorne builds to a more active enthusiasm for his calling than his question—What do you think of my becoming an author?—might initially imply. At the same time, however, the couched terms of his writerly ambitions seem to address preemptively maternal doubts about the vocational choice. Hawthorne imagines for his mother his attainment of respect, even as he knows this is not the profession she wants him to choose. Mrs. Hawthorne is hoping for a minister, lawyer, or doctor.[2]

Almost thirty years later, in "The Custom-House," Hawthorne's introduction to *The Scarlet Letter*, he hears generations of his ancestors jeering through history at his chosen calling: " 'What is he?' murmurs one gray shadow of my forefathers to the other. 'A writer of story-books! What kind of a business in life,—what mode of glorifying God, or being serviceable to mankind in his day and generation,—may that be? Why the degenerate fellow might as well have been a fiddler!' "[3] In "The Custom-House" Hawthorne still carries a marginal sense of his profession's legitimacy, and he emphasizes openly the naivete of writers who expect the reading public to respect them. His co-workers at the custom house have taught him something: "It is a good lesson—though it may often be a hard one—for a man who has dreamed of literary fame, to step aside out of the narrow circle in which his claims are recognized, and to find how utterly devoid of significance, beyond that circle, is all that he achieves, and all that he aims at."[4] Hawthorne's co-workers and forefathers have doubts about his business or calling, precisely because they see it as neither a business nor a calling. Writing fiction makes no money; it also fails to serve the greater good; it has little practical relation to the world. In the self-deprecations that punctuate his literary career, Hawthorne himself reveals a sense that authorship is less than a fully desirable or secure profession, even as he practices it as a form of self-definition. With some hope, more resignation, and very little defiance, Hawthorne seems to say in the passages above that he will write for a living, even as he senses the improbability of making a living or gaining professional respect by doing so.

Hawthorne would not have been so anxious about professional legitimacy twenty years before his first letter, because there existed no profession of authorship to be anxious about. As William Charvat and others have evidenced, the antebellum period marks the transition of authorship's normative mode from the avocational to the professional, from authorship as a genteel and financially irrelevant hobby to authorship as a career organized by increasingly complicated market mediations. For Charvat, a confluence of primarily material circumstances made this transition possible and perhaps inevitable. One should realize, of course, that writing neither professionalized nor commercialized overnight and that modes of avocational writing continue into the present. But Charvat's central points—that the emergence of copyright protection, an expanded reading public, and increasingly sophisticated ways of printing, marketing, and distributing texts fostered a change in the relations between writer, publisher, and reader—remain indisputable. By the mid-nineteenth century a more commercialized publishing industry found its economic base in an increasingly democratized audience. For the first time, writers could at least imagine economic self-sufficiency through their writing, but had new obligations to satisfy commercially oriented publishers and a buying public.[5]

The significance of this transition cannot be summarized or fully realized as a change in the material conditions under which literature is produced. It was also a transition of consciousness, of the possibilities of self-definition available to writers during the period of emergent professionalization. We know, for example, that the move from avocation to profession is intertwined with authorship's conceptual evolution from teaching or public service to entertainment for an increasingly leisured middle class of readers. Cathy Davidson argues that fiction writers of the republican period had to contend with the virulent antifictionalist stance of New England's elite that saw novel reading as a degenerate practice. For Davidson, this transition of the authorial from a tutelary function to one more focused on entertainment and commercial viability was already unfolding prior to 1800, and it served to mark the decline of established New England elites. Somewhat differently, Nina Baym's reading of mid-nineteenth-century reviews suggests that even as audiences looked increasingly to literature for entertainment, critics continued to search for didactic lessons. In *Woman's Fiction*, Baym adds, "that instruction is not at cross purposes with entertainment," provided the moral lesson is engagingly presented as relevant to the lives of a given readership. In fact, Ann Douglas's *The*

Feminization of American Culture argues that the simplistic moral virtues of sentimental Christianity in fiction appealed to an expanding middle class, allowing this literature to displace the complicated theological didacticism of the Puritan tradition. Lawrence Buell, while acknowledging a softening of the moral prescriptions of the republican period, also emphasizes that virtually all writers—from Emerson to Stowe—maintained a sense of didacticism refigured as salable entertainment. Buell claims that by the antebellum years a tutelary emphasis partially "stands for the transition to the commercial" and for writers' needs to understand the market contingencies within which they worked.[6]

This book is less concerned with the confrontations and accommodations made between a Calvinist and an "entertaining" aesthetic per se than it is with understanding that the increased demand for salable entertainment, for pleasing an expanded and unknown audience in its moments of leisure, fostered a new consciousness of authorship as an increasingly commercialized and professionalized mode of work, even as authors had little idea of what it meant to write professionally. Most centrally, this study explores the ways in which antebellum authors rhetorically reconstructed their newly professionalized work by mediating it through other forms of labor. By understanding antebellum authorship as structured primarily through rhetorical paradigms of work, I organize antebellum writers and literature in largely unprecedented ways. We have become accustomed to structuring literary fields on several grounds ranging from generic distinctions to gender exclusivity to affiliations with particular intellectual strains and philosophical schools. Each of these means of organization tends to ignore that writing is one form of work among many, that authorship requires definition—not only intrinsically or absolutely, but conditionally and relatively—as one part of a larger discursive understanding of labor and economics.

Indeed, the project of understanding authorship and its relation to other types of work became particularly urgent and complicated during the antebellum years of industrialization and literary commercialization as so many forms of work changed markedly.

In order to solve a crisis of self-understanding, antebellum authors created paradigms of relation between their own work, industrial labor, slavery, white-collar work, and craft production. These relationships tended to reflect violent ambivalences about the potential benefits and problems of authorship's and the industrial economy's emergent structures of labor. At the same time, the positioning of other modes of labor as figures for writing seized upon and helped to create relative valuations of different kinds of work both within and beyond the literary realm. As I understand it in this book, figuring authorship became a way of defining writing's place within a newly arranged hierarchy of labor as well as a way of ordering the increasingly complex literary profession itself.

One might reasonably debate whether a professional or genteel mode of authorship provided more enabling freedoms for the writer, and authors themselves seemed to wonder about this during the antebellum years. For successful authors, the emergence of the market as the determinant of relationships with readers and publishers promised economic independence and social prestige unavailable within the genteel framework. Writers could realize themselves precisely as professionals who performed no other sorts of work and who were respected, in public terms, primarily for the work they performed. But such potential advantages might be weighed against the dependence on the reading public and its tastes for one's livelihood and for a commercially legitimated sense of authorial self. In addition, authors had to assess the meaning of a newly anonymous relationship with their audiences as expanded systems of production and distribution increasingly attenuated their connection. Finally, if the attainment of a professional identity was possible, we would also have to recognize that it was by no means secure. Then as now, surely more authors failed than succeeded in their attempts to support themselves through writing. One would, then, want to consider the meaning and consequences of these difficulties as well as the advantages that obtained within a normative conception of professional writing, pointing, for example, to the manifest insecurity Hawthorne feels because his writing might fail to support him, might fail to gain him the acknowledgment that he hopes for.

But if authorship seemed an unlikely choice of profession even at the moment it emerged as a profession, economic self-sufficiency (glossed as commercial success) was hardly an aspiration or a standard of achievement shared by all antebellum authors. If the promise of sales, an expanded reading public, and professional respect gave writers something new to shoot for, it also gave them something to shoot at. Professionalism provided a means to self-understanding both in the acceptance of and resistance to it. In *Culture and Society*, Raymond Williams points out the contradictory but mutually dependent evolution of literature as a trade and the heightened imagining of the artist as a "Genius," "a special kind of person," the one who "perceives and represents Essential Reality . . . by virtue of his master faculty Imagination."[7] Among British romantics the insistence on the primacy of inspired artistic autonomy grew out of a defensive need to see the authorial profession as something more than a mere commercial trade even as it began to be reorganized very much along those lines. It was also born of the desire to make of art and the artist a repository of the values—imagination, individuation, independence—most seriously threatened by the emergent urban industrial order that came "to think of man as merely a specialized instrument of production."[8]

Lawrence Buell's overview of antebellum authorial professionalization notes that this conception of romantic authorship identified by Williams "started to become a major influence in New England at the time when professionalism also started to become a viable option."[9] One does not have to look too hard to see the truth of this. If, for example, throughout "The Custom-House" Hawthorne seems anxious and even defensive about his incapacity to realize himself as a self-supporting professional, he also has moments in which he scorns commercial success in his trade and implicitly invokes alternative measures of authorial accomplishment. We find one famous example of this antiprofessional Hawthorne, a Hawthorne who has a higher calling than popularity or commercial success, in his preface to *The Marble Faun*.

[The book is only] addressed nominally to the Public at large, but really to a character with whom he felt entitled to use far greater freedom. He meant it

for that one congenial friend,—more comprehensive of his purposes, more appreciative of his success, more indulgent of his shortcomings, and in all respects closer and kinder than a brother,—that all sympathizing critic, in short, whom an author never actually meets, but to whom he implicitly makes his appeal whenever he is conscious of having done his best. . . .
Unquestionably, this gentle, kind, benevolent, indulgent, and most beloved and honored Reader did once exist for me, and (in spite of the infinite chances against a letter's reaching its destination without a definite address) duly received the scrolls which I flung upon whatever wind was blowing, in the faith that they would find him out.[10]

Hawthorne writes for an audience of one; his successes are not to be measured in commercial terms; it may even be that the appreciation of his work lies wholly beyond the capacity of a reading "Public," even as Hawthorne acknowledges that such a "Public" does exist. What we can see here is Hawthorne's consciousness of the conditions of professional authorship as a mode of self-definition—even his relationship with his ideal reader is mediated through the market in such a way that he will never actually meet this person—while he rejects these conditions (the satisfaction of the public, the understanding of himself as commercially motivated) as irrelevant to his authorial success. Hawthorne is only one example of the simultaneous pursuit and refusal of commercial success as the measure of artistic success. We will see this characteristic split between commercial and aesthetic values take shape in Herman Melville and Henry Thoreau as well.

These sorts of conflict stand at the heart of the antebellum authorial consciousness, at the heart of a complex moment when American romantics and others came to understand the professionalization or commercialization of authorship, not as an isolated change in the meaning and status of their work, but as one part of broader changes in the arrangements of labor during the years of American industrialization. I will argue throughout that it matters very much which forms of labor authors choose as models to represent their own work, because through such choices they structure the process of professionalizing authorship within an industrializing economy. So, for example, if authors invoke or accept models of industrially rationalized labor or trade to describe their own work, that would point to an embrace of both the market as the site of literary relationships and the commodification of labor we typically associate with industrialization. On the other hand, if authors choose highly individualized, independent figures gifted with a kind of romantic "Genius" to represent artistic endeavor, that would suggest a disaffection with professionalization and the increasingly centralized urban-industrial order. Indeed, it would place authorship implicitly at odds with the rigidly rationalized modes of production developing in these years.

This book studies precisely that kind of rhetorical choice. It is a study of the constructed and positional meanings of antebellum authorship and the discourse through which these meanings were created. By "discourse" I mean to include any shared, coherent, and historically specific arrangement of verbal expression or cultural practice that serves to structure or define the terms of an understood social "reality." A discourse operates with various levels of intention and direction. Thus, I find some fairly heated and direct rhetorical alignments of writing bestsellers with the mass production of goods at a factory. But at other times I argue for discursive constructions of labor and authorship that appear more obliquely, as a shared way of thinking that emerges from interpretive readings of avowedly "literary" works within a cultural frame that makes itself most visible elsewhere—in political pamphlets, institutional structures, and so forth. Accordingly, literary texts appear beside documents and practices that fall outside the conventional bounds of literature: campaign speeches, free-labor pamphlets, copyright adjudication, and physical fitness movements. Only by bringing these heterogenous materials together does this book establish the paradigms of mediation through which antebellum authors reconstruct the relative meanings of their own and other sorts of work.

Implicit in the figurations of authorship presented here, then, is a simultaneous restructuring of both authorial labor and the work outside it, the work through which writing is figured. Though I am clearly most concerned with the meanings of authorial work, we simply cannot grasp the significance of a comparison relating a particular kind of work to authorship if we do not understand the cultural meanings that the comparison might bring to bear on the calling of the writer. Moreover, it should be noted that the connotations that accompany other labors are themselves by no means transparent or neutral outside their relationship to literary work. This study assumes that the meanings attached to work are not stable but created, and created in such a way as to satisfy historically specific anxieties about the status, nature, and value of particular kinds of activity—especially particular kinds of authorship.

This book emphasizes a history of authorship that is materialist in its emphasis on the economic contingencies of authorial work, committed to discourse analysis in its emphasis on the capacity of a shared and discernible cultural logic to render itself as a social reality, and radically individualist in its belief that writers and their personal circumstances tend to inflect paradigms of understanding to suit individual sensibilities and needs. In short, while it seems inarguable to me that the capacity of writers to imagine the terms of their labor is limited by observable material conditions and available cultural paradigms, I remain sufficiently romantic to believe in authors as individuals capable of mediating and inflecting these conditions in meaningfully individualized ways.

The most fundamental economic contingencies that preoccupy this study ought to be evident by now, but what were the paradigms of labor within which literary professionalization took its meaning? Any single answer to this question will tend to over-schematize the field of discursive possibility by drawing programmatic boundaries. Indeed, several enriching books on antebellum authorship have each attempted to interpret all or part of it through a single paradigm of work and market relations. Mary Kelley's *Private Woman, Public Stage*, for example, provides an excellent account of the psychic costs paid by women writers ("literary domestics") who violated normative expectations of feminine privacy to write publicly. Kelley's book understands the work of the twelve women authors she studies as spiritual ministration, subtle evangelism, or mothering, carried out in the popularly mediated form of the sentimental bestseller.[11]

Reaching very different conclusions, Walter Benn Michaels and

Michael Gilmore have described the work of authorship as a labor that bears no very concrete relationship to any particular form of work, but which is, nonetheless, defined largely by its place within the commodification of labor that is integral to the market-mediated consciousness of emergent urban industrial capitalism. "What kind of work is writing?" asks Michaels. "It is the work of at once producing and consuming the self, or, what amounts to the same thing, work in the market." For Michaels, the work of writing is the work of constructing, consuming, and reconstructing the self. And this authorial work never takes place outside the cultural system, the market consciousness, in which it is created. In *American Romanticism and the Marketplace*, Michael Gilmore notes the "ambivalent reaction" of American romantics "to the extension of the market." Through their efforts to find an authorial mode somewhat resistant to an ethos of exchange, claims Gilmore, romantic works "acquired their distinctive qualities." Where Michaels believes it is impossible for writers to imagine themselves beyond the economics of capitalism, Gilmore insists that the effort to do so produced at least partially resistant authorial styles.[12] More recently, and with a more persuasively concretized sense of antebellum labor, Nicholas Bromell has studied the representations of work in mid-nineteenth-century culture and the relationship of them to various authorial modes and genres. For Bromell, "work at this time was understood primarily by way of the distinction between manual and mental labor, which rested in turn on an assumed dichotomy of body and mind." Furthermore, he adds, "The dominant view of work regarded it as valuable and rewarding to the degree that it was made up of mentality and excluded the effort of the body."[13] Bromell presents an array of sources that do draw distinctions between mental and physical work of various kinds and that do, indeed, privilege the intellectual. Yet to understand antebellum labor only in this way erases some of the historical variety of work that Bromell might hope to articulate.

A few questions present themselves: Were not different forms of manual and nonmanual labor differently privileged? One needs to know something about the status of particular types of manual labor relative to one another, because, for example, the prestige, rewards, and daily conditions of craft and industrial work could be considerably different. Similarly, bureaucratic work often took place in far different material circumstances and carried with it measures of cultural value far different from those accruing to authorship. If a "dominant" culture privileged the mental, then what are we to make of longings for physical activity among the socially privileged (a question I address in Chapter 3)? Should not a paradigm privileging the mental suggest a fairly unequivocal embrace of authorship as a profession, even though, as the doubts of Hawthorne's family have indicated, writing had no such unequivocally privileged position? Bromell concludes his study by pointing out that "most of the writers . . . discussed in this book . . . found inadequate the nineteenth century's paradigmatic distinctions between manual and mental labor."[14] He is utterly persuasive on this point, but the almost uniform departure from the paradigm points to the troublesomeness of accepting it as inclusive rather than to the dominance of its cultural deployment.

These works are especially fine examples of attempts to discover the relationship between authorial and other sorts of work at the dawn of America's industrialization and literary professionalization. I am indebted to each of them, but I also believe that they share a methodological problem. Attempts to understand the multifarious and surprising figurative comparisons between writing and other sorts of work through single paradigms cannot fully account for these mediations in their varied forms of expression. The relationship of antebellum authorship to other modes of work has tended to be thematized by critics into the explanatory power of single constructs.

The most recent treatment of the relationship between antebellum labor outside of and within the literary realm clearly follows in the steps of these other works. Cindy Weinstein argues persuasively that the antebellum audience's and author's uneasiness with allegorical characterization is discursively linked to an anxiety about the reduction of real people to mechanized versions of humanity. A type of narration that had been widely practiced and respected prior to the romantic period (in the work of Dante, Milton, and Spenser, among others) came under new scrutiny for failing to develop fully complex and multifaceted personalities at precisely the moment when the routinized labor of an industrializing economy threatened to mechanize workers and make flat characters of them.[15]

Though convincing in her description of why allegory may have fallen to the margins in the nineteenth century, Weinstein is less persuasive when she suggests that "any manifestation of labor [including authorship] seemed to resonate with the ambiguous status of industrial labor" and, therefore, that authors sought to eliminate signs of authorial work from their texts, participating in an "aesthetic ideology" that emphasized "an ideal of invisible labor."[16] The argument hinges upon the paradigmatic understanding of all labor as potentially mechanized, as industrial labor because it takes place within an industrializing economy, an economy whose dominant discourse of labor always returns to the idea of mechanization. The following chapters, however, suggest that antebellum authors and others made gender- and class-based distinctions among types of work, and that specific forms of labor appear conspicuously to draw attention to authorial and other types of work that are not typically thought of as "mechanical."

While relying on the work of these critics who have explored the constructedness of antebellum authorship, I take a different approach. This study explores the rhetorical relationships between authorial and other specifically named forms of labor, primarily as these relationships are expressed in conventionally literary texts. It finds the basis for discussion of these labors less in a single overarching thematic of labor and more in an exploration of the material conditions and intertwined rhetorical meanings that particular forms of work communicate. Moreover, while I am committed to exploring dominant discourses of labor and authorship, I also hope to reveal the simultaneous and often dialogic presence of residual and emergent discourses that help to define any dominant vision. If writers are culturally constricted in the metaphors of labor that they choose to figure authorship, it is also important to note that a range of choice exists within that restricted realm. I accept the notions that the economics of authorship are part of a larger industrial-capitalist system in which subjectivity is constructed (as Michaels would), that one paradigmatic distinction within this system is between the manual and the mental (as Bromell argues persuasively), and that these constructions are strongly inflected by gendered conventions (as Kelley makes apparent). However, I am finally concerned to understand specifically and with some sense of their multiple implications the relationships between, for example, authorial and industrial work, authorial and slave work, authorial and craft work, and authorial and white-collar work as each exists at a moment of historical transition. Even more to the point, I am concerned to understand the ways in which the rhetorical construction of authorship and other forms of work come to be mutually reinforcing and necessary to their social meanings and functions.

By presenting multiple paradigms for the understanding of the mediated relations between authorial and other sorts of work, all of which were simultaneously operative during the antebellum years, I capture not only the indisputable move of the authorial into the realm of the professional, but also the unevenness, the uneasiness of this move. The study provides a sense of the conflicted and even contradictory complexity with which antebellum authors and others reconstructed forms of emergent labor. It reveals, in short, the cultural consciousness of what various forms of labor meant in relation to authorial work.

It would be naive to think that I have exhausted the full range of labors upon which authors could draw to structure their own work. This book, like all books, is selective in the questions it brings forth and the textual evidence it interrogates. It is organized as four discrete but interpenetrating chapters, each of which discusses the discursive relationships between authorial and other types of work. Each chapter could stand on its own as a treatment of the paradigms and rhetorical values associated with particular modes of work and the relevance of them to writing. At the same time, the four chapters make implicit and explicit reference to one another, and only by reading the whole can the complexity and variation of antebellum attempts to figure the meanings of authorship be grasped.

The matter of selectivity raises more complicated questions, some of them inextricable from the matter of organization. Each chapter places conventionally extraliterary texts beside conventionally literary ones with the idea that the two might shed light on one another and that taken together they present the most persuasive claims for the existence of discursive paradigms that extend beyond the "literary" realm. In blurring the boundary between text and context, I treat the "literary" and "extraliterary" alike as vehicles for the construction and institution of particular systems of value, even as I persist in an old-fashioned distinction between these sources. I insist that while all texts work in concert in the formation of discursive paradigms, "literary" writers think more about writing than others and, therefore, that their texts are more fully and commonly suffused with figurations of this work. Although I find complicated and provocative figurations of labor outside the literary realm, when it comes time to understand the relationship of these figurations to authorial work and the process through which they are mediated as representations of authorship, I turn to "literature."

Issues of selectivity and organization also intersect in the arrangement of texts within given chapters. Rather than grouping texts into chapters by traditional divisions of genre, less traditional divisions of gender, or even by concentration on single authors or texts, I have aggressively and actively tried to cross such boundaries. I do so to emphasize that the paradigmatic understandings and mediated interrelationships of work discussed have implications that can be best understood by allowing them to expand and grow somewhat organically. I want to show that particular modes of mediation between authorship and other labors matter not for one author but for many, not for one gender but for both, not in one genre but in several. While I use categories such as "domestic authorship" or "romantic authorship" to clarify the specific position of writers relative to particular paradigms of mediation, I emphasize more fully the importance that various authors whom we normally segregate did invoke differently inflected versions of the same mediated understandings, that they structured their writing through shared or competing conceptions of labor that included but were not limited to considerations of gender and literary form.

In combining and attempting to see simultaneously the relationship of canonical romantic and more recently enfranchised (particularly "domestic") writers to the same rhetorical paradigms, this book is again at odds with most work that has been done on antebellum authorship. Gilmore's and Charvat's books concentrate only on male writers, and primarily on the canonical romantics of the American Renaissance, though some of Charvat's best work is on Henry Wadsworth Longfellow and James Fenimore Cooper. Bromell's more wide-ranging effort discusses Hawthorne and Rebecca Harding Davis's shared relation to the work of writing in one chapter, but the remaining eight chapters that discuss particular writers separate the male and female, the canonical and the non-canonical authors whom he studies. Kelley's *Private Woman, Public Stage* and Coultrap-McQuin's *Doing Literary Business* are devoted solely to describing a female version of professionalization. In all of these works, the male romantic writers tend to have their conception of authorial labor formulated by confrontations with the marketplace and the commercial values it represents, while the women writers envision their work as a form of maternal or domestic labor and are also (generally) ambivalent about the restructuring of authorial relationships through the market.

Although this book relies upon some of the distinctly gendered conceptions of authorial work presented by these and other critics, it also suggests that historically coincident forms of writing had more in the way of shared focal points of self-imagining than we have typically been led to believe. It argues crucially and by example that when we organize authorship around constructions of antebellum labor, texts that we normally separate come to address shared anxieties about professional writing. Moreover, this regrouping of texts and writers across familiar boundaries makes visible the terms of authorial consciousness and positional understandings of writing that have remained obscured by segregation.

A study such as Gillian Brown's *Domestic Individualism* has already begun to question the rigidity of the borders between the separate male and female spheres, between the romantic and the domestic in antebellum writing and culture. Brown, while she does not have much to say about the construction of authorship itself, underscores the extent to which domestic forms and values penetrate romantic ideology and vice versa. Brown's book forces us to think of typically separated literary realms as interpenetrating, as working with and within many of the same cultural contingencies to create various possibilities of self-definition that depend on the fusion and interdependence of realms too often understood as wholly distinct.[17]

This is not to say that we ought to abandon useful and meaningful classificatory distinctions. The idea of the canon is useful in this study precisely in that it serves to avoid the homogenization of the literary, the creation or implication of a realm in which all writing is not only equal but essentially the same. I am perfectly willing to accept that romantic and domestic writers, who compose what Gillian Brown calls with some skepticism the "two disparate literary movements [that] seem to emerge in the 1850s," worked toward different modes of authorial self-definition.[18] I even believe that the "classic" texts are a better and more sophisticated group according to particular standards of aesthetic value. But such considerations of aesthetic form and merit, while certainly worth contemplating, are not the primary concern of this study.

Rather, I am interested in the possibility that distinctions (and similarities) of authorial self-understanding may be most meaningfully visible when they evidence themselves as divergent (or similar) positionings relative to and mediations of the same mode of work. In Chapter 1, for example, we can see most clearly what it means to be a romantic writer and what it means to be a sentimental writer when we see both "types" of writing taking up positions relative to industrial work. Here I consider Hawthorne's and Melville's different attempts to cast women's sentimental or domestic writing as mass production, even as they make exorbitant claims of individuated expressive power for themselves. As a particularly dramatic example of the refusal of women writers to have their literary work cast as industrial production, I draw from the *Lowell Offering*, a mid-nineteenth-century journal of what we would now call women's sentimental literature written by industrial operatives. Chapter 2 undertakes to merge Harriet Beecher Stowe, Hawthorne, and Harriet Jacobs into a shared understanding of authorial celebrity as it is mediated through slavery. Just as abolitionists began to cast slavery as most horrible for emblematizing an economy in which human beings rather than goods were exchanged, these three authors come to imagine literary audiences bent on the trade and consumption of authors themselves.

If Chapters 1 and 2 focus on the negative associations authors make between writing and modes of disadvantaged labor such as industrial work and slavery, Chapter 3 takes up the question of what it means to see authorship's position relative to the increasingly white-collar work of an emergent middle class. I argue that middle-class privilege carried with it an anxiety about the removal from republican valorizations of manual labor. Middle-class workers attempted to redress this anxiety through an elaborate discourse that reconstructed physical labor as physical fitness. Thoreau and Hawthorne borrow a form of this logic that sets authorship outside both the realm of professionalism and manual work by seeing authorship itself as a figurative embodiment of manual labor, while Susan Warner fantasizes about the possibility of removing herself not only from manual labor but from the work of writing.

I close in Chapter 4 with a discussion of Edgar Allan Poe's, Fanny Fern's, and Hawthorne's relationship to copyright laws and conceptions of literary property. The chapter makes an appropriate end, because it stresses that for all the efforts of writers to imagine their own work through the work of others, disruptions of these mediations constantly occurred. Copyright law simply did not (and does not to the present day) interpret the work of authorship as creating the same sort of rights in property created by other, particularly materially productive, labors. For all the analogizing and materializing in the world, mid-nineteenth-century courts simply did not understand authors as possessors of a strongly materialized intellectual property.

My goal in the juxtaposition of the various authors and sources in each chapter is not the sinister or laudable one (depending on one's perspective!) of doing in the canon. I do mean to say, however, that the concerns of canonical authors and their terms of self-definition were not always uniquely their own, and I give extensive play to conceptions of authorial work that emerged from domestic or sentimental writing.

This study also puts forth alternatives for organizing antebellum authorship beyond splitting it along the lines of literary form or gender. We might structure authorship by understanding its position, not in a literary vacuum of aesthetic form or as an almost ontologically imagined gender difference, but as one part of a more broadly changing landscape of work that is, to mix in a metaphor of labor, constantly under construction. But to do this, we will need to understand as primary the relationship that authors of various "types" imagined their works to have to other forms of labor. We must understand the various paradigms of work through which an understanding of writing might have been either limited or enabled. Beginning on this path leads inevitably to unfamiliar readings of and associations among antebellum texts and authors, but even more importantly it points to the possible and constantly shifting understandings of work that authors drew upon to cope with—to figure out—the terms of their own emerging profession.

CHAPTER ONE

Industry and Authorship

*Hawthorne's Mob, Melville's Maids,
and the 'Lowell Offering'*

Thoreau's Pencils

More than fifty years ago, F. O. Matthiessen pointed out that Henry Thoreau persistently thought of authorial work in terms of the labor that surrounded him: "The depth to which [Thoreau's] ideals for fitness and beauty in writing were shaped, half consciously, by the modes of productive labor with which he was surrounded, or, in fact, by the work of his own hands in carpentry or pencilmaking or gardening can be read in his instinctive analogies."[1] Matthiessen makes the statement almost offhandedly, as if it were obvious that Thoreau should and did seize equally upon carpentry, pencilmaking, and gardening as tied to authorship. To some extent, of course, Thoreau's journals and *Walden* do almost self-evidently liken building a house (carpentry) and growing beans (gardening) to the work of writing, but pencilmaking will surely strike Thoreau's casual readers as disconsonant.

Matthiessen must have assumed that people would be familiar with Thoreau's biography. Henry Thoreau was much more than superficially involved in pencilmaking over a period of more than fifteen years, from the mid-1830s to the early 1850s. Pencilmaking was his father's vocation, but John Thoreau had barely eked out a living. Then, after his son Henry entered the shop, pencil manufacturing became markedly more profitable.[2]

Henry Thoreau changed the family pencil business and, in fact, at certain periods became almost utterly consumed by his efforts to improve it. He told Ralph Waldo Emerson that even after working full days at the shop, he would dream about the various machines he had invented. In order to compete with the makers of pencils of superior quality imported from the Faber Company in Germany, Thoreau instituted an entirely new process of production. Rather than continuing to push a slow-drying lead-based paste into the split halves of a wooden shell that would only later be glued together, Thoreau negotiated an agreement with a nearby glass factory to obtain from overseas a new kind of clay. He added this clay to the graphite mixture and brought ovens into the workshop. Thoreau baked the lead hard in the new ovens, and invented a saw for cutting it to precise specifications. He bored holes in the wooden shells. The lead could then be jammed into the wood, saving time and numerous inefficient steps. Even after this, however, the lead was too gritty for Thoreau. Accordingly, he invented an entirely new machine for grinding the lead into an unprecedentedly fine powder. He later developed a technique for baking the lead dry in pieces of precisely the right size and so eliminated the inefficiency of cutting them afterwards.[3]

By the late 1840s the Thoreaus had expanded their shop into what might properly be called a small factory, a long row of sheds. They were not rich but had made plenty of money to buy a house. The Thoreaus had become one of the premier pencil makers in Massachusetts, perhaps in the United States, and won several citations in honor of their product. In 1844 Emerson told a friend that the Thoreaus charged seventy-five cents a dozen for their pencils. In 1849 Thoreau brought one thousand dollars' worth of them to sell in New York. The arithmetic suggests that, without bulk discounts that would only have increased the number and without some other significant change in price, Thoreau planned to sell on one trip alone almost 16,000 pencils.[4]

With this biography in mind, we might understand why Matthiessen mentioned pencilmaking alongside carpentry as a prominent labor in Thoreau's life; but what is more difficult to comprehend is why, if we can agree that Thoreau did "half-consciously" form and even express analogies between other, biographically less central modes of production and his writing, he refused or neglected to liken pencilmaking to authorial work. The answer to this difficulty must be, of course, that work in the pencil factory had different associations for Thoreau than the work of carpentry or gardening, that he thought of it differently, as somehow less like authorship, and that the three sorts of labor ought not to be grouped so casually together.

The Thoreaus' pencil factory was not an industrial enterprise of the same type or on the same scale as the mills in Lowell or the shoe factories in Lynn, Massachusetts, but it nonetheless shows Thoreau pushing the family enterprise toward the enormously complicated and broadly cultural reorganizations of production that we now summarize as "industrialization." As historians have pointed out, these restructurings occurred piecemeal and in smaller workshops something like Thoreau's as well as in the more conspicuous factories of the antebellum period.[5] Pencilmaking in the Thoreau factory came to include newly invented and specialized machines and tools; the family must have hired others to help them; production was accelerated and took place on an unprecedented scale; Thoreau traded internationally to obtain his materials; the pencils were advertised and sold beyond strictly local markets and, as I have said, Thoreau even saw the Faber Company of Germany (a surviving tradename to the present day) as one of his primary competitors.

The Thoreau enterprise, in short, seems to have remained a family business until its demise, but it very clearly was not the same business it had been when John Thoreau, working for marginal profits in his shop, had struggled to make ends meet. It also very clearly was not the fully self-contained, independent, and essentially unprofitable labor of house building and bean farming by Walden Pond. Rather, it was a commercially oriented enterprise of mass production. Moreover, the long hours required to make the shop profitable must have disagreed with Thoreau and the lead powder that escaped from the grinding machines into the air can only have aggravated the chronic weakness of his lungs. Thoreau constantly sought to escape the pencil factory by working as a surveyor, as a school teacher, as Emerson's handyman and, of course, as an author. Economic necessity, however, repeatedly drove him back. For Henry Thoreau to reject pencilmaking as a trope for authorship, simply put, was for Henry Thoreau to reject very specifically any figurative relationship between his writing and his highly personal experience with the emergent conditions of industrializing labor.

I begin with the conspicuous absence of pencilmaking as a trope for writing (especially conspicuous in light of Thoreau's willingness to use gardening, carpentry, and countless other forms of work in this way) only because it is a fairly transparent example of the tendency of certain antebellum authors to distance the figuration of their literary work from emergent forms of industrial labor. Thoreau, however, serves only as an entry point. This chapter, on the whole, is devoted to several more elaborate and deeply submerged treatments of the rhetorical relationships between industrial and authorial production. Indeed—and this is the central point—it seems to me that we might see revealed in the figurative patterns of industrial analogues for writing (or the conscious avoidance of them) not only the emergent structure of a rapidly expanding literary market, but also one of the discursive means through which authors themselves struggled to structure their position within that market.

This chapter hopes to answer particular questions about who used industrial tropes for authorship during the antebellum period and what kind of writing these tropes were meant to describe. In answering these questions, more widely significant ones crop up. What sort of structural definitions, discriminations, and differences do writers bring into play when they invoke the work of the operative to describe the work of the writer? How does such an image function within a larger system of differences to construct varied (and differently privileged) visions of literary work? The more one thinks about such questions, the more clear it becomes that when writers invoke other forms of work as figures to describe writing during the antebellum years, they are seeking to set out the relationship of their own work to other types of labor evolving during America's early period of industrialization. But these figurations also work to structure the emerging profession of authorship itself through a complicated mingling of class and gender discriminations. The following chapter, then, works not only to uncover the use of industrial tropes for writing, but to insist that such tropes implicitly organized and hierarchized an expanding literary world through invocations of class and gender differences made particularly acute by increasingly depersonalized modes of industrial work.

Class, Gender, and Authorship

A number of literary critics and historians have told us that at the moment of craft labor's industrialization, the American economy in general and the literary marketplace in particular expanded dramatically. In the eighteenth century, according to William Charvat, authorship had been primarily an elitist hobby. Joel Barlow and the rest of the Connecticut Wits, for example, had written primarily for one another and their social peers, with no hope of making or desire to make a profit, much less a living, from their literary work. By the mid-nineteenth century, however, authorship had become at least potentially viable as a self-supporting profession. James Fenimore Cooper, Charvat suggests, was "the first American writer of imaginative literature to make a living from his work."[6] Lawrence Buell, borrowing his typology from Raymond Williams, also pinpoints the antebellum years as the period in which the "commercialization of letters led to an increasingly diverse and complicated set of mediations between author and public." Buell emphasizes that after 1830 writers increasingly became "market professionals" hoping to make an independent living from their work rather than writing largely from avocational interest.[7]

As my introduction outlines, the emergence of a commercially driven literary industry created perceived opportunities and liabilities for authorial self-realization. On the one hand, those successful in the new arrangements obtained an economic independence and a wide-ranging professional respect unimaginable to earlier generations. On the other hand, to accept the market as the appropriate location and arbiter of authorial accomplishment meant that one relied on and had to please an increasingly anonymous reading public distanced by the mediations of commerce to attain one's sense of professional legitimacy. Accordingly, we find many antebellum writers—particularly those unsuccessful in commercial terms—seeking out self-understandings alternative to those grounded in commercial success.

The tendency of most recent criticism has been to separate this emergent professional and commercial literary realm into two smaller and discretely gendered domains, one occupied by female, sentimental, or domestic writers, the other occupied by the familiarly canonized and male romantics of Matthiessen's *American Renaissance*. The logic of this separation must be imported from—or at the very least is consistent with—historical work on the antebellum period that details the emergence of radically separate "spheres" of male and female social and cultural activity within the emerging Northeastern middle class. Nancy Cott and Carol Smith-Rosenberg, for example, have made compelling cases for a private, mid-nineteenth-century female realm by detailing the intimacies, opportunities, and restrictions afforded by, to use Cott's phrase, a "cult of domesticity," or to use Rosenberg's, a "female world of love and ritual." In this by now widely known work on the culture of domesticity, the mid-nineteenth-century woman's sphere emerges as centered upon the home and the family, on a private, noncommercial domain in which women share emotional intimacies even as they are marginalized economically by a professional world that increasingly privileges men as breadwinners. Where women tend to the spiritual ministrations of the middle-class home and cultivate sentiment, middle-class men find themselves increasingly separated from the home and family by the movement of work away from the house.[8]

When feminist literary critics have sought to restructure antebellum authorship, to open the closed canon of the American Renaissance to women writers, they have typically invoked the spatial metaphor of separate spheres that Cott, Rosenberg, and others have made familiar. Women's writing emerges from these canon-expanding enterprises as something ontologically discrete from the male, romantic forms of writing that academic study has long privileged. Jane Tompkins, for example, argues for the centrality of the sentimental text in the mid-nineteenth century, and she does so by insisting that this female mode originates from an exclusively women's social situation radically different from that occupied by romantic writers. Where the writers of the classic American Renaissance might privilege individuality and literary complexity, the writers of what Tompkins calls "The Other American Renaissance" privilege shared feelings and appeal to intimacy and emotion. The logic of Tompkins's position dictates that men could not, by virtue of their nature or social position, write in the mode she associates with sentimental power.[9]

Other critics, most notably Nina Baym and Susan Harris, have suggested that women's literature not only has its own set of sociopolitical concerns but also its own narrative forms. Baym and Harris both describe versions of "master plots" or "cover stories" that guide women's novels but are never explicitly evidenced in men's writing. For Baym, "all woman's fiction shares the same story of 'trials and triumph'" and "men did not compose in this genre."[10] Woman's fiction tells the story of young women overcoming the unfairnesses to which the women reading the novels might themselves be sensitive. More than Baym, Harris commits herself to uncovering the subversive form of women's novels. According to Harris, the conventional stories of, for example, "trials and triumph" are structured with underplots that feature women exploring the bounds of acceptably feminine behavior. The structural triumph of women's novels in Harris's account is that they feature submerged suggestions of "women's a priori capabilities for self-determination."[11] In these arguments, the social entanglements and constructedness of middle-class womanhood lead not only to particular resistances to and complicities with ideological expectations, but also to recognizable and even generically distinct aesthetic forms.

Mary Kelley and Susan Coultrap-McQuin give us a third approach to describing the separate, gender-determined spheres of literary endeavor. They argue that domestic literature of the mid-nineteenth century reflects the psychological and social negotiations of women who idealized the privacy of a woman's separate sphere even as they entered the public realm by virtue of their authorial acts. Coultrap-McQuin argues that popular women writers "could be comfortable with their own literary aspirations," while Kelley emphasizes the strongly ambivalent "dual identity" of the domestic novelists, but rather than focusing primarily on the novels themselves both critics detail the cultural and biographical conditions of women's writing within the increasingly commercialized publishing industry.[12]

Judith Fetterley has pointed to many strengths and weaknesses in the writing on nineteenth-century American women's literature. A primary strength of this criticism is that it undertakes an obviously significant and ongoing recovery of long-ignored women's writing. Moreover, debates about the political subversiveness or conservatism of these works can only make us think more carefully about what we include and exclude from cultural centrality in our study of American literature and history. Though we may never resolve the debate over the patriarchal or matriarchal politics of texts such as *Uncle Tom's Cabin*, the proliferating readings of them force us to acknowledge their crucial place in the production of mid-nineteenth-century sociability, politics, and aesthetics.[13]

Fetterley's critique of the scholarship, however, sounds at times as if the act of recovery can only succeed through a kind of assertive advocacy, through a relatively uncritical praise of women's writings and the women who wrote them. Fetterley laments "an asymmetry in certain recent work, the disproportionately negative as opposed to positive assessment of these writers." She laments that many recent critics have attacked nineteenth-century women writers for their complicity with and participation in a sentimental, middle-class ethos that establishes itself largely at the expense of those outside it—the working classes and racial others. While acknowledging at one brief moment that "there is much to critique in the texts of nineteenth-century American women writers," Fetterley seems to prefer celebrating these texts as products of a purified and positive gender difference to critiquing them as manifestations of middle-class dominance.[14]

My own sense, then, is that Fetterley's critique repeats a difficulty present in much of the criticism she evaluates. In treating women's writing as a separate literary preserve we threaten to structure the antebellum literary world almost exclusively and transparently through a privileged notion of gender difference within an emergent and potentially uninterrogated middle class. In other words, while we debate the relative aesthetic and political merits of gender-exclusive male and female literary realms, our debates and understanding of masculine and feminine authorship threaten to break down into (and preserve) gender-determined confrontations in a bipolar literary world. Even more problematic, sealed within this middle-class world of gender difference, class itself might be obscured as a category of difference, as a constantly deployed force of discursive distinction that functions in conjunction with gender to create models of authorial subjectivity.[15]

A number of recent theorists and historians of class and labor have pointed to the danger in a debate that collapses critical analysis into a nearly gender-exclusive fashioning of difference, and some recent work on literary domesticity recognizes its barriers and functions as much in terms of class privilege as gender difference. For Laura Wexler, domesticity becomes an instrument of middle-class imperialism as freed slaves of the postbellum era are educated into its values of piety and submissiveness. Amy Lang has argued that domesticity's attempts to structure social life in terms of gender difference serve to mask an overwhelming class coherence that excludes factory operatives and others from its midst.[16]

These newer formulations seem helpful, because, as Ava Baron has put the matter succinctly, "If gender is conceptualized [and reified?] simply as two categories of contradictory interests, it has little explanatory power."[17] Rather, Baron, profoundly influenced by the work of Joan Scott, suggests that categories of gender and class might work simultaneously to define and create one another, to create systems of meaning functioning simultaneously in several different dualistic (or multipolar) realms. We would thus need to understand that antagonisms or constructions of difference appearing to be grounded in distinctions of gender might also work meaningfully through symbols of class. The rhetoric of gender, in other words, might be figured through the rhetoric of class discriminations and confrontations and vice versa. Furthermore, the discourses of gender, class and other differences may all work simultaneously in harmony or conflict to construct particular cultural and material realities.[18]

Such observations noting that gender is only one discursive category within an elaborate system of confrontation and cultural difference are extremely helpful when it comes to imagining the terms of mid-nineteenth-century authorship. We will be reminded, I hope, that individuals hold several cultural identities simultaneously, and that confrontation might take place between men and women, between male and female authors, at any one of these points of identity. The final truth about both the sentimental (female) and romantic (male) authors of the mid-nineteenth century is that they work through and construct middle-class authorship upon a relatively narrow field of class similarity as much as upon gender difference. If we must debate whether given gender-determined literary groupings tend to be radical or conservative, to produce aesthetic achievements or artless botches, we should also note that the texts produced within such groupings work toward consolidating and contesting a particularly middle-class cultural sphere of the literary. They work, in other words, toward defining the space of emergent, middle-class professional authorship through certain discriminatory categories of understanding, and gender is only one of them.

If we understand versions of mid-nineteenth–century writing not to have an ontological or reified separability purely in gendered terms, then we will realize that the sentimental and romantic modes of authorship in the mid-nineteenth century are not so much separable from one another as they are mutually necessary and interdependent in the project of defining an increasingly professionalized authorial realm. Accordingly, the establishment of difference between these modes of writing, the battle over what will constitute the profession of authorship in the years between 1830 and 1860, is finally a conflict that finds some expression in gendered confrontation, but that is also about contested (and uneasily shared) class position. The differences between these texts arise not from the need or desire to occupy wholly different social terrain, but from the desire of various writers to construct and occupy the same middle-class social space. The conflict over that space, the contesting definitions of difference and deviation from it, are, accordingly, imagined not only in terms of gender but also in terms of class discriminations and polarities. In short, when male romantic writers such as Hawthorne and Melville come to dismiss or attack female, domestic, or sentimental writers of the period, they do so not only, and maybe not even primarily, by accusing them of womanly emotionalism, hysteria, or intellectual incapacity. They imagine them simultaneously as a mass of working-class factory operatives who have no legitimate claim to the individuated imagination and autonomy of a romantic and independent agent of creativity. On the other hand, when sentimental writers construct their own vision of authorship, they not only rely on their femininity to suggest moral and emotional authority, but specifically invoke images that divorce that femininity from working-class modes of labor and production. For the writers of the *Lowell Offering*, a magazine produced by women industrial operatives, literary work becomes a way of denying a working-class or proletarian identity and asserting instead ideas of middle-class-bound cultural achievement.

The general if not uniform antagonism of Hawthorne and Melville to women writers of the period is well documented. Hawthorne and Melville both gained moderate degrees of commercial success with particular books, but their work, on the whole, never approached the popularity of the bestselling domestic novels, and by the mid-1850s, they clearly resented the commercial success that they found themselves unable or unwilling to achieve. Hawthorne's infamous letter deploring the "mob of scribbling women" is, perhaps, the most often quoted literary letter of the antebellum period. Melville's mix of envy and contempt for sentimental authorship was perhaps most elaborately worked through in *Pierre*, a novel that seems to approach sentimentality only to fail miserably, maybe even parodically, to achieve it. *Pierre*, after all, though Melville described it as "calculated for popularity," features incestuous love and almost open disdain for the taste of the reading public. As those familiar with Melville's career know, *Pierre* was so abysmally unsuccessful in the market and greeted with such hostility by the critics that Melville found publication of his subsequent work more difficult than ever.[19]

It is useful to remember that highly personal and professional interests and jealousies might have motivated any condemnation, implicit or explicit, of the best-selling domestic novelists, but such condemnations fulfilled not only personal or individual needs. Rather, Hawthorne and Melville at once channeled and reinforced the rhetorical energy of culturally grounded class and gender differences in an attempt to define the emerging and amorphous figure of the literary professional. In other words, I hope to make increasingly clear that Hawthorne and Melville rhetorically entangled the best-selling work of the literary domestics with, to approximate Matthiessen's phrase from the beginning of this chapter, a surrounding mode of production, the disindividuated labor of the industrial operative. Furthermore, this entangling worked out not only a personal distaste for and envy of popular writers grounded specifically in gendered discriminations, but reinforced and helped to create more broadly constructed visions of the relationships among class, gender, and authorial work.

The figure of the industrial worker as an immediate reality and the conception of such work as degrading and disindividuated appeared at more or less the same historical moment as the best-selling novelists themselves. The factory operative's dehumanization and the degradation of craft labor during the first decades of industrialization have been voluminously documented. Sean Wilentz, for example, has described the centralization, mechanization, and routinization of labor in New York City sweatshops and factories and summarized these developments as "the bastardization of craft." Independent printers, he points out as one example, were threatened by the economies of scale, capital investment, and marketing power of larger publishing houses, as the steam press, electrotyping, and stereotyping began to make the skilled work of press operators and typesetters obsolete. Similar evolutions took place in shoemaking, clockmaking, and gunmaking to name only a few of the more conspicuously industrializing trades.[20]

Labor and cultural historians, however, have only begun to explore the potential force that the figure of the industrial worker might have carried beyond the boundaries of his or her own class situation and degradation. What did the factory operative signify to other types or classes of workers? How did these workers define themselves against such disindividuated labor? Phrased in this way, the questions are extremely broad, but the problem might be made more manageable for a discussion of authorship: How did antebellum writers construct the continuities and differences between the increasingly mechanized and working-class-bound labor of the operative and the ideally individualized and middle-class independent labor of the professional author?

Simply put, the emergence of the industrial worker and the conception of mass production as degrading and disindividuated made the operative a potentially powerful and damning figure for (and distortion of) commercialized (and sentimental) modes of literary production. To condemn particular sorts of literary work as mass produced, as the products of industrial labor, became a way of attacking and dismissing the importance of that work. It ought to be noted at the same time, however, that the creation of analogues between industrial and any particular mode of authorial work was far from inevitable. That is to say, the analogies formed between industrial or working-class labor and authorial work existed most crucially as ideologically charged cultural figurations, as naturalized or constructed comparisons that imposed order on an unfamiliar literary world. The literary work of the domestic novelists, after all, no matter how widely it sold in this period, was not industrial work. As craft labor industrialized, authorship within the middle-class market professionalized; as craft labor more and more came to be dominated by the time and work disciplines of mass production,

professional authorship came to be guided more and more by entrepreneurial concerns, by the individual author's attempt to negotiate and make a financial success of his or her relatively independent labor within the publishing industry and the literary market.
Though a number of recent critics have, like some of the authors I
will explore, attempted to insist on the parallels between emergent
industrial work and commercial authorship, to do so is to make an
improbable historical claim, one that must render utterly abstract
the day-to-day realities of two very different types of work.[21]

But if authorial and industrial work had evidently divergent paths
of historical evolution, it was exactly these divergences that figurations of authorial labor as industrial labor sought to eliminate. By
likening certain types of commercialized authorial work to the disindividuated work of mass production, these types of writing could
be dismissed as unskilled, degrading, and disindividuated industrial
work. Moreover, to condemn writing as the work of mass production was to damn it to a kind of subliterary or even antiliterary
status, to place it on the lowest imaginable rung in the increasingly
hierarchized literary market. Finally, for male writers to characterize women's writing as industrial work was to call into question the
very grounds of or justification for domestic authorship. For, as critics of domestic writing almost unanimously agree, the popularity
of these women authors rested largely upon the role of cultural and
spiritual guardian granted women within their increasingly separate
sphere of middle-class domestic life. The ideology of domesticity
dedicated itself to the creation of the nuclear family with an exaggerated and naturalized version of the mother and wife as the unique
source of moral and religious authority. Domestic fiction, we now
know, with its representations of just such women and their families, was unquestionably a part of this particular class and gender arrangement, and the women who wrote the domestic bestsellers functioned in part as well-known embodiments of its primary tenets.[22]

But if middle-class writers of the middle-class domestic novels
turned out to be working-class laborers more engaged in mass production and commercial success than in spiritual and moral ministrations, it might become more and more difficult to value the writ-

ing they did. The very basis of domestic or sentimental authorship, in other words, could be called into question by positioning such authorship as a form of industrial rather than familial or spiritual work. To say this is to begin to answer the question of which sorts of literary work were cast figuratively as industrial work and to hint at some of the discursive functions undertaken by authorial-industrial analogies. But the dynamics of such analogies are extremely complicated and meaningfully varied in their details.

Fiction Factories

Michael Denning and others have shown that comparisons between authorial and industrial labor were most direct and apparent not within the realm of middle–class authorship at all, but, rather, in middle-class critiques of the extensively circulated story papers, penny press, and dime novels that began to emerge alongside, or perhaps more appropriately, in the shadows of the domestic and romantic fiction of the antebellum period. For, as the authors of best-selling sentimental fiction and those authors we now associate with the American Renaissance emerged in their own overlapping but gender-specific middle-class cultural milieus, dime novels and sensationalistic story papers dominated the working-class literary sphere. From the late 1830s and 1840s, such publications evolved with bursts of phenomenal success and failure until nearly the end of the century. As Denning points out, not only did these stories find their primary audience within the working class of artisans and industrial workers, but their politics (particularly those of the many "mysteries of the city" written by George Lippard and others in the 1840s and 1850s) tended toward political advocacy of the worker and condemnation of the very middle class, the very political order, so deeply inscribed and idealized in more sentimental fiction.[23]

What is intriguing for my purposes about this particular mode of working-class fiction and political reportage, however, is not only that it often implicitly (and sometimes explicitly) took up the cause of the working class, but that the actual production of dime novels and story papers came increasingly to be viewed within the middle class as a kind of working-class or industrial labor in its own right. For, as Denning points out, throughout the second half of the nineteenth century, from Edward Everett and others in the 1850s to Edward Bok in the 1890s, "the writing of dime novels was viewed by literary figures as an extraordinary kind of industrial production."[24] The mode in which working-class fiction was produced, in other words, seems to have been identified with both the occupational status of its readership and the politics that this fiction tended to advocate.

At some level, of course, the analogy between industrial production and cheap story production was simply descriptive of this writing as it would not have been of the popular domestic or emerging "higher" literature of the same period, and this reality ought not to be overlooked. Dime novelists, including Lippard, seem typically (though not universally) to have produced more work in less time according to a kind of rationalized standard than authors popular in the middle-class cultural sphere. Moreover, as the century wore on, cheap-fiction writers were increasingly alienated from their final product as it appeared in print. By the end of the 1860s, for example, any number of anonymous writers might have produced stories under a shared name for a given publisher who held not only the copyright in the manuscript but a legal trademark right in the name under which the authors wrote. Dime-novel writers tended to be miserably paid, and were expected to produce on a rigorous and often gruelling schedule.[25]

But the likening of dime-novel production to industrial modes of work through the rhetorical emergence of what Denning and Quentin Reynolds before him have called "fiction factories" was not solely a matter of historical or objective observation. Rather, it was a way of figuring authorship. What the rhetorical birth of the "fiction factory" begins to suggest is that industrial analogues for literary production—particularly when issued from within the ranks of middle-class culture—were, from the start, a way of branding and dismissing particular types of literature and literary production as subliterary, a way of containing working-class fiction by dismissing it as mass-produced, unskilled, and routinized work unfit for higher minds.

Hawthorne's Mob

If fiction-and-factory analogies had some important relevance as descriptions of the way in which dime novels and other pulp fiction were actually produced, they had, as I have been suggesting, relatively little apparent application as descriptions of the fiction produced by the domestic novelists or by authors such as Hawthorne and Melville. As a number of literary historians have made clear, the best-selling domestic authors of this period could receive substantial pay for their manuscripts and became celebrities within their cultural sphere. Authors such as Melville and Hawthorne, while experiencing some conflicts with publishers at various points in their careers, could never be said to have entered into the kind of scheduled and rationalized labor that dominated the cheap-fiction business.[26]

The question that arises, then, is what ought we to make of industrial analogues for literature produced in ways that bore absolutely no (or very little) similarity to the rationalized modes of production increasingly operative in the sphere of cheap stories and nascent mass manufacturing? What, in other words, would we make of attempts to figure the middle-class domestic fiction of the antebellum period in something like the "fiction factory" terms that cheap fiction was dismissed? The answer is that we would certainly have to recognize such figurations as ideologically freighted, as designed to establish a certain (rather low) place for that literature.

It should not be surprising, then, to find such an analogy between commercially successful sentimental authorship and mass production within the writings of Nathaniel Hawthorne, a man notorious for his condemnation of the "damned mob of scribbling women." Hawthorne's letter undertakes the kind of rhetorical transformation of women's fiction into a depersonalized form of mass production that I have been discussing. Furthermore, it should not be surpris-

ing that when it came time to imagine the terms of his own literary
production, Hawthorne chose as the appropriate figure not industrial but, rather, notably outdated and highly aestheticized types of
craft labor.

We have learned only recently that for more than a century literary critics have mistakenly accepted Hawthorne's gripe as a fair
dismissal of a diverse and important group of novelists, but to know
this is not necessarily to understand the rhetoric that has given this
passage such power as a statement of the women's literary inadequacy. That rhetoric and its historical situation are exactly what
interest me:

America is now wholly given over to a d——d mob of scribbling women
and I should have no chance of success while the public taste is occupied
with their trash—and should be ashamed of myself if I did succeed. What
is the mystery of these innumerable editions of the Lamplighter, and other
books neither better nor worse?—worse they could not be and better they
need not be when they sell by the 100,000.[27]

Raymond Williams tells us that in England "mob" had a specific
class history and rhetorical function that have been generally taken
over by "mass." The "mob" suggests "gullibility, fickleness, herd-
prejudice, lowness of taste and habit." To group individuals as an
anonymous and disindividuated mob has been a way for dominant
classes to lump together, render invalid, and distance themselves
from the tastes, interests, and activities of lower and generally working (increasingly proletarian) classes.[28] "Mob" and "mass" surely
have a similar rhetorical history in the United States, a history that
we might see, for example, in the late eighteenth century, with
Thomas Jefferson's famous expression of distaste for the unedu-
cated, impoverished, and disindividuated laborers in urban workshops and factories: "The mobs of great cities add just so much to
the support of pure government, as sores do to the strength of the
human body."[29]

But Hawthorne's use of "mob" only begins to suggest the extent
to which he obliquely invokes the working class, and particularly
the routinized work of industrial mass production, to describe his

"scribbling women." Hawthorne's anonymous mob of novelists—
and critics have never been entirely certain as to which individuals he meant to include—produces nearly interchangeable manuscripts, one "neither better nor worse" than another, and these
manuscripts, in turn, are produced and sold by the 100,000 in "innumerable editions." Origination, to the extent that Hawthorne acknowledges it, is merely unskilled scribbling. The production Hawthorne complains of in this passage is almost infinite reproduction,
yet he grossly exaggerates the scale on which such reproduction
actually occurred. While it is true that the bestseller emerged on an
unprecedented scale in the 1850s, by 1855, the year of Hawthorne's
letter, only one novel had sold more than 100,000 copies, and it
was *Uncle Tom's Cabin*, not *The Lamplighter*. Furthermore, Hawthorne not only obscured the fact of writing behind a hyperbolic
vision of the text's reproduction, he also ignored the individualizing
fame that accompanied commercial success. Hawthorne may have
been unwilling or unable to name the women he condemns, but personal appearances, biographical details, lucrative publishing contracts and, perhaps most crucially of all, the names of best-selling
authors served to identify and market the individual bestsellers and
the writers of them.[30]

If I am reading Hawthorne's letter at all faithfully, one of its main
rhetorical thrusts works to collapse the actual writing, the actual
origination of domestic fiction into that fiction's reproduction. It is
as if, for Hawthorne, no such thing as an original, a manuscript,
exists, only an endless stream of uniformly produced products. To
say that this critique is grounded in an opposition between the idea
of the individuated artist and the process of mass production is,
perhaps, to say the obvious. What is necessary to observe, however, is that the analogy between domestic literary and industrial
work can be formed at a rhetorical level almost wholly apart from
the observable, historical conditions of domestic authorship. That
is to say, Hawthorne's comments carry force not because they describe the realities of literary production in the domestic sphere,
but because they borrow from and perpetuate freighted analogies
available to him within the industrializing society.[31] They are an at-

tempt to deploy paradigmatic or discursive constructions of industrial labor specifically to define the non-industrial work of women writers. They suggest the creation and deployment of a cultural paradigm to define and create a social reality, even though that observed social reality might be inconsistent with this particular representation of it.

Such paradigms, such discursive understandings, we have become increasingly aware, function through assertions of difference and distinction from a presumed norm, an always assumed and already privileged standard of comparison or judgment. It is, accordingly, through such discursive constructions that privileged, normative, and moral standards assert themselves while other behaviors and values are established as deviant, threatening, or valueless in relation to them.[32]

What makes Hawthorne's letter so interesting as I understand it is that we have for so long and so insistently misunderstood gender to be the only important category of difference in it. We need to realize, however, that Hawthorne, when it comes to creating standards for authorial work, figures gender difference through an implicit class difference and vice versa. In fact, for Hawthorne to condemn women writers, it almost seems absolutely necessary for him to think of them simultaneously as not middle class, as mass producers, as operatives in a fiction factory. In this sense, this figuration demonstrates clearly to us that antebellum authorship, even in its gendered tensions, needs to be thought of in relation to class position. The power of Hawthorne's condemnation rests exactly on its ability to interlock and intertwine the idea of women's writing with industrial production.

To say, however, that Hawthorne speaks here of a definition of authorial worth that operates simultaneously in class and gendered terms might only be to beg a further question. Why should Hawthorne organize a model of distasteful writing exactly along these lines? Why would this peculiar and by no means imperative interlocking appear to be so necessary, obvious, and opportune to Hawthorne? What did it mean to unite femininity and industrial labor?

If, as I have said, industrial enterprises increasingly incorporated craftsmen into processes of large-scale production, Hawthorne's letter demonstrates his sensitivity to the significance of women's absorption into industry. As both operatives and outworkers sewing in their own homes, women served increasingly during the antebellum years as an important pool of labor for industries from textile production to shoemaking. This inclusion of women in industry featured its own set of cultural tensions and anxieties that Hawthorne exploits.

One central oddity in antebellum industrial labor was the extent to which operatives and owners struggled to preserve already established gender roles within the industrial process. Mary Blewett, for example, tells us that well into the 1860s, women in the shoemaking industry had clearly defined work that kept them firmly dependent on more skilled male workers. In fact, in an extraordinary continuation of gender conventions, women's specialized work of "shoebinding" was extremely slow to enter the factory or workshop at all. Rather, it continued to be performed as outwork, not just in the home but very specifically in the kitchen. Furthermore, working in a kind of sidesaddle fashion, the woman "did not straddle a shoemaker's bench. She used a new tool, the shoe clamp, which rested on the floor and accommodated her long skirt and apron while providing a flexible wooden holder for leather pieces." [33]

Sidesaddle shoebinding in the kitchen for large industrial enterprises stands as a relatively minor and highly specified example of a broader point about women's industrial work: the movement of women into antebellum industry remained palatable only as long as women's labor invoked established norms of gendered behavior. The example of shoebinding, in other words, ought to illustrate the implicit tensions between femininity and industrial labor; it ought to make clear that a working-class identity, should it fail to be structured in just the right way, always threatened a feminine one.

The textile mills in Lowell, Massachusetts, awaken us to this awkwardness on a considerably larger scale, and they begin to suggest how the literary might be deployed to overcome the tensions between industrial work and femininity that I have described. In order to attract and retain their workforce, the owners of the Lowell mills, the Boston Associates, made a concentrated effort to present Lowell less as an industrial-capitalist enterprise of mass production and profitability and more as a sort of home-away-from-home for their female employees. The Boston Associates and those supporting them insistently declared that the operatives in their factories would be protected by benevolent paternalism, and in the 1830s and 1840s they built boarding houses, instituted strong moral codes for behavior in and out of work, and sponsored various social and cultural activities for their workforce.[34] The *Lowell Offering*, a literary magazine written wholly by factory operatives but influenced and financed by the Boston Associates, repeatedly represented work in the mills as an opportunity for young rural women to make some money that they might bring home to help support their families while experiencing guarded freedom in their early adulthood.[35]

From 1840 to 1845, then, the *Offering* broadcasted for the most part the vision of an idyllic and independent life of the "factory girl," carefully constrained by the familial and paternalistic boundaries of benevolent corporate concern. Operatives filled the earliest numbers of the magazine with stories, poems, and autobiographical accounts of young women who arrived at Lowell, became highly cultured through corporately sponsored events, earned money, and yet retained their sense of a daughter's filial duty. Sarah Bagley, in "The Pleasures of Factory Life," assured the *Offering*'s readers that the factory girls were "not without a guardian."

> We are placed in the care of overseers who feel under moral obligation to look after our interests; and, if we are sick, to acquaint themselves with our situation and wants. . . . In Lowell, we enjoy abundant means of information, especially in the way of public lectures. The time of lecturing is appointed to suit the convenience of the operatives; and sad indeed would be the picture of our Lyceums, Institutes, and scientific Lecture rooms, if all the operatives should absent themselves.
>
> And last, though not least, is the pleasure of being associated with the institutions of religion, and thereby availing ourselves of the Library, Bible Class, Sabbath School, and all other means of religious instruction. Most of us, when at home, live in the country, and therefore cannot enjoy these privileges to the same extent; and many of us not at all.[36]

In Bagley's 1840 article, the Lowell mills offer more of home than home itself could provide, and the article is obviously written to characterize the mills in these terms. To leave the countryside for the factory is not to change radically the gendered conventions of behavior, it is to live them in some sense more fully than they could be lived at home even as home itself stays actively on the mind. Bagley's column stands as one among many in the *Offering* that manages at once to insist on the comparability between the mill town and the home left behind while implicitly asserting continued dedication to the original household and its conventions.

Harriet Farley's series, "Letters From Susan," for example, tells the story of a woman who feared "coldness, or at least entire indifference, in this city" only to discover that her landlady, Mrs. C., an employee of the mills, watches over her carefully in place of her parents, introducing Susan to other respectable and friendly "factory girls." This series of letters, not only in its content, but in its very epistolary form, negotiates delicately the ambivalences produced by leaving home, finding an appropriate substitute for home, and insisting on the persistent, continuous connection to home through the written words of the letters.[37]

What the Boston Associates and the *Offering* almost never openly mentioned, however, were the actual details of the often grueling labor at Lowell or the increased independence from family that seems in reality to have motivated so many of the operatives to migrate in the first place. Thomas Dublin's detailed social history demonstrates that elaborate networks of familial attachment did ease "the shock of adjustment both to work in the factories and to the novel urban setting."[38] Letters to and visits from home maintained the bonds between the women workers and the home they left behind. But Dublin also argues that the women who went to the mills removed themselves from the family as they gained an increasing economic freedom. Moreover, the private correspondence of Lowell operatives frequently indicates this growing independence. Sarah Hodgdon, for example, received this message in a letter from her sister Elizabeth: "You say you want to come home when we all think you have staid long enough, but we do not know better than you or so well either when you have earned as much as you will want to spend."[39] This suggestion that the mill worker herself is working for economic independence and might be the best judge of when she has obtained it suggests that the ties between home and work were strained by a practical self-sufficiency.

In addition, published writing by the operatives in other magazines often attacked the *Offering* and the notion of the woman worker's subordination to family and corporate paternalism. So, while the *Offering* might have insisted in its best sentimental and domesticated voice that "Woman must be the mother and that fount of 'deep, strong, deathless love,'" the *Voice of Industry*, a radical labor magazine also written by operatives, sounded considerably different: "[Women] have at last learnt the lesson that a bitter experience teaches, that not to those who style themselves their 'natural protectors' are they to look for needful help [in improving the conditions of labor], but to the strong and resolute of their own sex."[40]

During the years of the *Offering*'s publication, operatives typically worked twelve-hour days, six days a week, of increasingly routinized and disciplined drudgery, frequently with some displeasure, and often with the goal of leaving rather than supporting family. The *Lowell Offering*, though, sought to preserve the rhetorical or very partial reality in which operatives remained traditional family workers with idealized moral strictures placed upon them, even as these workers became increasingly proletarianized.

These stresses between the labor of life at Lowell and the *Offering*'s attempt to create an alternative to it finally erupted into direct, printed conflict in 1845. Toward the end of the *Offering*'s run, even this journal found it increasingly difficult to represent factory life as family life and, as Herbert Gutman claims, "Even the *Lowell Offering* testified [though I would say only occasionally] to the tensions between mill routines and rural rhythms and feelings." One writer, for example, complained that the noise of the mill rang in her head even after her shift, adding ambivalently that "now I do not mind it at all. You know that people learn to sleep with the thunder of Niagara in their ears and the cotton mill is no worse."[41]

The *Offering*'s strain in maintaining its vision of factory life finally led to rupture over the workers' movement throughout the 1840s to limit the work day to ten hours. Originally, the *Offering* had declared editorially, "With wages, board, &c, we have nothing to do," but by 1845 Harriet Farley editorialized in support of the ten-hour movement.[42] In the same year, Sarah Bagley, at one time the author of the *Offering* essay, "The Pleasures of Factory Life," publicly accused the magazine of refusing to publish articles on the actual conditions of labor at Lowell. The *Offering*, said Bagley, was "controlled by corporation influences."[43] In 1845, in a telling change of rhetorical emphasis, the *Offering* ceased publication and the primary organ for the operatives' writing became the labor-oriented *Voice of Industry*.

In one sense, the history of the *Offering* is a history of the magazine's hotly contested political stances on the place of women in industry. Viewed from this perspective, the contents of the magazine alone suggest its ideological value and mission: present the Lowell mills as an agreeable place consistent with the culture of domesticity under the supervision of a paternal corporate order. Indeed, once this purpose became untenable, once Farley herself was editorializing on behalf of the operatives' interests at the expense of the Associates, the *Offering* quickly went out of print.

From a slightly different vantage point, however, the *Offering* alerts us to and embodies a peculiarly important effort to demonstrate the possibility of women's simultaneous involvement in and establishment of identity through two apparently discrete social activities: writing and industrial labor. The numerous improvement circles, moral regulations, and literary groups fostered by the Boston Associates made plain that these workers' identities were to be found as much in the sphere of cultural achievement as they were in the sphere of material production for an anonymous corporate entity. The *Offering*, in short, by establishing its contributors as capable of producing domestic and sentimental writing located these contributors outside the realm of the lower and working class. This representation of the *Offering*'s staff (and by extension of the "mill girls" for whom they supposedly spoke) was effective because these two identities—female factory operative and author of the sentimental—were, as I have pointed out, in deep cultural and economic conflict. To manifest the operatives as writers, in short, was to insist upon their identity as something other than degraded operatives.[44]

Nathaniel Hawthorne, of course, makes no direct reference to the work at Lowell or its representation in the *Offering*, but we can see in his rhetoric a complete reversal of the Boston Associates' strategy for making women's industrial work palatable and even familiar. The Boston Associates sought to quell the cultural anxieties about the movement of young women into the industrial workplace by obscuring their work of disindividuated mass production, by presenting the mill workers as having the more acceptable and still personalized feminine interests of their family and cultural activities very prominently in mind. Hawthorne, by contrast, takes what had become by the mid-nineteenth century one of the few marginally acceptable modes of middle-class female labor—domestic or sentimental authorship—and turns it into an industrial enterprise, the type of depersonalized and proletarian labor that the Boston Associates sought to obscure. In the end, one could say that the Boston Associates and Hawthorne both understand the necessary antagonism between industrial labor and literary work, only they deploy these understandings very differently. In one case, the Associates want to bring the literary into the factory where it may not "naturally" belong. In the other case, Hawthorne wants to bring the factory into the literary, where it also does not "naturally" belong.

Hawthorne's entangling of the domestic work of best-selling female authorship with industrial labor is thus effective not only in its invocation of a deskilled laboring class. Rather, it is also decisively damning to the extent that it reconfigures the domestic construction of female authorship to render this work akin to the labor that brought many women into the industrial workplace and took them away from more traditional concerns in the home. It undermines, in other words, the associations with domesticity that made female authorship not only acceptable but successful in antebellum America, substituting instead the vision of women working in mass production that the culture at large and the Boston Associates in particular attempted to suppress.

Hawthorne's Decorative Work

I have been trying to suggest that the "mob of scribbling women" integrates for Hawthorne the commercial success of women in the literary market with industrial production, that it equates women's authorship with the unskilled, routinized, and "unfeminine" work of the factory. Hawthorne, however, did not see his own work in this way, and his fiction makes that fairly clear. If Hawthorne identified commercial success with industrial labor, his stories also persistently identified artistry with the skills needed in residual modes of craft production.

Hawthorne's fiction includes at least three major characters whose artisanal work becomes intertwined with artistry: Hester Prynne in *The Scarlet Letter*, Owen Warland in "The Artist of the Beautiful," and Drowne in "Drowne's Wooden Image." Each of these characters is a different kind of craft laborer: Hester sews, Warland makes watches, and Drowne carves figureheads. At the same time, each of them produces one work that crosses from the realm of the artisanal into the realm of the artistic: Hester sews her extraordinary "A," Warland builds his mechanical butterfly, and Drowne carves one exceptional sculpture.

A repeated logic, language, and representation of craftwork that slides toward art in isolated circumstances penetrates all of these self-referential fictions. In *The Scarlet Letter*, for example, we read of Hester's gifts as a seamstress. Hester sews "deep ruffs, painfully wrought bands, and gorgeously embroidered gloves." Her "handiwork" becomes "what would now be termed the fashion."[45] When Hawthorne speaks of Hester's sewing for the community we find words such as "fashion," "handiwork," "labor," and even "toil." She performs this work for "emolument" or a "subsistence" (82–83). But when Hawthorne describes Hester's "A," his vocabulary changes. The "A" makes manifest the privileged and heightened sensibility of the artist, Hester's gifts as an isolated seer: "Walking to and fro, with those lonely footsteps, in the little world with which she was outwardly connected . . . she felt or fancied that the scarlet letter had endowed her with a new sense" (86). If Hester is a gifted artisan when she sews for others, she has the artist's privileged and exclusive sensibility when she sews her "A."

"Drowne's Wooden Image" and "The Artist of the Beautiful" are preoccupied with exactly the same sorts of distinctions. Robert Danforth, the blacksmith of "Artist," is a hybrid of the deskilled industrial worker and a kind of supercraftsman. Danforth pounds metal with a mindless, brutal, and repetitive hammering. Owen Warland is never an embodiment of mechanical necessity, but before he makes his butterfly, Warland's work is only frivolous craft production. Warland makes "pretty shapes in wood, principally figures of flowers and birds."[46] Hawthorne distinguishes this labor from the moment, the singular achievement, that transforms craft into art. Hawthorne surrounds Warland's butterfly with words such as "ethereal," "higher sphere," "immortal," and upon its completion describes Warland as "the artist [rising] high enough to achieve the beautiful" (474–75). In "Drowne's Wooden Image," the familiar pattern recurs. Drowne begins by making figureheads that are "manufacture[d]." His work is "skillful" or "distinguished" (307–308). By the end of the story Drowne has carved a single figurehead that might be called a "masterpiece," or a "vision matchlessly embodied." It is "the very spirit of genius" (313–14).

I want to emphasize not only the difference between the work that Hawthorne describes through a vocabulary of craftwork and the work that he insists is artistic, but also the continuities between craft and art within this imagistic pattern. The point, in other words, may not be that craft is radically and completely discrete from art in Hawthorne's writing, but that his craftworkers do very much the same sort of skilled manual labor in both cases, even as that labor comes to resonate with very different sorts of meanings. Whether Hester sews her "A" as a gesture of inspired defiance or sews ruffles for the guardians of the Puritan state, she still sews. Whether Owen Warland tinkers with watches or tinkers with butterflies, he performs the same sort of work of manipulating mechanical miniatures. When Drowne carves figureheads and when he carves "sculpture," he is still carving.

Critics typically understand these figurations as tending almost uniformly to emphasize a decisive disjunction between craft and art grounded in a mystical and mystified notion of inspiration. Nicholas Bromell, for example, argues that these stories demonstrate the tension between the manual (craft) and the mental (art) operative in the antebellum years. In his reading, the heterosexual desire for women's bodies inspires Warland and Drowne to move from craft to art. Warland is driven by his bodily "desire for the lovely Annie Hovendon." Drowne attains the stature of the artist when "an aristocratic lady of rank" for whom he yearns models for him.[47]

Bromell reads wonderfully the paradoxes and tensions of an artistic (mental) labor that grounds itself in intensely physical, bodily longings, but he fails to acknowledge the extent to which a specific form of physical labor itself—not just sexual longing—penetrates Hawthorne's representation of artistic endeavor. These stories show us not only that artistic work can be distinguished from craftwork by its intangible, immaterial, inspired, or intellectual qualities; they also show us that craftwork consistently veers toward the artistic. This may be particularly evident insofar as none of these craftworkers, even in their less inspired moments, ever undertakes the sort of labor that might be conventionally distinguished from the artistic by virtue of its utility. At the very least, they are all workers in what we might now call "decorative arts."

If we approach this persistent habit of craft labor's to trend toward the artistic in historical terms, as part of Hawthorne's attempt to position and reconstruct his authorship relative to industrial work, the continuities between craft and artistic work become as important as the disjunctions. We know that industrial labor became culturally available at this moment as a representation of unskilled and routinized work partly because it began to displace artisanal modes of skilled production. This should not be taken to mean, however, that all forms of artisanal labor ceased to exist. One reason for what Sean Wilentz calls "the persistence of tradition" in craftwork was that industrialization was uneven, conquering some areas of production before others.[48]

A more important reason for craft's persistence in the case of Hawthorne, however, is that artisanal labors displaced by industrial production could and did begin to resituate their place in the expanding market. Craft production may have been bastardized during the antebellum period by industrialization, but it also redirected itself in many cases toward the exclusive production of luxury and ornamental rather than primarily utilitarian commodities. My point is not that ornamental crafts were nonexistent before industrial production, but only that industrial production rendered many modes of craftwork obsolete as utilitarian occupations. Rather than standing as a primary or dominant mode of utilitarian production, craftwork was resituated as a residual and lingering mode of nearly aesthetic work.[49]

How does Hawthorne capitalize upon this reconception of craft labor in order to construct a different place and nature for his authorial work than the one he carved out for the work of the "scribbling women"? One has only to consider collectively his artisan-as-artist figures. Drowne works on figureheads, and when it comes to producing fairly routine products that share a "family likeness," Drowne has a peculiar gift for success and a reasonable degree of skill (308). This rather routine production is not, of course, industrial labor, but it is a whole different kind of craftwork than the sculpting of the one truly beautiful figure that he creates. Not coincidentally, the artistic figurehead takes considerably more time, is the only one readily distinguishable from his others and, perhaps most significantly, it is the only figure for which Drowne rejects the hundreds of dollars that he might receive. Hester Prynne similarly produces any number of highly skilled and marketable nonutilitarian items through her sewing and embroidery, but the "A" is the one that truly stands out as artistic and it is, again, the only one that is emphatically not for sale. Finally, Owen Warland makes watches, beautiful ones of "pinchbeck, silver, and one or two of gold" (447), but none of them seems to work. They do, in fact, according to the man Warland served as an apprentice, "derange the whole course of time" (448). The purpose of Warland's watchmaking, like Drowne's carving and Hester's sewing, is not utilitarian but ornamental. All the same, his craft does not fully achieve artistic status until he turns to the mechanical butterfly, a work wholly apart from any possibility of bringing him profit.

We can see first and foremost that Hawthorne's consciousness of craft is post-industrial, that he has recognized or absorbed the idea of craftwork as a residual and ornamental as much as a utilitarian labor. We might then say that Hawthorne recognizes that the marketability of craftwork is based upon its residual and luxury status in the industrial marketplace. But, as the figures just discussed also make clear, it is not, in Hawthorne's logic, simply the cultural relocation of craftwork to the ornamental that moves such work into the realm of the artistic. For artistry becomes entangled with ornamentally motivated artisanal work only in isolated instances.

The situation is extremely complicated. By articulating the transition from craft to art in Hester's "A," Drowne's one sculpture, and Warland's butterfly, Hawthorne imagines artistic work (and by implication his own authorship) as entangled with the artisanal only when the artisanal removes itself from the possibility of success (or even sale) in the market. Artisanal labor, to the extent that it survived, did resist the disindividuation, mechanized production, and economies of scale that Hawthorne invoked to dismiss the mob of scribbling women. Artisanal labor did not, however, fully separate itself from the market. Rather, it resituated itself in nonutilitarian terms. What we see in Hawthorne's invocation of the artisan-as-artist, however, is not only the revaluation of craft goods in an industrializing market. It is, rather, the invention of an idealized mode of production in which artisanal market-oriented concerns utterly vanish in the name of art. The artisanal becomes artistic not by virtue of its actual evolution in the market toward ornamentation but, as Hawthorne somewhat differently imagines it, by virtue of its complete rejection of market value.

The group of figurations I have been discussing has at its heart not only the working out of a synonymy between industrialization and commercialization but the thorough separation of true art from any sort of market-determined valuation. Yet these antimarket figurations obscure as much as they enlighten. They are self-idealizations more than reflections of any reality, because "artistic" authorship generally has a market or commercial life of its own. Hawthorne was constantly both involved in and retreating from his own promotion, a marketing campaign that presented him very much as the antimarket artist. Richard Brodhead describes in detail Hawthorne's ambivalence about the market, and the way that his publisher, James Fields, used that ambivalence to promote him as a man of artistic rather than commercial ambitions. Fields, for example, published the tale of how he had been compelled to rip the manuscript of *The Scarlet Letter* from the hands of the uncertain and reticent genius in order to bring it into print.[50] Furthermore, as James Wallace has argued, the extent to which Hawthorne expressed distaste for the scribbling women might very easily be seen as the extent to which he was ambivalent about the commercialization and publicity emerging in his own authorial career. Wallace claims convincingly, for example, that the immodesty, the marketing of cheap emotions, that Hawthorne despised in his "scribbling women," he also feared and loathed (but recognized) in his own work and life.[51] By the time of his infamous gripe, Hawthorne was a fairly well-known writer—though, as I have been at pains to make clear, well-known on *artistic* rather than enormously popular terms. Furthermore, he remained throughout his career notoriously jealous of his privacy, even as Fields more and more publicly marketed his shyness. The extent to which Hawthorne could distinguish himself from the "scribbling women" through metaphors such as those I have discussed above, is, finally, the extent to which he could also distance himself from what he might not have liked about his own market life.

For Hawthorne at a purely personal level, the pushing to polarities of market-oriented (industrial) and artistic (artisanal) literary production clearly served a compensatory function that allowed him to construct or imagine an idealized version of his own literary career along several axes of difference from the popular female writers of the 1850s. Hawthorne's figurations, however, are not only personal. They also participate in a cultural effort to resolve insecurities about the whole matrix of social change and alienation that accompanied industrialization and literary commercialization. Hawthorne embraced industrial labor as a figure for supposedly degraded female authorship, because such work had been made culturally available to him as a degenerate form of craft production and as a threat to women's established domestic and familial roles. At the same time, he embraced artisanal work as potentially close to the artistic, because such work could be newly imagined in terms of its capacity to survive many of the restructurings of labor that accompanied industrialization or, shifted slightly but meaningfully, that accompanied the restructurings of literary commercialization.

Melville's Self-Imaginings

I have been arguing that Hawthorne's envy of or distaste for the professional success of the domestic authors as well as his broader absorption and deployment of cultural anxieties about industrial labor and womanhood informed certain of his figurations of authorship and artistry. Hawthorne built and absorbed his idea of authorship through constructions of difference that aligned, on the one hand, the working class, the commercial, and women's writing and, on the other hand, the artisanal artist, the noncommercial, and his own writing. This particular alignment of forces was not, however, unique to Hawthorne. Herman Melville also formed his authorial identity partly through an opposition to women's writing grounded in the figuration of class and gender difference, particularly in "The Paradise of Bachelors and the Tartarus of Maids." This diptych portraying gentlemanly bachelors indulging in leisurely camaraderie in one half and pale, ghostlike women churning out mass-produced paper by the ream in the other obviously contains an attack on the degradation of the industrial worker strongly focused on that worker's, particularly the female operative's, mechanization and exploitation. We might thus say, as we did for Hawthorne, that the widespread cultural reaction against the displacement of preindustrial markets and modes of work is one inspiration for Melville's story, but to do so will not explain his particular mediations. Why, one wants to ask, does Melville particularly use a female workforce to raise his objections and why does he situate these workers very specifically in a paper mill?

At some level, the answer to these questions is biographically obvious: Melville visited a paper mill only a few years before writing his story, and his journals and letters show that the mill (like his visit to the Temple in London) left some impression upon him.[52] Further-more, as Elizabeth Renker has recently argued, Melville may, in his "maids," have been working through a psychologically deep-seated hostility toward the women upon whom the production of his writ-ing and his domestic unhappiness depended. By the mid-1850s Mel-ville approached functional blindness, could no longer see clearly enough to write his own words, and relied upon his wife to tran-scribe them. Renker suggests that Melville profoundly resented this dependency in both his writing and his everyday life, and she details his hostility toward his family, going so far as to suggest (without really proving) that Melville routinely beat his wife.[53]

One can have little doubt about Melville's rancorous familial re-lations, but neither the biographical detail of his visit to a paper mill nor the possibility that he beat his wife can account for what we find in "Tartarus." Nor will it be adequate to understand the story wholly as Michael Rogin does, as Melville's impassioned as-sault on emerging industrial capitalism, its gendered separation of labor, and its system of class domination. Rogin is surely right to say that "Tartarus" calls into question and implicitly satirizes the idyllic innocence, paternalism, and sentimentalization of women's factory work that we have seen in the *Lowell Offering*, but "Para-dise" and "Tartarus" are not purely anti-industrial rants any more than they are rants purely against the women in Melville's family and against his dependency on them.[54]

Melville addresses the intersection of gender and class difference in this diptych, but does so not primarily, to use Philip Young's strong phrasing, to express a "curse on the enslavement of females to mills . . . a social consciousness [that] Melville never for a moment reveals in the story." Rather, Melville, as Young goes on to imply, is most concerned about the conditions of his professional life and the interference created by the demands of his family and his own biology. "Tartarus" is, in Young's words, "a revelation of the depth and passion of the author's frustration . . . [with] the 'metallic necessity' that governs reproduction of the species." According to Young, "Tartarus" dwells figuratively on Melville's frustration with his own sexual urges and the consequences of them—his wife's pregnancies and his children—which interfere with his complete and utter ambition to write. For Young, "Tartarus" makes unavoidable metaphorical reference to the conditions of Melville's authorial practice and the painful interference with it brought on by his intransigent sexual needs and their biological consequences.[55]

Young turns us in the right direction, though he overstates the case against Melville's political consciousness when he suggests that "Tartarus" "never for a moment" reveals a distaste for the industrialization of female labor. Such social concerns need not preempt the provocative insight that this diptych is also about the work and conditions of writing. "Paradise" and "Tartarus" do ruminate on authorship, but these ruminations are more complicated and less purely autobiographical than Young (or Renker) suggests, even as they are also less politically abstract than critics such as Rogin tend to suppose.

"Paradise" and "Tartarus" present two models of authorial labor that depend on intersections of class-based labor and gender distinctions. On the one hand, as we shall see, the bachelors suggest a literary model based on genteel male camaraderie; on the other hand, the "maids" emphasize a new facet of the now familiar intersection of industrial work and women's writing. In the end, Melville rejects both of these models as unsatisfactory.

By the time Melville wrote "The Paradise of Bachelors and the Tartarus of Maids" in 1855, twelve years after the publication of his first novel, *Typee*, his literary self-identity had already undergone a meaningful transformation. I have already mentioned that by the time of *Pierre* (1852) Melville had built his authorial sense of self partly upon his rejection of and difference from sentimental writing. Myra Jehlen has suggested that by the 1850s Melville "assumed himself as a writer" in a fully artistic and individualized sense, an assumption of self that domestic novelists did not and may not have wanted to make. Susan Coultrap-McQuin's work on the careers of women writers buttresses Jehlen's point. Coultrap-McQuin makes plain that the writers she studies were concerned to "integrate their female values and behaviors into the pursuit of their literary careers." These women sought out "genteel publishers" with whom they could maintain relations grounded in "familial spirit" and often "paternalistic relations." [56]

As Herman Melville's biographers recognize, he underwent a dramatic shift away from any model of gentility, paternalism, or even reasonably polite sociability between 1848 and 1852. The author of *Typee* and *Omoo* (Melville's first novels) devoted himself to popularity, to writing adventure novels that he hoped would suit the public taste. For Melville, to be an author was, originally, to write, to publish, and, most importantly, to sell books. The early Melville is, to use the writer's own words, "calculated for popular reading, or for none at all." [57] In the labored composition and belabored philosophizing of *Mardi*, however, Melville, in his own words, "began to feel an incurable distaste" for this earlier self-conception; he began to push it aside, and to focus his energies on literary immortality. No writer is more motivated by a self-conscious ambition for greatness than Melville in the early 1850s. By the time Melville takes up his almost obsessional and exhausting work on *Moby-Dick*, the common readers whom he had once calculated to please have become his enemy, a malignant public hostile to him. Writing to R. H. Dana, he claimed to reject the value of "acres & square miles of the superficial shallow praise of the publishing critics." [58]

Melville's antimarket posture, however, was cut through by an anger and outrage that the market would not accept him on his own, newly discovered terms. In other words, if Melville rejected the market, it must also be noted that the market rejected Melville, and his bitterness about that is not even disguised. In numerous letters to Hawthorne from this period, Melville's antagonistic feelings toward the tastes of the public shine through: "What I feel most moved to write, that is banned, — it will not pay. Yet altogether write the *other* way I cannot. So the product is a final hash, and all my books are botches."[59]

Melville must have meant several things at this point in his career when he spoke of writing "the *other* way." His new literary posture was predicated upon the rejection of the older, cheerful, adventure novels in his literary past, but it was also, as he imagined it, very specifically predicated upon the rejection of the sentimentality and femininity of the literary women who came to dominate the marketplace of the 1850s. Melville imagined himself competing for space in the market with and losing badly to what he thought of as other, mawkish, "feminine" fiction. His recognition of commercial defeat and the simultaneous claim to an individual and artistic superiority imagined in gendered terms becomes clear in a letter to Sarah Morewood, a friend of the Melvilles in the Berkshires:

Concerning my own forthcoming book [*Moby-Dick*] . . . don't you buy it — don't you read it . . . because it is by no means the sort of book for you. It is not a piece of fine feminine Spital fields silk — but is of the horrible texture of a fabric that should be woven of ships' cables and hausers. A Polar wind blows through it, & birds of prey hover over it. Warn all gentle fastidious people from so much as peeping into the book — on risk of a lumbago & sciatics.[60]

In this paragraph Melville understands himself and his work as strongly, even dangerously, individuated. He sees what the blind eyes of a conspicuously feminized reading public cannot. Melville now writes to share intimate connections with individually intelligent and sympathetic readers such as R. H. Dana and Nathaniel Hawthorne, but has lost interest in the public taste. Furthermore, Melville's separation from the public is achieved through images of exaggerated masculinization. His writing resembles "ships' cables and hausers"; it is opposed to finely spun and feminine "Spital fields silk."

In constructing a radically independent and individualized sense of himself, Melville paradoxically relied on his literary and more broadly cultural surroundings. He persistently invoked an array of cultural understandings of masculinized individuality to separate himself from that culture. To catalogue in detail all of the resources on which Melville drew to construct his newly independent, masculine authorial self would be a book unto itself. Wai-chee Dimock, for example, has pointed out that Melville's fascination with his own individuality is "informed by a tradition of property rights" stemming from John Locke and the idealization of possessive individualism. Quentin Anderson has argued that "flight from [shared] culture, from the institutions . . . of associated life" is the quintessential expression of an American "imperial self." More recently, David Leverenz has detailed the culturally ingrained fears of commercial and sexual inadequacies on which Melville's masculine self-understanding is conspicuously based.[61]

What interests me here, however, is not so much that Melville created the sense of his own strongly independent authorial labor through various forms of positive identification with particular cultural traditions. Rather, I want to insist that Melville's conception of a radically independent authorship depended not only on the acceptance of shared values, but also upon the rejection of other modes of authorship that he experimented with in his career and saw operative around him: the more or less cheerful and amusing writing of the *Typee* period and the sentimentality that he could not achieve as anything but a parody in *Pierre*. In "The Paradise of Bachelors and the Tartarus of Maids," Melville's rejections of both literary gentility and literary domesticity become ways of asserting his authorial identity through a discourse of difference as much as identification.

Like Hawthorne, Melville identifies women's authorship with industrial production but, unlike Hawthorne, Melville finds himself unable to recover a mode of labor adequate to represent his idealized authorial role. Part of the grimness in this diptych lies in the hopelessness for Melville of discovering appropriate authorial analogues, in his inability to imagine an ideal authorial mode in 1855. "Paradise" and "Tartarus" present the story of a dual rejection of authorship figured through class and gender-specific metaphors. And after rejecting the bachelors and rejecting the maids, the only mode of authorship imaginable to Melville is grounded in the act of rejection and renunciation, in the act of positioning himself as outside the arrangements that both halves of his story represent.

Genteel Bachelors

"Paradise" and "Tartarus" tell the stories of agreeable bachelors and dehumanized, female industrial operatives, and any reading that fails to recognize the pleasure of the lawyers at Temple Bar and Melville's sympathy for the laborers in the paper mill cannot be taken terribly seriously. At the same time, both of these stories obliquely call up with some distaste particular models of literariness. In "Paradise," genteel literary dabbling is heavily ironized. In "Tartarus," as we shall see, the maids of Melville's mill are not only pathetically dehumanized factory workers, they are also the disindividuated mass producers of quasi-literary texts.

We already know that by the mid-nineteenth century the model of elitist and avocational literariness was increasingly displaced by more popular and professionalized modes. At the same time, of course, such class-bound constructions of the literary did not simply vanish. Rather, they, like craft labor after its displacement as a dominant mode of production, remained residual in resituated forms. Hawthorne signified his sensitivity not only to the shifting meanings of craft labor and its potential for helping to fix the meaning of authorial work, he also provided one of the great antebellum figures of the displaced but enduring genteel writer. In Miles Coverdale, Hawthorne develops the character of a writer who no longer writes, a paralyzed minor poet with authorial ambitions most conspicuous for their outdatedness. From the very beginning of *Blithedale*, Coverdale greets us as a poet working in archaic forms. He never understands writing (or any other occupation) as the means to a livelihood, as the profession it had become. Rather, the literary life forms Coverdale's sense of his own leisure, his ability to separate himself from the necessity of labor or any kind of commercial involvement. For Miles Coverdale, the literary is never financially contingent and his ambition is never to have a mass audience. Rather, the literary signifies erudition and a set of genteel habits.

Herman Melville's bachelors have much in common with Hawthorne's Coverdale, and it may be that Melville had Miles Coverdale in mind when he wrote "Paradise." Indeed, Melville might have seen Coverdale as emblematic of an entire tradition of gentlemanly, anglophile authorship that had Washington Irving at its American fountainhead. Early in Melville's career, Irving had advocated Melville and the publication of *Typee* to his English publisher John Murray but, by 1850, years before he wrote "Paradise," Melville had disavowed any affiliation with Irving and the vision of writing that he embodied. He dismissed his one-time sponsor as merely "popular and amiable." Irving, Melville claimed, owed his reputation to "the studied avoidance of all topics but smooth ones." [62] While Irving surely had a profound sense of his own commercial motivations and the money he might make from writing, he did concentratedly strike the pose of the gentleman dabbler in the literary. Consider, for example, his self-described mode of authorial practice in "The Author's Account of Himself," a kind of introduction to *The Sketch Book of Geoffrey Crayon, gent.*: "I have wandered through different countries, and witnessed many of the scenes of life. I cannot say that I have studied them with the eye of a philosopher; but rather with the sauntering gaze with which humble lovers of the picturesque stroll from the window of one print-shop to another; caught sometimes by the delineation of beauty, sometimes by the distortions of caricature, and sometimes by the loveliness of landscape." Irving, as Crayon the gentleman, goes on to say that he has found himself "disposed to get up a few [literary sketches] for the entertainment of my friends." Even Irving's epigraph for the sketchbook invites comparison to Melville's uncommitted bachelors: "I have no wife nor children to provide for. A mere spectator of other men's fortunes and adventures, and how they play their part; which methinks are diversely presented unto me, as from a common theater or scene." [63]

Melville's bachelors are men of literary sensibilities of the nonconfrontational, dabbling, self-satisfied sort, men who understand literature as an avocation rather than as an aggressive form of self-expression, men who subscribe to Irving's self-presentation. For the bachelors, literature exists more as an artifact marking a social position than as demanding work to be meaningfully undertaken. Melville's bachelors are "men of liberal sense, ripe scholarship in the world, and capacious philosophical and convivial understandings." They "linger in the ancient library . . . turn over pages of the Decameron . . . [and peruse in the British Museum] costly books without a duplicate."[64] They nickname one another Benedick and Socrates. Their temple is the perfect haunt for "a lounging gentleman and bachelor, a quiet unmarried literary man" (319). Dr. Johnson, Charles Lamb, and "hundreds more of sterling spirits" have gathered there (319). Reading, writing, and alluding to literature seem to be almost as common as (if somewhat less conspicuous than) eating at the Temple.

As Perry Miller has described in detail, the publication and popularity of *Typee* in the late 1840s very quickly brought Melville into a rather genteel set of his own, a group of socially distinguished New York literary Democrats that went by the name Young America. Young America was most conspicuously headed by Evert A. Duyckinck, a man who took it as his mission to establish a particularly American high (and marketable) literary culture. Duyckinck surrounded himself with authors and editors whom he thought might help him achieve this end. Duyckinck's conception of literary artistry, however, could not, in the long run, tolerate the extravagances of Melville's work once it turned toward *Moby-Dick*. Duyckinck found *Moby-Dick* the work of a self-indulgent egotist and began to put distance between himself and the author whose entry into the literary world of New York he had once sponsored.[65] A full summary of the convolutions and shifting allegiances within Young America is impossible here, but I want to note with some emphasis that the years between 1850 and 1855, the time of "Paradise"'s publication, saw Melville increasingly becoming a literary outcast. The conviviality of Melville's New York set, even his later-blooming friendship with Hawthorne, had more or less disintegrated.

With this in mind we might understand why Merton Sealts notes that the representation of genial bachelors is a persistent one in Melville's writing, and also that it persistently carries nostalgia for the kind of camaraderie and companionability that Melville frequently touched but never enduringly grasped throughout his literary career. Genial bachelors, Sealts points out, appear in works from *Mardi* to Melville's very late work on the incomplete collection of *Burgundy Club* sketches, and Sealts is convincing in his claims that Melville's darkness and democratic rages generally exist beside a fondness for more or less polite but intimate male companionship.[66]

In "Paradise," I am then suggesting, Melville obliquely and fondly remembers not just his visit to London but his own, less isolated literary past, a past that suggests the literary as a genteel vocation shared by men, even if it has some economic motivation. But if "Paradise" suggests the possibility of a literary geniality and comradeship in both a personal and historical authorial past, we must also note the distaste for "Paradise" implicit in the ironic juxtaposition of "Tartarus." In fact, as Sealts points out, "Paradise" and *The Confidence Man*, published only one year after the diptych, ironize "geniality" and the possibility of true camaraderie more heavily than any other works in Melville's career.[67]

The essential trick or shock in reading "Paradise" is that the bachelors' self-indulgent and elitist activities of all kinds have entirely different meanings before and after one reads the second half of the diptych. For, upon first reading, the Temple seems an entirely pleasant location of more or less innocuous fraternal camaraderie. Many critics have pointed out the intense homosocial bonding of "Paradise" and delight in picking out titillating images of the phallus, the vagina, the anus, and the penetrating of the first into the others. According to Bruce Franklin and Robyn Wiegman, for example, entry into the cloister of the bachelors is described "via the landscape of the male homosexual act." The "deep glen" of the temple is "a symbolic anus" penetrated by the narrator.[68] Wiegman goes on to argue that "Paradise" and "Tartarus" work to expose the class- and gender-based oppressions on which male camaraderie is constructed in an industrial capitalist order.

Wiegman is surely right to say that the diptych exposes a problematic social structure grounded in homo-erotic exclusivity. For, after we see "Tartarus" it becomes impossible to accept joyfully the homosocial and hedonistic pleasures of the genteel bachelors.[69] What Wiegman and other readers of this story miss, however, is what I take to be central: the place of the literary, of "literariness," in defining the bachelors' shared social position. The grounds of their homosocial fraternity lie as much in a shared sense of literary life as they do in the figurative representations of sexual acts: "The thing called pain, the bugbear styled trouble—those two legends seemed preposterous to their bachelor imaginations. How could men of liberal sense, ripe scholarship in the world, and capacious philosophical and convivial understandings—how could they suffer themselves to be imposed upon by such monkish fables?" (322).

I take it that the irony in such a comment about the bachelors in light of the conditions at the Devil's Dungeon mill must be somewhat biting. These quasi- or even pseudo-literary men of "liberal sense," and perhaps even more outrageously of "ripe scholarship in the world" are, in reality, almost stubbornly ignorant of it—not just separate from the pain of Woedolor mountain, but blithely unaware of and completely unsympathetic toward the dehumanizing aspects of industrialization.[70] The point is not just that they are men who consider themselves to be educated even in their ignorance. Nor is the most engaging interpretive point to be made about a supposedly veiled sexuality that one can hardly avoid seeing anyway. Rather, the decisive bonding experience for this fraternity rests in their shared ability to conceive of evil and misfortune as wholly circumscribed by a genteel literary imagination that defines real-life tragedies as frivolous literary forms. "Pain" if it is not a "preposterous legend" can only be conceived of alternatively as a "monkish fable." If we read this passage with a touch of the irony to be instilled by "Tartarus," we begin to see not only an attack on industrialization in its most broadly defined terms, we also see that the model of literary gentility and homosociability emblematizing the lawyers' social status (and Melville's early career) has distasteful implications of elitism, callousness, political unawareness, and self-indulgence, all of which are, I think, at least as central to this shared experience as the suggestions of anal penetration. Perusing the *Decameron*, lingering in "ancient libraries," and nicknaming one another Benedick and Socrates serve at once as bonding experiences and emblems of a shamefully self-absorbed and isolated class solidarity.

The place of literary gentility and companionability within "Paradise" and the resonances of such a model in both Melville's career and the culture at large now begin to emerge. Melville may have been nostalgic for a more comradely literary past, but he was, we can be sure, also embittered by his rejection—by Duyckinck's failure and by the public's failure to understand his prophetic sense of self. The idea of genteelly shared, male authorship had come to seem impossible in the market-driven literary world of the 1850s that had exiled Melville from its community. But this model of the literary must also have seemed frankly undesirable in its intellectual facility and dishonesty, in its political irresponsibility as it is represented in the diptych. In the next year, the extremity of Melville's cynicism about the impossibilities of fraternity and the guise of gentility that masked larger social cruelties would erupt still more violently in *The Confidence Man*. Here literature, intimacy, friendship, and breeding become part of a metaphysical con game in which sincerity is sacrificed utterly to self-interest. In the end, where Nathaniel Hawthorne was able to retrieve an idealized mode of artistry through residual modes of ornamental craft labor, Melville much more bleakly calls up personally and historically residual modes of genteel, masculinized literariness only to find them as distasteful as Hawthorne found commercialized, "feminine" (and implicitly industrialized) modes.[71]

Laboring Maids

This is not to say that the commercial, sentimental, or industrial have any appeal to Melville as an alternative to the Temple. When our bachelor narrator moves from "Paradise" to "Tartarus" the man of leisured letters perusing invaluable manuscripts becomes a businessman concerned with printing "an incredible quantity," "hundreds of thousands," of seed packets. The seed packets, of course, though they are legibly marked, are not literature, and that is the point. In "Tartarus" industrial modes of production and work exclude any notion of genteel or even meaningful literary activity, instead emphasizing alienated and disindividuated mass production by a particularly female and sterile workforce. The envelopes, in fact, are not even printed at the mill. The narrator has come to buy strictly blank paper that will only later, in a different location, be "stamped and superscribed with the nature of the seeds contained" (324).

The industrial process at the Devil's Dungeon mill clearly capitalizes on cultural anxieties about industrial dehumanization at large and, in particular, on the dislocation and dehumanization of women, but more than the fear of domesticity's displacement by factory work penetrates "Tartarus." For Melville, industrial work and machinery clearly increase the capacity for material reproduction but also destroy absolutely the organic, generative power of the women. The great papermaking machine at the mill, in fact, seems itself to perform a kind of birthing, as the paper passes through it and is extruded in a mechanistically precise and telescoped gestation period of nine minutes rather than nine months. The maids of Melville's mill are capable of industrial production but seem divorced from human reproduction. Their bodies have become cogs in the industrial process rather than generative forces in and of themselves: "At rows of blank-looking counters sat rows of blank-looking girls, with blank white folders in their blank hands, all blankly folding blank paper. . . . The girls did not so much seem accessory wheels to the general machinery as mere cogs to the wheels" (328).

To say that "Tartarus" presents us with a dehumanized, sterilized, and frightening version of femininity is not, of course, to say anything terribly insightful or original.[72] One must, however, recognize this depiction to understand fully the complex and even opposing pulls that emerge in this story's alignment of female industrial labor with debased modes of literary activity. On the one hand, Melville is clearly sympathetic toward the operatives, perhaps more in sympathy with these women than with the bachelors of "Paradise." On the other hand, I am suggesting that beneath this pity lies a subtext denying not only in biological but in artistic terms the idea of female originating power. The extent to which Melville imagines these operatives as exploited workers is the extent to which he explicitly and consciously sympathizes with them. The extent to which he associates them with a quasi- or even antiartistic mode of literary endeavor is the extent to which his anxieties about the commercial success of the "scribbling women" informs the particularities of this anti-industrial expression. In other words, when Melville is seen to be writing an anti-industrialization polemic, the operatives in the Devil's Dungeon mill have all of his sympathy. But when we understand that the mill is another site on which class and gender arrangements figure largely as a discussion of the literary, Melville's sympathies become more clouded and complex.

If the seed packets (and the absence of seeds in them) begin to suggest the generative sterility-in-mass-production, the incapacity of those in a female workforce to conceive, the antigenerative quality of this work becomes still more apparent when we consider in greater detail the paper that the mill produces. The mill pours out prodigious quantities of blank paper, but sheets in this mill are strangely perceived as and called "blank" even when they are imprinted. The narrator asks Cupid, his ironically named guide, about the paper: " 'You make only blank paper; no printing of any sort, I suppose? All blank paper don't you?' 'Certainly; what else should a paper factory make?' " (329). Only moments before this question and answer, however, the narrator has told us that some sheets in the factory are not, strictly speaking, blank:

In one corner stood some huge frame of ponderous iron, with a vertical thing like a piston periodically rising and falling upon a heavy wooden block. Before it—its tame minister—stood a girl, feeding the iron animal with half-quires of rose-hued note paper, which at every dab of the piston-like machine, received the impress of a wreath of roses. . . .

Seated before a long apparatus, strung with long slender strings like any harp, another girl was feeding it with foolscap sheets, which, so soon as they curiously traveled from her on the cords, were withdrawn at the opposite end of the machine by a second girl. They came to the first girl blank; they went to the second girl ruled. (328)

The mill makes something other than blank paper, but the power to mark paper is utterly transferred to the phallic piston-pressing machines that are fed by passive women operatives. Again we see a strong figurative denial of the women's active role in any process of individuated origination or willful production, even as the mill produces thousands of stamped sheets. These sheets, to put the matter bluntly, are not "blank" in every sense of the word, but blank only insofar as their markings are part of the industrial process of manufacture. The rose paper is "blank" because all rose paper has mechanistically imprinted roses; ruled paper is "blank" because all of it is uniformly ruled.

Cupid and the narrator define this paper as blank not because it is, not even because the mill does "no printing of any sort," but because, as this story imagines it, blankness can be altered only through specific sorts of printing or inscription. It would seem that sheets are no longer "blank" only when they have been marked by some means discrete from the paper's manufacture, only when the paper becomes primarily an object to be looked at or read rather than one to be written upon or stamped. The women and the factory, quite obviously, do no writing or printing of this particular sort. Rather, "Tartarus" suggests that meaningfully legible texts and acts of writing simply do not or cannot emerge through mechanical production on an industrial scale. If the lawyers occupy themselves with precious manuscripts that have no duplicate, the factory operatives can produce only blank uniformity and empty seed packets, while themselves becoming mechanized ciphers.

Melville imagined a paper mill and a specifically female workforce not because either of these particularities was necessary to a critique of industrial evolution at large or, for that matter, necessary to a generalized critique of gender relations within an industrial capitalist order. But these women engaged in the mass manufacture of illegibly or meaninglessly imprinted paper do have a rather specific reference to Melville's anxiety about female literary capacity and commercial success. He places within the factory a group of female automatons who produce antiliterary paper, marks that need not even be noticed because they are not the right kinds of strongly individuated and individualistic writing that Melville claimed as his own.

What becomes difficult to comprehend in the workings of such a figuration is the extent to which Melville must simultaneously imagine commercially oriented, nonindividualistic female writers as unskilled industrial workers while coming to the verge of feeling some sympathy with the predicament of the domestic authors in the cultural marketplace as they themselves imagined it. For, as I have repeatedly emphasized, Melville did not admire the work of best-selling women authors, and his conception of meaningful literary production is, over and over again, masculinized. But if Melville imagined the women writing in "Tartarus" as industrial operatives, he must simultaneously have imagined them as victimized by the processes of industrial production that he seems more willing to question. In this sense, Melville's understanding of the domestic writers' cultural situation is considerably more complex and ambivalent than the understanding suggested by Hawthorne's "scribbling mob." For, as Melville imagines it, the antiliterary mass production of the paper mill is not simply unskilled and disindividuated, it is unwilled by and thrust upon the operatives (or writers).

This element of victimization, of forced production, was as much a constituent element of middle-class women's literary work as the more familiar domestic values that inform it. In fact, as Mary Kelley and Susan Coultrap-McQuin have made clear, it would be no exaggeration to say that the notion of productive reluctance, of the insistence that writing for commercial success was a kind of forced labor, recurs as a biographical theme in the lives and works of domestic novelists. In *Ruth Hall*, for example, Fanny Fern's highly autobiographical narrator, Ruth, proclaims broadly and universally that "No happy woman ever writes." As Kelley explains, what this really means is "No happy woman ever writes *for a living*." [73] In the world of *Ruth Hall*, the work of writing is work forced upon the mother and wife by the loss of a husband, her abandonment by her own parents, and an economic structure that refuses Ruth the possibility of providing for herself and her children in any other adequately profitable way. "No happy woman ever writes," Ruth says to her daughter, stating purely and simply the forced and unwilled nature of her labor, its antagonistic relation to the very model of wifely, motherly, and privatized womanhood that would be more ideal.

Fanny Fern herself as well as Ruth are so striking in their representation of women's writing as originating in a forced departure from more ideal conventions of domestic womanhood only because this self-representation repeats with remarkable regularity (though not uniformity) among popular women writers of the antebellum years. Over and over, writing comes to be imagined by these women as a compulsory act of partly unwilled generation. It is not only Fanny Fern who presents professional writing as an undesirable financial imperative, as a necessity thrust upon women forced into public for self-support. E. D. E. N. Southworth's autobiography reinforces this model of self-representation. Looking back to her motivations for taking up the pen, Southworth described her separation from her husband and failure to support her children adequately through teaching and other types of work. Finally, "broken in spirit, health and purse . . . with my two babes looking up to me for support," Southworth began to write. It is not a happy choice for Southworth to begin writing any more than it was for Ruth Hall. It is, rather, a compelling duty that entails unpleasant sacrifice of her health: "The time devoted to writing should have been given to sleep or fresh air."[74]

Mary Kelley tells us that the trajectory of Susan Warner's career followed somewhat similar lines. Warner's once prosperous family fell upon financial ruin when her father, a lawyer in New York, lost much of the family money in the panic of 1837. As early as 1839, Warner noted in her journal that she was thinking about writing for money. By 1850, she and her sister, Anna, had come to feel a demanding need to write prolifically. Their journals are filled with activities such as correcting proofs in poor light because the family could not afford to buy lamp oil. Warner reports that she wrote because she could not abide "living on nothing, or on borrowed money." When creditors threatened to foreclose on the family home, the Warners forced themselves to produce still more abundantly: "So we worked [to pay the debt]. . . . Big books, little books; now and then an article for some paper or magazine." Similar journal entries appear elsewhere: "Work, work, and get off the last of the copy and the preface," wrote Susan. Or, "Feel I must work and ought to be brave. Must be economical too, to make our funds last till we can get another book out."[75]

I describe this self-imagined paradigm of compulsory professional writing not to suggest that women writers were industrial slaves who had everything in common with Melville's factory women. For if the posture of reluctance and compulsion was very real, it was also highly opportunistic and enabling rather than restricting in some crucial ways. The domestic novelists of the mid-nineteenth century were not industrial operatives, but seized upon this language of reluctant authorship to enter the profession on terms that could be acceptable to their sense of themselves as privatized individuals. Melville's "maids," then, should not be seen only as his attempt to attack the best-selling women by imagining mass production and literary activity as ontologically exclusive of one another. Rather, they should also be seen as Melville's own absorption and working out (however drastically he misunderstood the details) of the domestic writers' own sense of their victimization and unwilling participation in literary production.

The degree to which Melville transformed the popular women novelists' reluctant production of literature into the forced and anti-literary activity of the Devil's Dungeon mill becomes most apparent when our narrator steps up to the "great machine" that presses pulp into blank paper. More and more, all that appears in the mill is the unwilled production of mechanized blankness:

It was very curious. Looking at that blank paper continually dropping, dropping, dropping, my mind ran on in wonderings of those strange uses to which those thousand sheets eventually would be put. . . . Then, recurring back to them as they lay here all blank, I could not but bethink me of that celebrated comparison of John Locke, who, in demonstration of his theory that man had no innate ideas, compared the human mind at birth to a sheet of blank paper, something destined to be scribbled on, but what sort of characters no soul might tell. (333)

The narrator here seizes exactly on "scribbling" as a trope for the creation of individuality, as a decisively generative act fully apart from the production of blankness at the factory itself. One point to be made is that scribbling, of course, is what the factory operatives cannot do. To this extent, Melville's depersonalization of the women in "Tartarus" is even more complete than Hawthorne's. Hawthorne imagined the mob as capable of human if illegible writing, but in the context of "Tartarus" it would seem that all attempts to construct an individualized identity through writing are denied.

The degree to which "Tartarus" wants to associate individuation with the actual act of writing or even scribbling becomes most clear, however, when we note that Locke's language differs meaningfully from our narrator's version of it: "Let us then suppose the mind to be, as we say, white paper, void of all characters, without any ideas:—How comes it to be furnished? Whence comes it by that vast store which the busy and boundless fancy of man has painted on it with an almost endless variety?"[76] Mixing metaphors with abandon, Locke tells us that the blank sheet is furnished, supplied, or painted on, but he does not explicitly mention writing or scribbling of any kind as constitutive of individuality. The difficulties with our narrator's version of Locke only grow because when Locke later returns to an image of printing on this blank page, it seems to be that—an image of physical impression, not writing or scribbling: "[One] will, upon taking a strict view, see that he has not any idea in his mind but what one of these two have imprinted; . . . And though the ideas of obvious and familiar qualities imprint themselves before the memory begins to keep a register of time or order . . ."[77]

Locke is not, of course, suggesting that understanding is mechanically or uniformly produced. Rather, he has in mind the possibility of singular impressions. Locke, in other words, imagines a type of printing that has no necessary metaphorical opposition to individuality and that can very meaningfully eliminate the blankness of an unmarked sheet. Accordingly, he does not need to rely on "scribbling," on writing by hand, as the only possible trope for meaningfully marking the blank page of the unconstructed personality. "Tartarus," on the other hand, because it is so concerned to imagine printing only as a part of a wholly inhuman and forced industrial process performed by female ciphers, must rely on scribbling as the means to individuation, the type of *writing* that the operatives do not perform.

The only instance of actual writing in "Tartarus" is followed by that writing's mechanical erasure. In order to time the papermaking machine, the narrator writes Cupid's name on a slip of paper.

Cupid then "adroitly dropped the inscribed slip on the incipient mass" of pulp. The narrator follows the slip, "inch by inch" through the network of rollers until an "unfolded sheet of perfect foolscap, with my 'Cupid' half faded out of it" emerges (332). The place of any attempt at authentically literary and personalized inscription in the factory is sealed. The narrator's "Cupid," already a ridiculous literary allusion, is immediately absorbed and obscured by the oppressive, blank-making machinery of the Devil's Dungeon mill. The industrial workforce of the Devil's Dungeon mill may indeed sympathetically expose the consequences for working-class women of an increasingly industrialized order. But it also deploys these figurations of class and gender difference as the groundwork to represent the lack of generative capacity, both verbal and biological, in women who produce reams of paper with no words worth reading for the literary market.

The *Lowell Offering*

Hawthorne and Melville had their own personal as well as larger cultural anxieties to work out at various levels of consciousness in the figurations I have been discussing, but female literary endeavor did not, of course, have to be entangled with disindividuation and the degenerated skills of mass production. For all of the self-deprecating modesty and sense of forced labor or necessity that recur in the comments and biographies of women writers such as Fanny Fern, E. D. E. N. Southworth, or Susan Warner, these authors did not seriously imagine themselves as anonymous or disindividuated industrial workers. They were authors of novels that later went into print, often were enormously profitable, and guaranteed not anonymity but a highly celebrated individuality.

But to emphasize the extent to which women writers aspiring to the expression of domestic ideals purposefully distanced themselves from the act of industrial production and the implicitly defeminized representation of womanhood that could accompany it, I want to return briefly to the *Lowell Offering*. It may be easy to imagine that writers who were not factory operatives seldom saw their work as industrial production, but what the *Offering* makes so clear is that the act of writing itself, the activity of literary production, could be used to prevent the fusion of womanhood, industrial labor, and writing that Hawthorne and Melville envision. In the *Offering*, writing is not tied to industrial work, but is imagined as the sign of the operative's class difference from laborers, even if these writers are laborers. Through the *Offering* the operatives seek to imagine themselves as middle-class women devoted to intellectual self-culture rather than as an exploited proletarian class, even as they become an industrialized workforce.

I have already suggested that the Boston Associates used the *Offering* as a kind of recruiting tool. The *Offering* presented relatively little of the sometimes grueling industrial labor in the mills, emphasizing instead the opportunity for the factory women to support their families while working in pleasant and culturally constructive surroundings. The *Offering* by no means met with universal approval, even among the operatives themselves. As should be clear by now, those workers who identified themselves primarily as exploited laborers, those who resisted the mill owners and wrote for the *Voice of Industry*, were particularly antagonistic to the representation of a fully preserved true womanhood at the Lowell mills.

But for those who worked consistently on the *Offering* from 1840 to 1845, the magazine clearly was, in and of itself, a literary enterprise demonstrating to the world "what factory girls had power to do" in the cultural rather than the materially productive sphere.[78] In displaying the mill workers as capable of and interested in authorship at all, the *Offering* made the claim that industrial life did not destroy, reduce to uniformity, or create machines out of the operatives. The Lowell workers, precisely unlike those in Melville's story, could write. One can find within the *Offering* historical essays on Joan of Arc, articles on the "antiquities" — "curiosities and works of art, bearing the impress of cultivated intelligence" — and highly sentimentalized poetry exhibiting all the markings of a middle-class, sentimental sensibility. An elegy to President William Henry Harrison, for example, speaks self-evidently of these cultural aspirations. The writer is clearly schooled in the elegiac tradition, so much

so that the poem is an exaggerated repetition of literary convention
and a strained demonstration of the writer's familiarity with it:[79]

> Gaze on your Ruler—well ye may,
>   And, statue-like refuse to weep;—
> There is about that shrouded clay
>   That bids refreshing tear-drops sleep.
>   There is, that lies for grief too deep.

The *Offering* could work as an ideological tool only to the extent
that it represented (and relied upon the cultural construction of) literary labor as something very different, even radically opposed to,
the routinized work of mass production. Whatever else one might
say about a poem such as the one above, it conspicuously declares a
perhaps unexpected capacity of the operatives to produce poetry at
all and a deep familiarity with, even an absorption by, the conventions of literary cultivation.

The authors of the *Offering* and those who reviewed it presented
the journal in just this light, as the unexpected and triumphant
emergence of the literary sensibility where one would, because of
industrial labor's demands, least have expected it. Charles Dickens,
for example, was notably surprised to find literature coming from
the factory: "Of the merits of the *Lowell Offering*, as a literary production, I will only observe—putting out of sight the fact of the
articles having been written by these girls after the arduous hours of
the day—that it will compare advantageously with a great many English annuals." [80] The epigraph on the journal's title page, borrowing
from Gray's "Elegy" to hint once again at the cultural achievements
of those in the factory, refers poetically to the strange and paradoxical emergence of literary production from the "dark caves" or
"desert" of the mills:

> Full many a gem of purest ray serene
>   The dark, unfathomed caves of ocean bear;
> Full many a flower is born to blush unseen,
>   And waste its sweetness on the desert air.

The paradox of the *Offering* is that in using the presence of the
literary to humanize life at the mills, even in publishing many stories

that idealized work there, the insistent contrast between literary and industrial work threatened to highlight the sometimes grueling conditions of the women's employment. The mill is, after all, likened to a desert; Dickens refers directly to "arduous labor"; and, perhaps most tellingly of all, not only does the afterword to the journal's first volume make reference to the "evils and miseries and mortifications attendant upon a factory life" just to dismiss them, the introduction informs the reader that "In estimating the talents of the writers [one should remember] that they are actively employed in the Mills for more than twelve hours out of every twenty-four. The evening, after 8 o'clock, affords their only opportunity for composition."[81] For the literary to function as proof of the operative's separation from the labor of the mills, that labor often had to be repressed but was always implicitly (and sometimes explicitly)·present in the background. The *Offering* was not to feature labor, but to make sure that labor remained absent or obscure while the process of cultural refinement stood in the representational foreground. It was, as I have said, the increasing encroachment of labor issues such as the ten-hour movement, the increasing tendency of women to be represented as "laborers" rather than as "writers" or "women" that finally led to the *Offering* ceasing publication in 1845.

But while the *Offering* continued, and as long as its editors imagined their literary work as opposed to the work of the mills, the magazine thrived. In saying that the women of the *Offering* by and large disassociated their literary from their industrial labor and identities, however, we should still understand that they do not, on the whole, embrace any model of independent and individualistic artistry. This individuation, of course, was the ideal of authorship that Hawthorne embodied in his artisan-as-artist figures and that Melville imagined as his own prophetic calling, but the authors of the *Offering* have more modest and communal interests:

Now we never expected to be considered oracles, instructors, modern Minervas, &c. We did not write for the Offering, thinking our assistance was needed to enlighten the community upon lofty or abstruse themes. . . . Yet if our "romantic stories" and "nonsense" have not this redeeming quality, they are certainly an innocent amusement for those who are too toil-worn to engage after their day's labor in profound disquisitions, or deep investigations.[82]

The contrast between industrial and literary employment is not, for the operatives, a contrast between metaphors of mass production and individuated art but it is a contrast between actually experienced labor and leisure. Furthermore, literary work is not a means of preserving the individual as such from the broadly depersonalizing evolutions of industrialization (a project, I have suggested, taken up by both Hawthorne and Melville). Rather, literary work is a means through which an industrially created group of laborers might consolidate their identity as a group outside the terms of that labor and its disciplines. The Lowell operatives never signed their work with anything more than first names, initials, or pseudonyms; they persistently defined themselves generically as operatives; only through historical research or by scrutinizing internal, textual evidence is it possible to speak of contributors to the *Offering* as individual authors at all.

At the same time, the publication of the *Offering* served quite obviously as a bonding experience apart from the operatives' labor, and those involved in it were insistent about describing the journal as "the organ of the factory girls," as "A REPOSITORY OF ORIGINAL ARTICLES, WRITTEN BY FEMALES EMPLOYED IN THE MILLS."[83] The authors of the *Offering*, we might then say, see themselves as a group of women writers and, in another capacity, as a group of operatives. They very definitely do not, however, see themselves as a group of operative/authors, the kind of mob that Hawthorne and Melville implicitly imagine mass-producing illegible texts.

In this emphatic separation of their authorial and operative identities, it should be clear that a primary way of describing women's writing, and a primary way in which descriptions were contested, had relatively little to do with gender as an exclusive category of analysis or self-understanding. Rather, what is central to the tropes I have been discussing is whether or not we are to understand gender differences working in conjunction with a class-based understanding and denigration of female authorship. The idea of womanhood, the writers of the *Offering* suggest, was hardly a shocking contrast to the idea of meaningful authorship. The idea that industrial work and authorship might exist in the same location, however, was truly a surprise and a sign of the operatives' elevation above that class situation.

I have been trying to emphasize throughout this chapter not only the complicated figurative relationships between industrial labor, authorship, and gender that developed in antebellum America, but several notes that will sound repeatedly throughout this book's coming chapters: a persistent cultural contrast between residual modes of artisanal and emergent modes of industrial work; the significance of a shift to an increasingly public and commercialized sphere of cultural production in general and literary production in particular; the newly emerging, but still inchoate and widely varying sense of what it meant for literature to become a marketable commodity on an unprecedented scale; the notion that constructions of authorship are seldom built upon a single duality but rather emerge from complicated systems of difference and likeness at multiple points of interdependent comparison. Finally, I have tried to make clear in general terms that literary figurations need not appropriate consciously or intact broadly conceived historical events to present individuated mediations of them.

Authorship did not become literally or historically an industrial labor but, if I have been at all convincing, it should be apparent that the evolution of industrial labor—particularly as it combined with gendered anxieties about writing—played a role in the way that specific writers figurally imagined and structured their labor, their self-conceptions, and decisive categories of difference or distinction. These figurations also matter, though, because their consequences extend beyond the isolated careers and instances discussed to organize possible meanings of antebellum authorial work. Gendered contrasts between literary work and industrial labor or, more broadly speaking, between artistic work and mass production, were in no way fully imperative, absolute, or natural, but the figurations that established the contrasts had enormous significance in forming functional and enabling mid-nineteenth-century notions of authorship.

In these figurations, we can see those thinking about the place and nature of authorship in an increasingly industrialized economy and increasingly commercialized literary realm. Provided we do not wholly overlook differences fostered by gender and class position among these writers, we could say simply and a bit too generally that authorship is imagined by Melville, Hawthorne, and those writing for the *Offering* as a privileged, anti-industrial endeavor during a period of industrialization. In this sense, we would be saying that these writers contend with large social events unfolding beyond their own writing, and they clearly work hard to articulate and maintain in their particular ways the differences between highly rationalized modes of mass production and authorial work.

But there is also a more complicated point at stake: industrial work is taken up by antebellum authors not as something already fully comprehended and exterior to their own work, but as a mode of labor in the process of being defined with varying possibilities for organizing the dominant meaning of authorship as it evolves from a genteel avocation to a potentially professionalized career. In this sense, industrial labor is not separate from authorial work, but has already intruded upon it as a trope that might be selectively and differentially deployed to hierarchize the gendered divisions of the literary world and one's place in it. From this viewpoint, we would have to see that writing came to be understood not so much as a deeply and inherently humanizing activity in the face of industrialization, but that industrialization itself could be invoked to suggest positional meanings grounded in the rhetoric of class distinction for various forms of "male" and "female" writing.

In other words, by the 1850s an emergent hierarchy of labor and class in the United States could be—indeed already had been—imported to help structure a professional literary realm that shortly before had been primarily the noncommercial province of genteel men. Industrial tropes for the literary helped to mark off and organize with gender and emergent class distinctions what had been for the most part defined as the prerogative of aristocratic social position. The new organization was, then, not only commercial, but beginning to become highly stratified into complicated oppositional categories: commercial/artistic, industrial/artisanal, female/male. The positioning of authorial work on particular sides of these and other slash marks is at once the work of industrial tropes for authorship and the indication that these oppositions (among others) had already begun to operate as organizing principles for the new literary realm.

This chapter has emphasized fragmentation and strategies of differentiation among antebellum authors in terms of class and gendered imagery, but other, very different paradigms could structure authorship in such a way that class and gender differentiation became secondary to an overwhelming anxiety about the newly market-mediated terms of the authorial profession. In my next chapter, I want to argue that writing for and being economically dependent on an increasingly demanding audience created anxieties that crossed the lines of distinction that industrial tropes seem to construct.

If my purpose were to create a perfectly coherent and programmatic vision of antebellum authorship, this second chapter would surely be, to some extent, an unravelling of the first one. But we should understand that while the tropes that concern me throughout this book reflect an obvious and even a sustained effort on the part of antebellum authors to situate their emerging and unfamiliar profession within an emerging and unfamiliar structure of labor, this effort could, often enough, lead them in contradictory directions. Any effort to recover a cultural history of authorship's representation ought not to be overly devoted to finding a monolithically comprehensible unity, but might instead strive toward the historically complex inclusion of a contradictory cultural consciousness that one would expect to find.

The coherence in the figurations that concern me throughout this book must be found in the effort of antebellum authors to understand the meaning of their work as it moved into the realm of the professional even as so many other forms of work in the United States were themselves emergent or unstable in their cultural meanings. In such a complicated cultural situation, with forms of labor understood as potential tropes usable for definitional ends rather than as central and established facts, we ought to expect and welcome contradictory glimpses into the processes of self-definition. With this in mind, I will argue in Chapter Two that writers working in vastly different literary genres, with vastly different social concerns, could unite when it came to imagining the problematic relationship of the antebellum author to the antebellum audience. They formed this union through their shared imagination of the relationship between slavery, celebrity, and authorship.

CHAPTER TWO

Eaten Alive

Slavery and Celebrity in Antebellum America

Celebrity

James T. Fields, the Boston-based publisher, recited this celebration of modern marketing and printing techniques to about six hundred authors and other celebrities—politicians, editors, publishers, ministers, and more—on September 27, 1855 at "The Complimentary Fruit and Flower Festival, Given to Authors, by the New York Publishers' Association":

> How slow and sure they set their types!
> How small editions ran!
> Then fifty thousand never sold—
> Before the sale began.
> For how could they, poor plodding souls,
> Be either swift or wise,
> Who never learned the mighty art
> Of how to advertise.

The publishers sponsored and hosted the extravaganza at the Crystal Palace in an attempt to ease—or at least disguise—tensions between publishers, booksellers, and writers. Suspended above the primary banquet table, enclosed in gaslights, one could read the publishers' tribute to authorship: "HONOR TO GENIUS." In the speeches following dinner, notes of shared economic interest were sounded, and the following day, reporting on the Fruit Festival in a story that made the front page, the *New York Daily Times* declared that if the antagonism between publishers and writers "ever had any existence, [it] has now completely passed away."[1]

The Fruit Festival did not, of course, end the economic tensions between authors and publishers. In fact, the staging of it, I want to suggest, may have helped to reinforce and construct a new kind of conspicuously public space for the celebrity, one which caused some discomfort for many antebellum authors. The event, in other words, was not only, perhaps not even primarily, an attempt to establish unity within the industry. The festival, in all its gaudy self-consciousness, was a publicity stunt, the presentation by the publishers of authors and other notables before their public. The publishers distributed color-coded tickets weeks before the sold-out event (then advertised the unavailability of and demand for these tickets) with instructions as to which entrances were to be used by the press, spectators, and guests. Three hundred celebrity-seeking fans, nine-tenths of them women, occupied the gallery overlooking the pavilion where dinner was served to the celebrities below. The art of advertisement was not entirely new in 1855 but, as Fields's poem suggests, it had achieved a sophistication and vastly expanded presence only shortly before, and the particular advertising strategy acted out in the Fruit Festival—the public appearance by the author as a celebrity in order further to promote that celebrity—may have been systematically used for the first time in America as a mass-marketing tool less than twenty years before, by Charles Dickens.[2]

The Fruit Festival was only one among many events and orchestrations of public appearance that began to construct a newly prominent and celebrated place for those working in the (broadly defined) cultural sphere. It was in the 1840s and 1850s that P. T. Barnum, perhaps the first to understand fully the potentialities of an emergent middle-class cultural market, emerged to promote himself and such divergent personages as tiny Tom Thumb and sweet-singing Jenny Lind. Religious figures such as Henry Ward Beecher (who attended the Fruit Festival) abandoned more and more the harshness of Calvinist doctrine in their attempts to promote themselves as prominent spokesmen to and for a middle-class public. Andrew Jackson's presidential campaign marked a quantum leap in campaign spending and was the first to rely on a nationwide network of party newspapers and publications to present its candidate as a representative man of the masses. During the antebellum period candidates began to publish widely circulated campaign biographies (such as the one Hawthorne wrote for Franklin Pierce) as a standard political practice.[3]

The literary market and the authorial celebrity emerged upon this cultural field of the publicized personality. Following the lead of William Charvat, a great deal of recent scholarship has detailed the social and technological developments that made the expansion of the literary market possible.[4] The emergence of a literate middle class, the passage of copyright laws, and improved technologies of reproduction and distribution all combined to bring authors into an unprecedented relationship with their audience. Whereas genteel modes of avocational authorship for a familiar social group had dominated literary work in the eighteenth century, by the second quarter of the nineteenth a professional mode of commercial literary work for an expanded and anonymous audience had clearly emerged. For the first time, successful authors became public figures in a mass market with all of the privileges and demands that accompany such status. They might be idolized and supported as figures of cultural eminence and employment, even as embodiments of political or artistic principles but, at the same time, the personal and professional activities of antebellum writers were increasingly dictated and disciplined by an anonymous public's demands and intrusions.

The shifting place of writers as they increasingly entered into a market-mediated, professional relationship with their audiences precipitated a struggle to understand, to figure out, this previously unfamiliar kind of work by imagining it through other modes of labor. This is not to say that modes of work other than writing were, during this period of emergent industrialization, any more stable and apparent in their meanings than was authorship. It is to say that many forms of work wanted definition during the antebellum years as the industrially oriented market economy emerged, and these acts of authorial analogizing helped to create cultural meanings on both sides of the metaphorical equation.

Figurations of authorship could, of course, be used to structure the emergent literary realm as deeply fragmented and hierarchized along the lines of class, gender, or genre. As my first chapter makes clear, antebellum authors could seek to assert the primacy of certain modes of authorial work at the expense of other types of writing and labor. But to say that the figuring of authorship during the antebellum years was dedicated solely to the creation of distinction, fragmentation, and hierarchy along class and gender lines would be to miss some of the important shared anxieties of antebellum authors. Accordingly, I want to suggest in this chapter that many authors whom we might normally thrust into very separate realms based on generic, gender, and racial distinctions—not to mention personal histories—merge strangely together when they come to contemplate the meaning of celebrity as it emerges during the antebellum years.

The newly found potential for celebrity, for the appearance of the publicized personality in the literary realm, was enabled by the expansion of the literary market. One ought to point, however, to something more than a merely quantitative growth in readership and access when it comes to understanding antebellum authorial celebrity. Though market growth was certainly important to the discussion that follows, a qualitative change also unfolded in the relationships between celebrated figures and their audiences during the antebellum years. A larger literary market with its increasingly complicated networks of production and distribution led almost necessarily to an increasingly anonymous relationship between authors and their readers. It was not just that authors wrote for a broader audience; it was also that this relationship to an audience was more fully mediated by all the contingencies of production and distribution that made texts widely available in the first place. Antebellum authors were read with notably less of a sense of a closed and knowable elite community than writers of the preceding generation, even as more broadly democratic and market-mediated communities of interest began to form their identities through reading.[5]

The Fruit Festival shows us, however, that increasing alienation and anonymity cannot by itself possibly be adequate to describe the qualitative shift in relationships between authors and audiences. Why is a crowd watching a celebrity dinner at the Fruit Festival if that crowd feels increasingly distant from the celebrities there? The oddity about events such as the Fruit Festival, about the staged personal appearances of well-known individuals, is that they bespeak not a sense of alienation from the celebrity born of an increasingly mass-mediated relationship, but the audience's feeling of entitlement to and desire for intimacy with the well-known.

In *The Frenzy of Renown*, Leo Braudy argues that as early as the 1640s the democratization of fame had begun to strip the well-known of their impressiveness or awesomeness even as it expanded the horizons of their notoriety. The Elizabethan theater was transformed during the age of Shakespeare from a hall in which the glory of actual kings was exhibited as they took their privileged seats in the audience to a hall in which the dramas of kingship were themselves played out on stage for the public to judge: "Kingship and rule [were] turned into a show in which one might play a good part or a bad one, but always a part, while the audience, usually the subordinates of the great, for a time bec[a]me their judges."[6]

This process of turning imperial fame into intimately exposed mass-cultural celebrity reached a pivotal point of development in the 1850s, as technologies of reproduction and organizations of mass distribution emerged. Braudy underscores in particular "the emotional intimacy that the [newly invented] photograph helped foster between the famous and their audience," but one ought to emphasize the entire apparatus of display and promotion that the Fruit Festival emblematizes. By the 1850s in the United States, fame was becoming increasingly democratized and redistributed by various culture industries (particularly publishing) as celebrity. The Fruit Festival suggests that with this new form of well-knownness came the audience's paradoxical presumption of and desire for intimacy with the well-known, even as the relationship between celebrities and their fans became increasingly mediated by strategies of commercial promotion.[7]

I am going to argue that anxieties about an exaggerated sense of intimacy assumed by an anonymous public's demands and intrusions brings together antebellum authors whom we might normally cordon off from one another along the lines of gender, genre, or race. This is important because it demonstrates first that figurations of authorship were not always as clearly divided along familiar lines of male and female, black and white, romantic and sentimental as we routinely think them to be. But it is also important because it is in figurations of the grasping audience that the anxieties of antebellum authors about the newly market-mediated form of their labor, about the new ways of creating and conveying prominence, are most plainly and even exaggeratedly made manifest. The figurations in this chapter suggest that antebellum writers often felt radically victimized by and powerless before the changing expectations of those for whom they wrote.

My specific argument is that authorial anxieties about the demands placed by the public on those occupying the increasingly conspicuous cultural stage came to be imagined in the unexpected terms of slave labor and slave economics. It was the presumption of access and intimacy in the cultural market combined with an increasingly strident abolitionist movement that made the analogy between authorial celebrity and slave work a cultural possibility. Speaking most fundamentally, the celebrity and the slave were united through their shared cultural configuration as consumable workers, laborers whose bodies, rather than their labor or production, were available for consumption.

But, as should become increasingly clear, this analogy depended upon selective inclusions and exclusions, complex and ideologically charged constructions of property and labor relations. For no matter how writers may have felt about celebrity work in the cultural sphere, it was not slave labor, and to imagine it as such required not only a particular construction of the celebrity's status but of the slave's as well. Celebrities who ventured into the cultural marketplace generally did so willingly, suffered no literal threats to their bodies, and profited economically by selling books, performances, and so forth. Slaves, on the other hand, went to market whether they willed it or not, were themselves objects of exchange, and had, of course, no chance to profit from this kind of marketability. If writers could come together by imagining themselves as enslaved within the market, such a figuration also necessarily threatened to diminish the very real suffering of the actual slave.

The fundamental difference between the celebrity as a famous *producer* of cultural commodities and the slave's status as intrinsically exchangeable is precisely that which was imaginatively obscured by figurations of the celebrity as slave. These figurations operated by imagining the slave (and the celebrity) as particular types of property whose greatest value to a master (or audience) lay not in any conventional or economically rational relation of exchange, but in the act of corporal consumption. The slave in these imaginings was not defined by his marketability but by the irrational noneconomy of the South, by the master's pleasure, desire, and need to dismember, rape, or otherwise attack and consume the body of the slave at any cost. The celebrity was defined not by the audience's desire for his or her cultural productions or by the possibility of economically profitable exchange between the celebrity and audience but, rather, by the audience's irrational drive to see, touch, hold, possess, and consume the celebrity body itself.

In order to reconstruct this mediated connection between the slave and celebrity I will enlist the help of what might, at first, seem to be a few unlikely texts: Harriet Beecher Stowe's *Uncle Tom's Cabin*, Nathaniel Hawthorne's *The Scarlet Letter*, and Harriet Jacobs's *Incidents in the Life of a Slave Girl*. I choose these books not because they are the only or even the most obvious locations in which celebrity was reconfigured via the dynamics of antislavery conceptions of the slave, but because they show just how deeply ingrained were the rhetorical and associative logic mediating the ties between slavery and celebrity. Furthermore, these texts very obviously cross our conventional bounds of literary genre and practice. Loosely speaking, Stowe writes within a "domestic" or "sentimental" framework, Hawthorne within a "romantic" one, and Jacobs's book is a "slave narrative."

My point is not to erase entirely these differences of authorial idiom, but I do want to insist that the emergent middle-class cultural market, the conspicuous public access to the celebrity that it created, and an increasingly prominent abolitionist movement were, in general terms, social preconditions for celebrity-as-slave figurations. Furthermore, while I will argue for the pervasiveness of these figurations, I do not mean to suggest that authorial intention played a necessary part in them. These figurations were variable within and among literary texts and invoked a submerged affinity that their authors did not fully understand. Accordingly, celebrity-slave figurations are by no means as explicitly articulated in the rhetoric of antebellum authors as were the industrial tropes that dominated Chapter 1. Rather, they present themselves as a repeated cultural logic that implicitly plays itself out in the structure of mid-nineteenth-century plots and characterizations. The expansion of the public stage in middle-class culture, authorial anxieties about it, and abolitionist rhetoric shared no immediate, intentional, or simple causal relation that authors themselves understood or deliberately articulated, but the social and historical simultaneity of these phenomena allowed for mediated, submerged, and figurative connections among them.

Slavery

The conception of the slave not only as horrifyingly exchangeable within the market but as a horrifyingly consumable property of the master existed at some level in almost every version of abolitionist rhetoric. It was, however, most readily apparent not in the terms of Garrisonians emphasizing pure moral or Christian outrage, but in the increasingly prominent attacks on slavery's political economy. I note this only because throughout the antebellum period a range of tactical disputes fragmented abolitionism, and it may help to locate the rhetoric that concerns me with some specificity. From the 1830s on, William Lloyd Garrison and his most rigorous followers tended to object to all official political participation, even voting, and Garrison, by 1842, was advocating the Union's dissolution. The Liberty, Free Soil, and Republican parties, on the other hand, were political organizations from their birth in the 1840s and

1850s and generally sought to work through the existing political system, sometimes seeming more concerned to prevent the extension rather than to achieve the abolition of slavery.[8]

By the 1850s the Republican party had begun to coalesce largely around the antislavery issue and gained enough popular support to win the presidency by 1860 with virtually no help from the Southern voting block. The Republicans, however, did not often express their disapproval of slavery in the terms of extreme moral distress that kept Garrisonians on the perimeter of institutional power. Rather, perhaps the key elements in both Free-Soil and Republican rhetoric relied on doctrines of political economy, on the valorization, the idealization, and the need to protect the productive and capitalistic impulses of the free and independent laborer. In 1856, for example, Cassius Clay told his audience, "The Northern laboring man could, and frequently did, rise above the condition [in] which he was born to the first rank of society and wealth; but [I] never knew such an instance in the South." Clay referred here to the impossibility of poor whites advancing in the South, but Horace Greeley reiterated the point of contrast in slightly different terms, emphasizing that slaves had no motivation to work because they had no chance to profit from doing so: "Enslave a man and you destroy his ambition, his enterprise, his capacity. In the constitution of human nature, the desire of bettering one's condition is the mainspring of effort." Henry Seward and others pointed out throughout the 1840s and 1850s that slavery not only stymied the individual workers in the South but, because it provided so little incentive for production, stymied the Southern economy as a whole. In touring Virginia he found "exhausted soil, old and decaying towns, wretchedly neglected roads, and, in every respect, an absence of enterprise and improvement." Slavery, he said, had driven the South to "the calamity of premature and consumptive decline, in the midst of free, vigorous and expanding states."[9]

Such rhetoric served, of course, not only to attack slavery but as a means of defining and idealizing by antithesis, if not with the utmost historical accuracy, Northern labor and society. Republican free-labor rhetoric emerged, after all, at precisely a time when

Northern industrialization led to many workers losing precisely the social mobility and economic independence that such rhetoric described. While slavery's apologists—most notably George Fitzhugh and John Calhoun—as well as Northern labor unions were insisting upon and bringing into prominent usage the term "wage-slavery," both Republicans and abolitionists largely refused to acknowledge any possible parallel between work in the North and Southern bondage. Northerners, the Republican abolitionists by and large agreed, had the opportunity for social advancement and empowerment, the power to profit from their labor, and the certainty of upward social mobility. As Abraham Lincoln put the matter, no worker in the North was "always to remain" a laborer. He explained, "The man who labored for another last year this year labors for himself, and next year he will hire others to labor for him." [10] Slave laborers, by contrast, did not own their labor, could not exchange it for profit, had no claim to any of the goods they produced, and had no hope of upward mobility.

At this point we might say, and abolitionists of all stripes did, that the central perversity in the political economy of the South lay simply in the fact that slavemasters exchanged laborers rather than labor and its product. This, in turn, had the effect not only of destroying ambition and creating a nonproductive work force, but also of ruthlessly compelling slave women to "breed" families that would then be fractured for the slavemaster's monetary benefit. Southern slavemasters, in other words, might have been (and were) attacked not so much for their refusal to recognize the virtues of profitable exchange in the market but, rather, for carrying certain highly selective principles of trade and production to their most outrageous extreme. In breeding and selling people for profit, in viewing slaves as capital or commodities to be produced and exchanged, the slavemaster reinscribed in grossly perverted terms the faith in profitable market exchange that underlay the Northern idealization of free labor. The slavemaster, from the abolitionist perspective, failed to understand that only goods and labor—not laborers—should be produced and exchanged. [11]

From the abolitionist perspective, however, slavemasters not only traded immorally in the wrong commodities but, finally and most alarmingly, failed to privilege exchange value and rational economics at all. For, in the logic of abolitionist political economy, the most horrifying transgressions of the slavemaster occurred not because the slave was exchangeable, but when the master ceased to honor the logic of exchange, choosing instead to exercise arbitrarily and irrationally his absolute right of property, his right to consume or destroy the slave regardless of the economic consequences.

We can find this horror of irrational, lustful, sadistic, and economically prodigal corporal consumption in any number of abolitionist critiques throughout the antebellum period.[12] Lydia Maria Child's *An Appeal in Favor of that Class of Americans Called Africans*, one of the earliest abolitionist considerations to emphasize political economy, set the tone in 1833. Child, while always recognizing the power of economic motivations, points out emphatically that slavemasters have been known to ignore them in fits of greed and passion:

But it is urged that it is the interest of planters to treat their slaves well. This argument no doubt has some force; and it is the poor negro's only security. But it is likewise the interest of men to treat their cattle kindly; yet we see that passion and short-sighted avarice do overcome the strongest motives of interest. Cattle are beat unmercifully, sometimes unto death; they are ruined by being overworked; weakened by want of sufficient food; and so forth. (26)

Child provides this insight in the midst of a lengthy list of the tortures to which slaves are routinely subjected, a list capped by the stories of two runaways. The first is taken to a barn and dismembered with an ax in front of the other slaves on the plantation. A fire is lit "in order to consume" the bones. Later that night when the master's wife asks him why she had heard such horrific screams from the barn, the master tells her "that he had never enjoyed himself so well at a ball as he had enjoyed himself that evening." Child's second runaway is torn apart by bloodhounds while the whites look on, "highly delighted to find the dogs so well trained in their business."[13]

What seems crucial to note is the implicit motivation behind both of these acts of corporal destruction. According to antislavery rhetoric, rather than privileging the rational, self-interested production or even the capital value of the slave, slavemasters and the political economy of the South fostered labor relations organized by the master's absolute power. The slavemaster's pleasures, perversions, and avarice, his delight not only or most alarmingly in purchasing, owning, and profiting unjustly from the slave, but his delight in attacking, destroying, and consuming the slave's body, structured the political economy of the South.

Little Eva

I begin with this brief discussion of political economy in the antislavery movement, because it represents almost transparently the cultural emergence of particular categories of labor and associated economic understandings. The captive laborer is defined not only by his commodity status, but by his *absence* from the activity of monetary exchange and, at his most extreme, becomes himself an object of economically irrational consumption. The free laborer, by contrast, is defined by the alienation and profitable exchange of his labor and product. One form of labor leads to a nonproductive, irrational, self-consuming economy while the other is productive, rational, and constantly expanding. I want to suggest now that these discursive or rhetorical categories penetrated antebellum culture well beyond the sphere of purely abolitionist concerns, and very notably penetrated the attempts of literary texts to situate figuratively the emergent conditions of celebrity work in the increasingly conspicuous public space of the middle-class cultural market.

The character of Little Eva begins to show us how authors might figuratively reinscribe and implicitly invoke the slave economy's dynamics of physical consumption to address the potentialities and dangers inherent in cultural celebrity at precisely the moment when that celebrity emerged so prominently. *Uncle Tom's Cabin* presents a host of characters who demonstrate the economic inefficiencies and concomitant threat of bodily destruction to the enslaved worker in the South. Simon Legree's mortal beating of Tom points out not only his cruelty but his profligacy and economic irrationality. Legree spends hundreds, perhaps thousands—Tom "only hears the last syllable of the word *'dollars'* "—to buy Tom but is finally left with a valueless corpse.[14] When George Shelby offers to purchase the body, Legree tells him, "I don't sell dead niggers" (591). We can see Dinah's inefficiencies in the kitchen as an emblem of the inefficiencies of the Southern economy: all that "hurryscurryation" and waste to produce just one meal. We can see that George Harris runs away because he is denied the right to his wages, sees his enterprise stifled, and, finally, feels his status as a consumable possession underlined and literalized by beatings.

Eva, however, introduces us to another type of consumable and corporally vulnerable worker, one much more closely aligned with the relationship of the celebrity to her audience in the public sphere of middle-class culture. Laura Wexler emphasizes that critics as divergent in their assessment of Stowe's literary value as Jane Tompkins and Ann Douglas tend to agree that authorship was for Stowe the act of extending private values, her domestic ideology, through cultural work, a way of instituting the values of the woman and mother in place of those authorizing the cruelties and injustices of slavery. Even though Douglas laments the rise of sentimental culture signaled by Stowe's novel while Tompkins celebrates the power of sentiment to effect reforms in a corrupt, patriarchal world, both critics take for granted sentimentalism's social force. Wexler herself assumes perhaps an even more extensive power of the sentimental to shape subjectivity according to its demands. For Wexler, the sentimental extends well beyond the middle class and is deployed as an "imperial project" molding the lives of African American and Native American students at the Hampton Institute after the Civil War. Recent readings of Stowe and the sentimental leave no doubt that *Uncle Tom's Cabin* effectively images forth and structures an ideology of middle-class sentimentality insisting on the virtues of women's religiosity, spirituality, sentimentality, and domestic guardianship; the major debates are over the extent of sentimentalism's domain and whether it ought to be admired or held in contempt, seen as resistant to patriarchy (the Tompkins view), as part of an oppressively dominant and kitsch, middle-class aesthetic (the Douglas position), or as a form of imperialism through which the middle-class extended its cultural reach at the expense of the less privileged (Wexler's stance).[15]

Mary Kelley's important work also acknowledges the role of Stowe's writing in the creation of middle-class morality, but adds an important emphasis. Kelley insists that Stowe's public extension of domestic influence occurred at some psychic cost and in contradiction to the very values of feminine privacy enshrined within the ideology of domesticity. For, as Nancy Cott and others have described the mid-nineteenth-century cult of domesticity, it is grounded firmly in a vision of women's role in the private sphere, in the realm of the home, and the purification of the spirit rather than in the realm of the public purification of politics. Caught between her self-understanding as an angel of the household—a mother, wife and spiritual guardian of the family—and her role as a writer, Stowe found herself experiencing profound anxieties over the celebrity, the public exposure, and the demands that her career as an author created. According to Kelley and others, domesticity and its conflicts with celebrity "provided the context in which [Stowe] pursued her career as a writer and the substance of her writing."[16]

Within *Uncle Tom's Cabin* itself, Eva's evangelizing, her cultural work against slavery, functions similarly to Stowe's public extension of domestic privacy. Eva seeks to mount a kind of moral attack on the slave system firmly grounded in the feminine and Christian virtues of domesticity by extending her private values into a domain more public than that of the immediate household; only by paradoxically bringing domesticity into the public sphere can Eva hope to influence not only her family but the plantation's hundreds of slaves, all of the South (she fantasizes about opening a Bible school to educate slaves), and even various wayward representatives of the North.

Eva, in other words, occupies (and seems, with her ambitions for reform, to have at least a limited sense of herself occupying) a public as much as a domestic sphere. She becomes, within the context of the novel, a young woman adored (and who knows she is adored), even revered and followed around relentlessly by the Au-gust St. Clares, Henriques, Topsys, and Aunt Ophelias in whom she tirelessly invests more and more of herself and by whom, in turn, she is tirelessly and more and more conspicuously revered, more and more viewed as a representation and embodiment of Christian and domestic influence.

Eva's investment in her followers and their grasping after her, one might originally think, have a purely spiritual nature. The cor-poral economy of *Uncle Tom's Cabin*, however, suggests that for Eva a purely spiritual dispensation is impossible. While her work may take place as something quite like a reconstruction of spiritual and domestic dispensation or aggressive reformation in the public realm, she suffers not spiritual but corporal depletion in the process. Her body is in constant decline as Eva's worshippers seek more and more from and of her. The more Eva offers of herself, the further she deteriorates until finally, in the novel's most-discussed scene, Eva's most conspicuous act of spiritual influence takes the form of explicit bodily dispensation: Eva passes out locks of her hair. Lynn Ward-ley has recently claimed that the tendency of *Uncle Tom's Cabin* to fetishize material objects, particularly those associated with or that are literally a part of women, "resonates not only with the Catholic faith in the power of relics, but also with Pan-African religions of the antebellum South." [17]

Wardley may overstate Stowe's awareness of and interest in the "West African understanding of the . . . practice of fetishism," [18] but she is surely right to insist that Eva's exertion of spiritual influence is inextricably tied to the literal offering of her body, a kind of incar-nation of the spirit that demands the explicit surrender of her body to her audience of admirers. Those in need of Eva's counsel cannot compromise her spiritual being through their worship, but in the desire for holy relics they might leave their living saint half-bald and bedridden. If Eva chooses to exercise the private authority granted her by the ideology of domesticity within a larger, more public do-main, first her illness and then her dispensing of hair suggest that her body will suffer the consequences; Eva will become, in her act of public influence, corporally available to those who actively, perhaps aggressively, long for her spirituality and insist upon a fetishizing intimacy with her physical presence as an embodiment of it.

Eva's corporal consumption, might, then, place her in some relation to West African cultural practices, but most importantly it situates her within the sentimental genre as an evangelical martyr whose body attains a sacred, celebrated status. By offering her body, Eva achieves her own salvation and seeks to enable the salvation of others. But while acknowledging Eva's martyrdom and the Christian resonances of it, we must also note that Eva's bodily dispensation carries other latent cultural references as well.

Situated as it is in the midst of a virulently abolitionist novel, the consumption of Eva's body aligns her metaphorically with the consumption of the slaves so prominently and repeatedly displayed in *Uncle Tom's Cabin*, the slaves who are so prominently and repeatedly a source of empathetic suffering for Eva. In the character of Little Eva, *Uncle Tom's Cabin* demonstrates not only that the bodies of slaves are consumed by the whip within the Southern economy but that female, Christian virtue cannot survive temporally in such a setting. Like the slaves, though in purely figurative and empathetic terms, Eva is physically used up within the economy of bodily consumption operative in the South.[19]

Yet if it is possible for us to situate Eva simultaneously in terms of both paradigmatic representations of the Christian martyr and the dynamics of human consumption in the South (one could, of course, with different emphases, place Tom in a similar way), we might also situate Eva in still one last cultural field. Eva is, as even her name suggests, an evangelist for, a public embodiment, repository, and conspicuous figure of, female, Christian, and domestic authority. If Eva is consumed by her fetishizing admirers, we must also note the willingness, even the eagerness, with which she (unlike the slaves) presents herself. Such a figure might have been unimaginable in the United States twenty years before *Uncle Tom's Cabin* but, as the Fruit Festival has already suggested, it was in the 1850s that women authors first found a huge audience anxious to share in their domestic visions and inaugurated the literary bestseller in the contemporary sense of the term.[20]

What needs to be clearly understood about the history of events such as the Fruit Festival is that they served the obvious commercial function of marketing various kinds of cultural production: books, plays, museum exhibitions, and so forth. The celebrities themselves were made available in the marketplace in terms and for purposes radically different from those guiding the exchange of slaves. At the same time, it is the cultural implications and associations, the way that celebrity availability was selectively *understood*, the anxieties it raised in the context of slavery and an increasingly grasping, appropriating audience, that I want to focus on.

For the celebrity to imagine *herself* as available and the audience as intruding upon her body was, in the context of antebellum America, for the celebrity to cast herself in a relationship to her audience emphasizing less the rational and profitable exchange of labor or its products and more the irrational desire of the audience to consume the celebrated body itself. In other words, the "commodification" or "fetishization" of the celebrity (as apart from her products) was extraordinarily peculiar to the extent that it privileged not the alienated production or profitable exchange of labor or goods, but the act of very literal self-presentation and the audience's pure pleasure and valuation in the act of consumption.

In some sense, then, "commodified" as we normally understand the term, may be a misleading word to describe the celebrity in the antebellum market. Once the audience valued the pure presence of the celebrity body more than any cultural production, the relationship between the celebrity and her audience could hardly be called "alienated" or exchange-based at all. It became a dynamic that privileged the consumption of the public person rather than the exchange of her goods or labor. It emphasized not the audience's desire to purchase cultural commodities, but their desire to possess and consume the celebrated body itself. Such a dynamic, I have tried to suggest, was antithetical to the Northern idealization of free labor, alienated production, and exchange, but could be (and was) readily observed in the slavemaster's irrational desire to possess and consume the body of the slave. The point of comparison between the slave and the celebrity lay not, as we might expect, in their shared "commodification" but, rather, in their *de*commodification; the comparison lay, in other words, not in the drive of the slave-master and audience to exchange the labor, products, or even the bodies of the slave and celebrity but, rather, in their drive to possess and consume at any cost the slaves and celebrities themselves. This dynamic of pure and economically irrational consumption (as opposed to profitable production and exchange) realized itself most fully when slaves and celebrities transcended the economic measure of their labor, when they became not workers or even objects in a rational market, but workers or objects irrationally desired, sacrificed, seized, or attacked.

Harriet Beecher Stowe, already uncomfortably established on a small scale as an author and domestic force prior to *Uncle Tom's Cabin*, would, after the appearance of that novel, have ever-increasing demands for public appearances made upon her, appearances about which she was notably ambivalent. When Stowe toured England, for example, enormous crowds turned out to see and hear America's most prominent abolitionist, acting out what one of Stowe's biographers calls "a national dementia." Upon her ship's arrival, Stowe was surprised to find hordes of spectators "very much determined to look" at her; Stowe wanted to attend a particular church service in London, "but dared not for fear of being recognized"; upon her entrance into one hall, Stowe felt the terror of a near stampede as one woman was almost trampled to death; finally, when it came to addressing her admirers, Stowe, retreating firmly into the conventions of domestic privacy, called exclusively upon her husband, Calvin, to speak for her. Calvin, in turn, described the mob as ever more grasping, intrusive and demanding: "I am tired to death of the life I lead here. All that was anticipated by the newspapers, & ten times more, has befallen us. From the lowest peasant to the highest noble, [my] wife is constantly beset, & I for her sake, so that we have not a moment's quiet." [21]

Joan Hedrick also suggests that this trip to London highlighted the tensions between Stowe's public and private self. Though Stowe had been conflicted about any publicity that accompanied her writing before *Uncle Tom's Cabin*, during her trip to London she grew still more "highly sensitive to her public image and did much to cultivate the outward posture of true womanhood." [22] Within only a few years on either side of Stowe's English tour, Susan Warner, Augusta Evans Wilson, Maria Cummins, and other women writers were elaborately marketed by their publishers as figures of moral authority, achieving the same kind of historically unprecedented public recognition as Stowe, even as they, like Stowe, attempted at times to retreat from it.

In the figure of Little Eva public appearance and spiritual investment in the public (particularly in the name of Stowe's own abolitionist cause) are transferred to and taken out upon the domestic figure's body. This reconfiguration of the work of public moral persuasion into an act of corporal self-sacrifice, was, as I have said, undoubtedly imaginable for Stowe partly in terms of Christian martyrdom. At the same time, I am suggesting that it was also imaginable through her personal and professional anxieties about celebrity. For Harriet Beecher Stowe, to imagine Christian martyrdom as the process of moral reformation was to imagine that martyrdom taking place on stage, whether that stage be Eva's bedroom or the lecture halls of London. Furthermore, to imagine martyrdom in the figure of Eva was to imagine that martyrdom developing alongside and in implicit comparison to the martyrdom and corporal consumption of the slave. In short, Stowe imagines in Eva the domestic celebrity as Christian martyr but, simultaneously, imagines martyrdom through (and figuratively mediates the differences between) the conditions and economics of antebellum slavery and celebrity.

Arthur Dimmesdale

Little Eva has shown us how the celebrity's willing offer of cultural goods in the market might be shifted slightly and re-imagined as an offering, in very literal terms, of oneself. Furthermore, Eva also demonstrates how this offering of self unavoidably obscured or effaced the relation of monetary exchange when, in implicit comparison to the slave, the celebrity's body was fetishized as a material embodiment of spirit or principle then revalued as an object of corporal consumption rather than a source of cultural production. My point is not, of course, that Eva *ought* to have gotten some money for her hair and otherwise been left alone but, rather, that such an imagining would be, given Stowe, thoroughly outrageous. For Harriet Beecher Stowe, the domestic celebrity and reformer was imagined not through the profits she made in the sale of her products but, rather, through the psychic costs and bodily sacrifice in performing her work of reformation.

None of this is to say that Eva's admirers are openly hostile in their fervid desire for her, but imagining the audience as aggressively rather than worshipfully intrusive might be the next step in imagining the audience as a kind of slavemaster to the celebrity, in imagining the dynamics of celebrity-audience relations operating outside the realm of rational production and market exchange. As we shall see, it is this kind of intrusiveness, an unspeakable need for exposure and intimacy, that Nathaniel Hawthorne imagines in the interaction between Arthur Dimmesdale and the Puritan public. For, we should realize, anxieties over the economy of personal appearance and the audience's "consumption" of the celebrity played themselves out on a much broader literary field than purely abolitionist or domestic works, even if the precise terms of the comparison between slavery and celebrity, the precise ways in which the celebrity was imagined to enter the market, were always shifting slightly, serving different authors to bring forth differently inflected concerns.

We know that Nathaniel Hawthorne had very little sympathy for or even constructive interest in abolitionism. *The Scarlet Letter*, moreover, takes place in the seventeenth century and would seem on the surface to avoid representations of slavery, free labor, celebrity, and other contemporaneous issues. A number of critics, however, have recently made plain that Hawthorne's seventeenth-century setting has extensive reference to mid-nineteenth-century culture and society, and particularly to the slavery question. Furthermore, it has become more and more apparent, as Sacvan Bercovitch has suggested, that slavery served as a crucial context (or even subtext) for literary work throughout the American Renaissance.[23]

That *The Scarlet Letter* might also be concerned with nineteenth-century celebrity has been persuasively suggested by Zelda Bronstein. Bronstein points out, for example, that while the narrator of *The Scarlet Letter* is at pains to make claims for the "piety, reverence, reliability, dignity, and sobriety" of the Puritans in contrast to the nineteenth-century public, these claims of greater Puritan dignity are continually undermined. The Puritan audience, for example, values not the "long-tried integrity" or "solid wisdom and experience" of Dimmesdale's mentor, John Wilson. Rather, they are smitten by and obsessed with Dimmesdale's looks, evangelical furor, and rhetorical flourishes. They react to him not with reserved acclaim, but with the fervid adulation bestowed on nineteenth-century evangelists and Jacksonian Democrats. In short, claims Bronstein, Dimmesdale's Puritan public "behaves in a manner that corresponds to the narrator's designation of the nineteenth, not the seventeenth century."[24]

The questions that concern me, then, are not whether *The Scarlet Letter* is interested in slavery and celebrity but, rather, the precise terms in which these interests become tied to one another. From the beginning of the novel, the penitential logic of the public in seventeenth-century Boston emphasizes its claim to the bodies of the town's most public figures, the sinners on the scaffold. These claims are registered not only by the gaze of the town but very notably through branding and whipping, the afflictions, together with rape, that most centrally emblematized the slave's physical abuse in antebellum America.[25] As the town waits for Hester to emerge from the prison, to see her as a spectacle, Hawthorne emphasizes the lash: "It might be that a sluggish bond-servant, or an undutiful child, whom his parents had given over to the civil authority, was to be corrected at the whipping-post. It might be that an anti-nomian, a Quaker, or other heterodox religionist was to be scourged out of the town, or an idle and vagrant Indian, whom the white man's firewater had made riotous about the streets was to be driven with stripes into the shadows of the forest."[26] Perhaps not coincidentally—the crowd at the Fruit Festival and most worshippers of the newly publicized workers in the cultural sphere seem to have been women—women "take a peculiar interest in whatever

penal infliction might be expected to ensue" (50). The matrons outside the prison door, however, do not want to see Hester whipped.
Rather, they think she ought to be branded. Says one of the spectators and disciplinary enthusiasts, "At the very least they should have
put the brand of a hot iron on Hester Prynne's forehead. Madam
Hester would have winced at that" (51).[27]

To the matrons' dismay, the town officials neither whip nor
brand Hester. In fact, she remains defiantly and famously robust
before this threatening public. The body of Arthur Dimmesdale,
on the other hand, though he never comes fully before the public
until the novel's end, is marked with both stripes from his penitential whippings and an "A" burned into or erupted from his chest.
Dimmesdale, it seems, need not even confess or take the scaffold
to be subjected to the tortures—with one notable difference—that
the matrons imagine for Hester. The difference, of course, is that
Dimmesdale's tortures are self-inflicted.

But what does it mean for Dimmesdale to adopt for himself precisely the corporal punishments that the public would inflict? One
has difficulty imagining this as a fully independent act, and I want
to suggest here that Dimmesdale's self-discipline is no such thing.
Rather, it is an apparent extension into and enactment of public
discipline in the most private areas of Dimmesdale's existence. Not
only does the minister whip himself for having escaped whipping
and exposure, his body, in a kind of autonomous eruption of the
"A," seems to understand instinctively the public's right to place a
brand upon it.

I am suggesting that we might see Dimmesdale's penitential process in a perhaps slightly but meaningfully unfamiliar way. It is not
Dimmesdale's sin that tortures him, or even his conscience in any
independent sense of the term. Rather, it is his own sense of the public's need—and, in the ethos of the Puritan community, the public's
right—to know everything about him, even as he attempts to violate
that right. In the character of Arthur Dimmesdale, *The Scarlet Letter* imagines the cultural celebrity (and sinner) as one who cannot
imagine any type of privacy or corporal self-possession, because he
carries within and enacts upon himself—even when resisting it—
the public's claim to his secrets and his body.[28]

We can see the dramatic power that internalized demands to realize himself as a public property have on Dimmesdale not only in the corporal punishments he subjects himself to, but also in his preaching. The minister returns obsessively to precisely what he would keep private, acting out his confession, his ascension to the scaffold, hundreds of times, even though the audience has no idea that he is doing so: "More than once—nay more than a hundred times—[Dimmesdale] had actually spoken! Spoken! But how? He had told his hearers that he was altogether vile. . . . They heard it all and did but reverence him more . . . [but] the minister well knew—subtle but remorseful hypocrite that he was!—the light in which his vague confession would be viewed" (143–44). As Dimmesdale imagines his penitence, only by condemning himself as vile in public can he attempt (however futilely) to assuage the guilt of having not been publicly exposed; similarly, it is only by whipping and branding himself that Dimmesdale relieves the anxiety of having not been whipped or branded. In short, it is only by enacting through his own hands and conscience in private the public's right of complete and corporal access to him that Dimmesdale avoids this access. In Lauren Berlant's terms, Dimmesdale "literalizes the machinery of conscience—the abstract memory of the juridical apparatus—burned into the mind of every citizen."[29]

Though Berlant is concerned only with describing the process through which Dimmesdale and others are absorbed into an idea of nation or community, her insight is clearly relevant to the project of figuring celebrity as slavery. In Dimmesdale, autonomy utterly vanishes as the private self becomes the scene of public discipline. The minister cannot imagine himself as independent from the public's right to his body, cannot even imagine any mode of alternative punishment, but rather attempts to satisfy public demands by adopting in private and secretive forms the public and corporal modes of discipline emblematic at once of the Puritan community and, in the context of the mid-nineteenth century, those punishments very closely associated with bondage.

Dimmesdale's story ends, of course, with both his greatest sermon and the removal of his robe, the exposure of his branded body in the marketplace. Critics have recognized that the location of this self-offering is pregnant with meaning, that, in Michael Gilmore's understanding, Dimmesdale realizes Hawthorne's anxieties about the expanding, increasingly commercialized literary marketplace: "The writer [Dimmesdale] 'dies' because he has to find some way to survive in what has become purely a relation of [market] exchange."[30]

But, if I have been at all convincing, we might ask not only whether Dimmesdale and Hawthorne were anxious about relations of exchange in the conventional sense, but whether Dimmesdale, as a public figure, was imagined to have any such relation with his audience. For the general oddity about the Puritan marketplace throughout *The Scarlet Letter* is not that it emblematizes any typical kind of commodification or commerce but, rather, that we never see any goods exchanged or purchased in it. The Puritan "marketplace," in fact, hardly functions as a market at all, but more as a location in which the bodies of sinners (and ministers) are offered (or offer themselves) for spectatorial (and sometimes corporally punitive) consumption. My point is that we can see in this marketplace not any realization of monetary or exchange relations between the public figure and his audience, but a relationship much more fully realized in terms of the public figure's corporal and spiritual sacrifice of self for consumption.

Eva has already taught us that this self-sacrifice need not be seen wholly as a process of victimization, though surely it might be seen partly in that way. The celebrity (unlike the slave) might, in fact, assert himself most fully in the act of self-offering. Indeed, Dimmesdale, like Eva, achieves expiation and relief from his spiritual and bodily suffering only by surrendering himself utterly to his public. Furthermore, in the case of Dimmesdale, we might note that self-offering seems to eliminate, or at least moderate, the idea of the intrusive audience. For once the celebrity wholly surrenders himself, the idea of the audience as intrusive, the idea of the audience as somehow wronged by the celebrity's withholding, and *The Scarlet Letter*'s most obvious figure for these ideas, Roger Chillingworth, cannot survive. At the same time, however, Dimmesdale and Eva both demonstrate clearly that anxieties about entering into the market as a celebrity were imagined through the erasure of market dynamics and motivations. Far from imagining the celebrity as one who markets his cultural productions for profit through personal appearances, Dimmesdale, like Eva, imagines personal appearance as purely and inevitably an offering and sacrifice of the celebrity body.

Hawthorne's sensitivity to the celebrity's "enslavement" appears not only in *The Scarlet Letter*, but also in *The Blithedale Romance*. Here, too, we can find the appropriative psychology of the audience that would violate the body of the celebrity figure. In the first paragraph of *Blithedale*, Miles Coverdale introduces us to Priscilla, a "celebrity . . . phenomenon in the mesmeric line." Priscilla seems literally to be held either in bondage or indentured servitude by her master (and promoter) Westervelt, who displays her—hidden behind a veil that her public yearns to remove. The relationship between Priscilla and her audience, particularly as it is worked out in Coverdale's fantasies of intimate encounter, is fully grounded in voyeuristic fantasies of sexual possession. According to Gillian Brown's blunt assessment of the psychology underlying Priscilla's celebrity status, her show is "a fetishistic erotic practice, a substitute for genital encounters." *Blithedale* reemphasizes in more sexualized, less explicitly violent terms the appropriative psychology of the audience, the irrational lust for intrusion into and possession of the celebrity body that seems to have no self completely closed to access.[31]

Nineteenth-century demands for public appearance and complete access to the celebrity figure had their literal and historical expression not in anything as gruesome as Hawthorne imagines in the dynamics of Dimmesdale's contrition or as outwardly bizarre as Priscilla's enslaved exhibition, but in the audience's demands to learn everything about the private lives of figures on the public stage. Nathaniel Parker Willis's *Memoranda of the Life of Jenny Lind*, used to help promote her tour, amounts to an extended report and example of precisely this psychology. Willis reveals many details about the life of Lind, including, quite prominently (one wonders if he recognized the irony), reports of her harassment by the public and her strategies for sheltering herself from such harassment.[32]

But perhaps the most amusing anecdote of the public's demands for complete access to Lind comes to us not from Willis but from P. T. Barnum. According to Barnum, when he and Lind arrived at her hotel in Philadelphia during the singer's 1850 tour, a crowd chanted beneath her balcony hoping for an appearance. Lind, apparently, did not feel up to greeting her fans, so Barnum dressed a "companion" (a maid or servant?) in the singer's clothes and sent her onto the balcony. "She bowed gracefully to the multitude, who gave her three hearty cheers and dispersed." [33]

Lind, Willis, and Barnum show us that in the real world of celebrity promotion, personal appearances and bodily exposure could be (and were) tightly controlled. The successful celebrity could, in a sense, retreat behind a protective veil to hide herself from the consuming public at any moment. We might, then, remember that *The Scarlet Letter*'s introduction, "The Custom-House," seems to postulate as ideal just this kind of controlled self-exposure and hiding. Hawthorne, after pointing out that the reader might (or might not) be interested in the author's biography, but that he as an author tends to present too much of his own, concludes that "Authors may prate of circumstances that lie around us, and even of ourself, but still keep the inmost me behind [a] veil. To this extent, and within these limits an author, methinks, may be autobiographical, without violating either the reader's rights or his own" (4).

This, then, is Hawthorne's immediate and explicit discussion of a civil, appropriate, one might even say polite relationship between the public figure in the literary market and his or her audience. The urge of the audience to know the public figure and the urge of figures to expose and offer themselves are both contained by mutually acknowledged "rights." The book is the book, and the audience has a right to it as a book, a fiction. The author's personal life (not to mention his or her actual person) ought not to be fully exposed.

Yet once we move into *The Scarlet Letter*, it is precisely and very immediately these rules, rights, and logic of autobiographical decorum that come into question and under attack. Dimmesdale, far from echoing Hawthorne's ideal of the self-veiling public figure, stands whipped, branded, emaciated, and exposed at the novel's end, and—what would to Hawthorne, with his notorious desire for

privacy, have been even more frightening—Dimmesdale has irre-
pressibly sought out and enacted through his own hands the corporal access that audiences might mistakenly understand as their
right.[34] In sum, rather than discreetly producing cultural commodities for profitable sale apart from the offering of self, Dimmesdale
participates in a rather different market dynamic, a dynamic in
which neither labor nor goods but bodies are most crucially brought
into the "marketplace," a dynamic, as Dimmesdale's scourge marks
and brand might readily suggest, that has its most powerful referent not in the commodification or alienation of labor but, rather, in
the physically consuming work and trade of the Southern slave.

Linda Brent

So far I have emphasized that the apparently distant phenomena of
the slave's consumption and the emergence of celebrity in the cultural, particularly the literary, sphere were brought into rhetorical
proximity by literary mediations or figurations that worked through
personal and more widely cultural anxieties. These mediations were
ideologically charged by particular understandings of labor and
property rights. Anxieties about celebrity aligned the audience with
the slavemaster and his non- or even antieconomic (and, to some
extent, *de*commodifying) desire to consume the laborer rather than
exchange goods and labor for rational profits.

We need to understand, then, that celebrities were not slaves
but, at the same time, that celebrity could be (and was) figuratively
imagined through particular inflections of slavery. In fact, it seems
to me that the reimagining of slavery in the purely literary terms
of celebrity rather than as a lived condition of bondage is worked
out repeatedly in antebellum slave narratives. It has become almost
axiomatic to say that slave narratives feature the quest for freedom
and literacy, apparently in the assumption that these two acquire-
ments bear some inescapable and unambiguous relationship to each
other, and it is clear enough, most notably in the *Narrative of the
Life of Frederick Douglass*, that the authors themselves often assert
this tie.[35]

I want to suggest, however, a somewhat different view of what literacy and authorship mean to the slave writer, particularly in the case of Harriet Jacobs's *Incidents in the Life of a Slave Girl*. Hazel Carby has pointed out what should be clear to any careful reader of Jacobs, though what she sees has been invisible to some others: *Incidents* is not a story of a woman who rises from slavery in the South to a blissful or even moderately contented freedom in the North, but a story in which Jacobs's life in the North suggests an altered form of bondage to economic imperatives and the domestic ideology of middle-class New England womanhood. Jacobs, in other words, escapes literal bondage in the South only to find herself figuratively threatened with reenslavement in the North. *Incidents* simply is not the story of escape to an unqualified freedom.[36]

I want to discuss at some length Jacobs's bondage within Northern economics and domestic ideology, but even more central to this chapter is the way that, like the novels I have previously discussed, *Incidents* situates the business of personal exposure, the gaining of a public personality, via penetrations, echoes, and reconfigurations of slavery. What *Incidents* makes more clear than these other texts is precisely that the resituation of celebrity as slavery is a process of mediation. In other words, affinities between revealing oneself intimately to the intrusions of the cultural market and becoming much more literally an object of consumption in the noneconomic mind of the slavemaster do exist, but most importantly at a figurative or a rhetorical level.

Several critics have noted that the autobiographical nature of the slave narrative and its scripted featuring of the horrors of personal experience for an audience always threatens to reproduce the objectification of self that the ex-slave might have hoped to leave behind. In other words, as William Andrews has noted, the generic expectations of white abolitionists who read slave narratives allowed relatively little room for the individuality of the writer, but emphasized instead the exposure of the broadly "institutional facts of slavery." These generic expectations led to the simultaneous erasure and over-exposure of the self. The slave writer was forced to "achieve credence by objectifying himself [or herself]" for the reading public. On the one hand, as Sidonie Smith puts it, this emphasis on representativeness tended to push the ex-slave into "a scene of writing that, like the scene of slavery itself, required the erasure of individual history and 'self.'" On the other hand, the demand for the revelation of actually experienced, intimate details of physical abuses from rape to whipping tended not to erase writers at all, but to expose the humiliating details of bodily violation and force them to be relived publicly. The very dynamics of the slave narrative and its generic expectations threatened to reproduce the kind of direct access to a deprivatized body—publicly displayed and accessible in literary terms—that I have been pointing to as emblematic of antebellum slavery and celebrity throughout this chapter.[37]

Indeed, the familiar perversions of slave consumption and economics are everywhere in Jacobs's *Incidents* and, by this point, they hardly need explication in any detail. Chapter 9, "Sketches of Neighboring Slaveholders," heavily edited by Lydia Maria Child, is a lengthy and mortifying list of the atrocities to which slaves were subjected.[38] One recaptured runaway, the son of "a valuable slave, named Charity" (48), is imprisoned and immobilized in a cotton gin and, perhaps, eaten alive by rats. Another is shot through the head. Others are whipped, burned, and torn apart by bloodhounds. Charity's son, in particular, suffers because of his master's financial recklessness: "[W]hat did *he* care for the value of a slave? He had hundreds of them" (49). Beside these scenes of physical torture stand repeated references to the slaves' "dreary week, toiling without wages, under constant threat of the lash" (193). As always, slave labor is defined by the economic inefficiency, by the lack of *exchange* in its threats to punish or consume the worker rather than promise him or her material rewards.

Jacobs figures the outstanding instance of the perverse desire to consume the slave's body and the economic irrationality of the slave system in the desire of Linda Brent's (Jacobs's pseudonym) master to seduce her. Dr. Flint's lust and megalomania, his desire to have Brent as a mistress, are so absolute that he affirms repeatedly, even when offered substantially more than the market value of Brent by her paramour, "that he cannot buy her for any money" (80). Even after her escape, when he no longer has any practical authority over her or the profits from her labor, Flint refuses to sell. Brent escapes coerced sex with her master but not the central dynamic of the slave as consumable property, the corporal availability of the slave, by offering herself as a lover to a different white man, by relocating, with some small measure of choice, the man who will possess and use her. But the final equation of captivity with physical deterioration is Brent's seven years spent hiding in an attic too small for her to stand up, an immobilization of her body much like the imprisonment of Charity's son within a cotton gin, and Brent loses for a time all strength in her legs and the ability to stand. It is, then, as I have been emphasizing, not only Brent's status as a commodity for exchange that emblematizes her slavery, but her master's refusal to make an exchange "for any [amount of] money." Flint is not interested in rational profit or production, but only in forms of bodily (sexual) possession.

As most important critics of *Incidents* agree, Brent appears as an ardent advocate of socio-economic moral relativism. In the view of *Incidents*, one simply should not expect the same behavior, with the same emphasis on the woman's protection of her sexual innocence, from enslaved women that one might reasonably expect from free women in the North.[39] Brent continually reiterates this point in her narrative, so much so that her quest for freedom becomes a quest for a socio-economic order in which she might possess a home and wages which, in turn, will signify her self-possession.

The quest for freedom, Christian virtue, and bodily self-determination, in other words, is utterly conflated by Jacobs with the desire to escape from the noneconomics of slavery, to escape her status as a consumable human chattel to the status of one who works, earns wages, produces goods, and, like the ideal free laborer, exchanges them for a home and the goods within it: "If slavery had been abolished, I, also could have had a home shielded by the laws; and I should have been spared the painful task of confessing what I am now about to relate" (54). In a different economy, Jacobs tells us, she would earn and buy a home. In a different economy, that home would be protected by laws and she would have avoided the compulsion to give away her body. Sexual morality or immorality,

Brent suggests, follows very directly from the economic imperatives thrust upon women. Brent is forced into her affair not because she lacks the moral character of the Northern woman, but because she is denied the right to earn and own a secure home.

Brent, however, finds that the geographical escape from the slave states cannot be equated with the achievement of free, productive, and profitable labor and the concomitant benefit of corporal self-possession. Her escape North turns out not to be an escape to any alternative economy. Her first act upon reaching free ground is to buy gloves and veils. The transaction, Brent's first participation in open commerce, takes on almost magical significance: "The shop-man told me they were so many levies. I had never heard the word before, but I did not tell him so. I thought if he knew I was a stranger he might ask me where I came from. I gave him a gold piece, and when he returned the change, I counted it, and found out how much a levy was" (159). The escape to the North is the escape to purchasing power and the familiarization with commercially determined exchange value, but it is also the escape to an arena where personal exposure in the market must be guarded against. Brent's first purchase is a double act of concealment from observation as well as an education in the free-market society: she must hide from the shopkeeper where she has come from in order to purchase gloves and veils which are a further concealment of her from public exposure.

The escape to freedom should ideally signify the escape to an economy where her body and self are no longer available to others, where she is able to adopt some kind of free and profitable labor, but the purchase of the veils suggests exactly the opposite situation, a market and society from which her history and body require concealment. The fugitive slave law, various other discriminatory Northern practices, and a continuous stream of letters from her former master persistently continue to define Brent as human property.

Recent critics of *Incidents* emphasize the extent to which the book assumes its readers to be Northern, white, middle-class women, and that Brent continually undermines the ideology of domesticity by which these readers presumably live. There is, of course, ample evidence to support such ideas. Brent addresses Northern women directly and explicitly within the text; she subverts the notion of absolute adherence to sexual virtue; her tone is not the retiring voice of the "true woman," but the assertive voice of the committed activist. For Hazel Carby, Brent's assault on Northern white women is enthusiastic; for Jean Fagan Yellin, who sees Jacobs trying "to establish an American sisterhood" with Northern abolitionists, the critique of Northern women is more tentative. In Yellin's view, Jacobs's conflicts were not with Northern women, but with men who defined and instituted the ideals of domesticity. Jacobs saw "true womanhood . . . not as a category of nature, but as a [patriarchal] cultural construct that functioned to justify [her] oppression."[40]

Somewhat differently from these critics, I would like to underscore that while Jacobs finds the absolute invocation of domestic ideology and, more particularly, its emphasis on sexual virtue disabling, she also demonstrates some degree of commitment to it as an ideal. In other words, implicit in Jacobs's plea for relativism is a plea that her extenuating circumstances be understood precisely as extenuating or mitigating what she still seems to understand as a transgression against proper conduct in an ideal social order. While Brent questions the absolute fairness of demanding bodily modesty from those who do not have control over their bodies, she plainly values the opportunity to be sexually modest as a sign of self-possession.

We can see Brent embracing this ideal of modesty, of retiring or even hidden sexuality and bodily presence when we understand the dynamics of her purchase of the veil and gloves. Brent can appear as a public figure broadcasting her sexual transgression, but only from behind a veil of privacy, and only by seeking to justify or keep from sight a sexual history that Northerners may feel all too ready to judge severely. The veil not only protects Brent's body from the market while allowing her to participate in it; the veil simultaneously shows Brent participating in the disabling domestic logic of the female body's purity and sanctity even as she all but attacks and confesses to violating such demands elsewhere in the narrative. The absolute valuation of chastity, says Brent, comes from those who "never knew what it is to be a slave; to be entirely unprotected by law or custom; to have the laws reduce you to the condition of a chattel, subject to the will of another" (55). But despite Brent's objections to any moral absolutism, it is also clear that the preservation of such chastity is a powerful sign of the physical self-possession she seeks.

Finally, through the purchase of her freedom from Flint's heirs by a sympathetic Northerner, Mrs. Bruce, Brent is liberated from her slavery, but, as she herself ambivalently acknowledges, to have her freedom purchased is simultaneously to recognize her continuing status as property and, at some level—her adoption of a pseudonym indicates this—the purchase does nothing to relieve the pressures of concealment and social captivity enforced by the domestic construction of her femininity. The purchase simply transforms Brent from a piece of property with value only in her (sexual) consumption to one with a monetarily measured exchange value, but she herself is still property. For Brent, there is no final escape to the evasive ideal of free labor, production, and social mobility. She closes her narrative with regrets that she has been unable to gain the ultimate sign of material success and social independence—a home—and with the claim that "[l]ove, duty, [and] gratitude bind me to [Mrs. Bruce's] side" (201). Brent remains free yet bound in new terms to and by her purchaser and Northern society, an incomplete participant in the materialistic quest for profitable, independent, productive employment and self-ownership.

As I have described it to this point, the impossibility for Brent of achieving an independent public existence in the North without simultaneously requiring the figurative and literal protection of a veil has very little to do with the specific work of any conspicuously public figure in the cultural sphere. This ambivalence about public exposure and its threats are, however, central to understanding Jacobs's sense of herself as an author, as a figure on the public stage. For, as Lauren Berlant has claimed, Harriet Jacobs stands first in a long historical line of African American women who have brought their tales of corporeal, particularly sexual, violation into the public in the hope of stimulating reforms that will eliminate such abuses.

Unlike most critics, however, Berlant emphasizes the ineffectiveness of Jacobs's gesture and rhetoric rather than its subversive power. For Berlant, the act of testimony against these violations of bodily intimacy and autonomy, these accessions to publicity in the name of reform, are almost always performed with extreme ambivalence, as if going into public were very much to re-experience at the hands of the audience the kind of bodily violations against which the women originally came to testify. In Berlant's words, "For all these verbs of resistance [in the testimony of African American women], the women represent their deployment of publicity as an act made under duress, an act thus representing and performing unfreedom [slavery?] in America."[41]

What we need to understand about Jacobs, then, is that the act of writing her narrative, of going public, places her figuratively into a new relationship in which she sees herself as threatened by dismemberment and consumption not in the corporal terms of slavery but in the figurative terms of specifically literary self-presentation to a voyeuristic public. The telling of her story becomes for Jacobs the simultaneous recognition that she has escaped the literal threats of slavery and that she remains vulnerable to the more figurative threats of attack and consumption posed by an anonymous audience to the (particularly female) author who ventures with her questionable past into the public sphere of literary production and confession. The fear for Jacobs is that bringing her story to the market makes her, rather than her story alone, an object in the market. The fear for Jacobs is the fear of an exaggerated intimacy with an anonymous and threatening audience. Jacobs, in short, seems to want to offer her book without offering herself. She seeks to gain her public voice, to become a public figure, but experiences again a sense that she is surrendering her bodily self into a kind of overly intimate, anonymous bondage that places her body on display.

The original title page of *Incidents* itself protectively veiled the text and author even as she displayed herself on its pages: it featured the name of Lydia Maria Child as editor, but Jacobs's name appeared neither there nor anywhere else in the story. The contemporaneous reader of the narrative, then, was told from the outset that while Jacobs's story was true, it was also on its face not told strictly or openly in her words, not even strictly about her but, rather, about the pseudonymous "Linda Brent." Jacobs's preface calls attention to this veil, then attempts to explain it away: "I have concealed the names of places and given persons fictitious names. I had no motive for secrecy on my own account, but I deemed it kind and considerate towards others to pursue this course. . . . I have not written my experiences in order to attract attention to myself; on the contrary, it would have been more pleasant to me to have been silent about my history" (1). I have elided a paragraph between these comments to emphasize the problem: on the one hand, Jacobs harbors no secrets on her own account; on the other, it would be more pleasant never to have broken her silence by writing the narrative. On the one hand, Jacobs wants to offer her story freely to her audience; on the other, she feels a threat in presenting her experience publicly and needs an editor—however small or large Child's changes were—to present herself at all.

Yellin's edition of *Incidents* makes these competing claims of concealment and exposure, of retreat from and participation in the literary market, highly visible. First, and perhaps most importantly because it was published with the narrative to authenticate its veracity, we need to read Amy Post's testimonial: "I repeatedly urged her to consent to the publication of her narrative. . . . But her sensitive spirit shrank from publicity. She said, 'You know a woman can whisper cruel wrongs in the ear of a dear friend much easier than she can record them for the whole world to read'" (204). Next, as Yellin notes, is a letter to Amy Post in Jacobs's own hand:

your proposal to me has been thought over and over again but not with out some most painful remembrances dear Amy if it was the life of a Heroine with no degradation associated with it . . . I had determined to let others think as they pleased but my lips should be sealed . . . when I first came North I avoided the Antislavery people as much as possible because I felt that I could not be honest and tell the whole truth . . . I feel that God has helped me or I never would consent to give my past life to any one . . .

if Mrs. Stowe would undertake it [to be a ghost writer or editor of the narrative] I should like to be with her a Month I should want the History of my childhood and the first five years in one volume and the next three and my home in the northern states in the second besides I could give some fine sketches for her pen on slavery [42]

If Jacobs—consistent with domestic anxieties about publicity—seems to feel a sense of violation and threat in making her experience public, she expresses simultaneously a clear vision of herself as a public figure, an author, a woman with a marketable story to tell. She moves within this letter to Post between the vision of the self as requiring protection from exposure to an audience and the vision of her story (in two volumes!) being dictated to and co-authored by the best-selling author of the century. It is difficult to imagine a writer who more than Jacobs in this letter seems acutely aware of the wisest way to bring her story and other "fine sketches" most effectively before the public—even if she is hesitant to do so (or imagines herself as incapable of it) under her own name.

Authorship, for Jacobs, cannot be seen only as an expression of her freedom, or of her participation in the dynamics of free labor, but neither can it be seen wholly as the continuation of the corporally threatening labor that she has left behind. For Jacobs, the act of authorship is linked at once to the liberating production of a text, a new form of offering a book rather than herself for sale, and the fear of offering herself openly, of putting herself once again—in literary rather than physical terms—wholly into the market. Jacobs uses the veil of the pseudonym and the editor as Brent uses the veil purchased on first arriving in the North, as a means of participating in and protecting herself from (now literary) consumption, as a means of venturing into public in a way at once shielded from and consistent with the domestic ideology and judgments about which she feels such obvious ambivalence.

In the literary market, however, Jacobs finally came to be more a seller of books than a buyer (or even really a wearer) of veils. Yellin tells us that after publication "Jacobs . . . was eager to promote her work," traveling and selling personally copies of the narrative, even gaining a "limited celebrity" among abolitionists. Jacobs then used this celebrity during the Civil War to perform and promote relief work with slaves and freemen behind Confederate lines.[43] In the last analysis, the cultural work of authorship in the public arena was undertaken by Jacobs much as it was for Stowe and, it seems, with a sense of the literal differences as well as figurative similarities between slavery and celebrity. To offer a book for sale was not, after all, to offer oneself for consumption. How, in the end, could a woman born a slave imagine public appearance as slavery? How, on the other hand, could she not feel some familiar discomforts? In the end, the hope of Christian influence, of lessening the literal, corporal abuses of slavery, pushed Jacobs to publication, to the offering of her private experiences and values in the public, cultural sphere, even if such an offering carried with it some psychic (rather than corporal) cost: "if it would help save another from my fate it would be selfish and unchristian in me to keep [the narrative] back."[44]

Misery

We are coming full circle, moving back toward the beginning of this chapter, the mixed feelings about celebrity and exposure in the cultural sphere that simultaneously gave prominent figures power over, while leaving them vulnerable to, the gaping fans with their color-coded tickets at events such as the Fruit Festival. While I would not, of course, claim anything like universality for the mediation of celebrity through slavery, the demonstrable breadth of such mediations suggests several major points about the consciousness that antebellum writers had of their work and their audience.

First, and most obviously, these figurations demonstrate an enormous and shared anxiety about an expanding but highly unfamiliar market-mediated relationship between the author and the audience. What is odd about that anxiety, however, is that it seems not to be grounded precisely in worries that market-mediated relationships will be purely anonymous and alienated, but in the worry that these relationships will be unalienated, ungrounded in monetary exchange as audiences seek greater and greater familiarities, exposures, and intimacies from public figures. What is odd about this anxiety, in other words, is that slavery rather than free labor becomes the figure for it. This culturally charged figuration, whether consciously invoked or not, demonstrates just how deeply and in precisely what ways many antebellum authors were troubled and uncertain about the new terms of their marketing and professionalization.

To note the depth and even violence of the worries I have reconstructed here would itself be sufficient to mark the importance of this figuration, but I also want to emphasize its breadth. We are used to organizing our literary study in such a way that it would be almost unthinkable that Stowe, Hawthorne, and Jacobs, given their admittedly different privileges of race, gender, and class, could ever be said to share anything important in their conception of authorial work. This discussion of slavery and celebrity suggests, however, that while it may be useful and even enlightening to think of writers as occupying different spheres, it may also be worth recalling the literary history, the market and consciousness-creating conditions that they might have shared at the moment of authorial professionalization and a broader industrialization. This is not to say, however, that these writers followed one common thought pattern, one formulaic and consciously articulated vision of the meanings of writing for a market-mediated audience.

Rather, I want to acknowledge that widely changing social and authorial conditions found widely identifiable but differently inflected expressions of consciousness through a central paradigm. If we pursue such paradigms, we might begin to see texts speaking to each other that we have tended to insist have no (or only antagonistic) conversation to hold. By allowing for the possibility—even more, by actively seeking out moments—of shared understanding of authorial work that cross familiar lines, we may come to an understanding of certain reactions to authorial professionalization that are, if not universal, so broadly present in the culture as to mark turning points or genuine watersheds in the experience of authorship.

This brings me to the final reason that it is important to note the mediations I have reconstructed here. The figurations of slavery and celebrity speak not only to the antebellum period, but mark the beginning of both a generalized dynamic and a specific way of thinking about celebrity/audience relationships that has persisted into the present day. Indeed, I would be the first to acknowledge that my readings have inevitably been influenced by retrospection, that it would not have been possible to see the past as I have without the benefit of a much more prominent celebrity culture in the present. The prominence in antebellum culture and society of the slavery question encouraged the kind of submerged representations I have discussed, but these representations of the consumable celebrity continue to echo into the present day when we hear public figures complaining, sometimes in what has become almost hackneyed fashion, about the demands of their public, or in their complaints that their agents and audience overemphasize commercial success or popularity at the expense of artistic, political, or personal integrity and privacy.

Consistent with the vanishing of slavery, we might then say, it is considerably less likely that celebrity would be constructed with any oblique or direct reference to slavery per se, even as the image of the celebrity's corporal vulnerability, dismemberment, or dispensation to his fans is constantly re-enacted and re-emphasized in any number of personal appearances, movies, TV shows, and sometimes, alarmingly, real-life attacks. Celebrities and their fans, in other words, still forget or overlook that venturing into the market for promotional reasons is not to offer oneself literally as public property. It is, rather, a way of promoting one's performances, books, artwork, and so forth. The specific dynamics of twentieth-century celebrity and entertainment lie well beyond the scope of this chapter, but I do hope to have suggested that certain contemporary expressions of ambivalence about adoration and fear of it as intrusive, even personally violating in the most intimate, bodily sense, owe something to, are anticipated by, and reach backward to uncover the antebellum period's hidden figurations of slavery and celebrity.

One of Stephen King's 1987 novels, *Misery*, made into a major motion picture, serves as a closing illustration, a demonstration of how these antebellum images might be made contemporary. Here a best-selling author is kidnapped by a crazed ex-nurse, his "number one fan," following his injury in a car crash. She demands that he write a novel for her. One of the captive author's major problems is that every time he misbehaves, Annie Wilkes, his fan, takes out an ax and chops off a part of him, an aggressive rudeness barely suggested by Eva's demure clipping of hair. The captor actually makes explicit reference to the disciplinary practices of overseers in South African diamond mines and, in a metaphor that antebellum authors would probably have scorned as distasteful, Annie Wilkes begins by lopping off the author's foot and cauterizing the wound with a blow torch.[45] This exaggerated and gruesomely self-conscious depiction of the audience as overseer shows, perhaps, both how accustomed we have grown to such images and how tactlessly self-inflating and direct they might become. What was a deeply submerged cultural expression of ambivalence about the institutions of celebrity in the antebellum period becomes, in the hands of Stephen King, shamelessly (if entertainingly) self-indulgent.

Finally, it seems worth noting that Kathy Bates, for playing the role of Annie Wilkes, won at our own perennial Fruit Festival, the Academy Awards, an Oscar for her performance. Kathy Bates, after playing the audience as slavemaster, stood before a worldwide television audience of her own and thanked them profusely. One hopes they remain on such good terms.

CHAPTER THREE

Healthful Employment

*White-Collar Work, Writing,
and Middle-Class Fitness*

Ill Health

My first two chapters have focused on the ways that mid-nineteenth-century authors deployed historically conditioned tropes of industrial and slave labor in their literary work to define the terms of their own inchoate profession. This project of figuring out the profession was particularly compelling and complicated because not only was the meaning of authorship unstable and unfamiliar in its transition from genteel avocation to market-oriented professionalism, but the meaning of many other forms of work also grew into unfamiliarity as the United States industrialized and veered toward the Civil War. By attaching particular ideological meanings to other forms of labor—particularly industrial and slave work—antebellum authors created charged analogies that described some of the potentialities and pitfalls of their emergent profession.

As a matter of critical methodology, it should now be increasingly clear that the re-creation of aspects of authorial consciousness for which I am striving is accessible only within literary works themselves. I am insisting on something other than an account of the materially observable conditions or the intellectual history that accompanied the professionalization of authorial work during the antebellum years. Rather, this study implicitly values as primary the cultural and personal consciousness of authorship as it is revealed in the figurative logic of literary texts. It is a history of figuration and discursive understanding that depends upon but is not limited to a history of materially knowable factors or familiar intellectual legacies.

Finally, while it would be artificially reductive to demand a uniform, consistent, or overarching understanding of what it meant to be an author circa 1850, we might still find particular shared but individually inflected paradigms that are deployed by a range of writers as they respond to the increasingly market-oriented, commercialized, and professionalized evolution of their work. What seems remarkable about the analogies, the paradigms of thought, that I have invoked up to this point, however, is the apparent divergence between the vehicle and tenor of them. Industrial work and slavery would seem to have very little immediate relevance to or obvious basis for comparison with authorial work, though authors do, in one way and another, create such mediated ties. The unlikelihood of these figurations may itself point to the strength of creative need, the urgent grasping for a figurative understanding that might clarify the position of authorial work within larger antebellum arrangements of labor.

Since the pitfalls and promises of professionalization are at the heart of the antebellum authorial experience, one might imagine that other professional and white-collar forms of labor would be more obviously and immediately available as figures for writing. If these figurations are efforts to situate the meaning of authorship's transition to the professional realm, then we might expect authors to be preoccupied with the meanings and consequences of professionalism itself. For, as we shall see, the emergence of white-collar work, of professionalism as a middle-class marker, occurs alongside the professionalization of the literary, and the meanings of this growth of a white-collar middle class are extremely complicated.

So, one might ask as this chapter's central questions, what were the meanings of white-collar work available to antebellum authors and how did they deploy these meanings to define their authorial situation? A letter written by Hawthorne to his long-time friend Horatio Bridge on February 4, 1850, one day after the completion of *The Scarlet Letter*, begins to provide some answers:

I long to get into the country; for my health, latterly, is not quite what it has been, for many years past. I should not long stand such a life of bodily inactivity and mental exertion as I have led for the last few months. An hour or two of daily labor in a garden, and a daily ramble in country air or on the seashore, would keep all right. Do not allude to this matter in your letters to me; as my wife already sermonizes me quite sufficiently on my habits—and I never own up to not feeling perfectly well. Neither do I feel anywhere ill, but only a lack of physical vigor and energy, which re-acts upon the mind.[1]

Hawthorne tells Bridge that his vague malaise is recent, a product of his too-exclusive devotion to the "mental exertion" of completing his novel. But if Hawthorne's nebulous illness was recent, we might also recognize it as a recurrence. For the symptoms he experiences at the end of his writing of *The Scarlet Letter*, a general lethargy of mind and body, are in some ways similar to the symptoms mentioned in *The Scarlet Letter*'s introduction, the symptoms that he claims to experience while working in the Custom House. While by no means absolutely debilitating, work in the Custom House causes headaches and severe lethargy. It leaves Hawthorne unable to think or imagine clearly; it leaves him unfit for any "intellectual effort." In attempts to cure himself of the "wretched numbness" inflicted by labor in the Custom House, Hawthorne takes up precisely one of the therapies mentioned in his letter to Bridge—extended "seashore walks, and rambles into the country."[2]

Readers even slightly familiar with Hawthorne know that he imagined work in the Custom House as everything that authorship ought not to be. Lengthy passages in "The Custom-House" describe the impossibility of writing while he works as a surveyor, and one sign of Hawthorne's debility is that he finds his imagination paralyzed. How is it, then, that these two rather different, even opposed labors lead to similar ailments with nearly identical treatments? Hawthorne, it seems to me, is imagining, and may even be physically experiencing, some connection between the managerial work of the Custom House and the work of writing even though he so clearly desires to separate them. For all the differences between the two types of work, both foster ill health insofar as they create what Hawthorne's letter calls "bodily inactivity." Both might be usefully complemented by recreation and exercise.

This connection between various nonmanual, white-collar occupations and all sorts of ill health was not peculiar to Hawthorne, and this chapter will explore the meanings of this connection for antebellum authorship, itself a form of white-collar work. Indeed, Hawthorne's letter and "The Custom-House" are only isolated expressions of a much broader cultural anxiety about the expansion of nonmanual work and material nonproductivity during the antebellum years. Social and cultural historians have recently pointed to an emergent middle class in antebellum America that defined itself partly in terms of its divorce from more familiar modes of manual work and material production, the independent craft and agricultural labor of eighteenth-century "middling sorts." This should not, however, be taken to mean that the emerging middle class divorced itself absolutely from the long-standing ideological valorization of the yeoman and artisan. This sort of ideological rhetoric came down to the nineteenth century most clearly, of course, in Thomas Jefferson's eighteenth-century celebration of the yeomanry, but also existed, as Sean Wilentz makes plain, "in an urban variation of the Jeffersonian social theme . . . a republican celebration of the trades."[3]

On the following pages I argue that certain aspects of emergent middle-class culture—most apparently the stump speeches of its political representatives and the writing of various health reform exponents—began to redefine and appropriate manual labor in ways consistent with the middle-class separation from the necessity or performance of it. In other words, particular areas of middle-class culture worked to alter, or at least obscure, particular areas of middle-class social reality. For even as middle-class work increasingly defined itself through its separation from the manual, middle-class culture worked to reunite in rhetorical terms middle-class occupations with traditional valorizations of manual work. The management of capital, as we shall see, could be represented as the work of one's hands, and agricultural and artisanal work could be reconfigured as forms of exercise for the otherwise "bodily inactive" worker.

What "The Custom-House" and Hawthorne's letter begin to suggest is that the work of authorship in antebellum America also has a particular place in this social and ideological history of middle-class emergence, that the work of authorship, however different it may be from work in the Custom House, also needed to be reunited with the virtues of physical activity, what Hawthorne, in a telling phrase, calls the "daily labor" of gardening.

On the following pages, accordingly, I argue both a broad and a more specific point. I suggest that a broad effort to claim the virtues of selected and idealized forms of manual activity and production emerged within middle-class culture even as the middle class decisively separated itself in the realm of lived, social experience from such work. This reunion of the physically leisured with bodily activity occurred, to some extent, across gendered lines, as reformers recommended exertion to middle-class women as well as men.

More specifically, I argue that the figurative physicalizing of authorial labor as the work of the artisan or yeoman was strongly male gendered and that we can see this in the work and lives of Hawthorne and Thoreau. Hawthorne's experiences at the Brook Farm settlement in 1841 and his writing of "The Custom-House" as well as Thoreau's experiences at Walden Pond and his writing of *Walden* attempt to reclaim for authorship the virtues and physical health persistently associated with manual labor and production. Hawthorne and Thoreau attempted this reclamation by mediating their representations of authorship through modes of idealized and residual manual work. In short, then, I hope to reconstruct a rhetorical history of the relationships between white-collar work, the middle-class transformation of physical labor into physical fitness, and a particularly gendered figuration of antebellum authorship.

From Work to Exercise

A number of historians have begun to mark the boundaries and habits of a recognizable if still emergent middle class in antebellum

America. Gary Nash tells us that in the urban Northeast of the republican period, social hierarchies tended to be structured by rank rather than by class. In the smaller cities of the late 1700s and even the early 1800s, work and social interaction took place in a "face-to-face" society, one in which professionals and aristocrats might routinely come into contact with and live beside craftsmen and less skilled manual workers. Such encounters, of course, hardly assumed the social equality of those of different ranks. Rather, they were ordered by fairly static, nonconfrontational conventions of assumed social deference and differentiation.

By the mid-nineteenth century, these face-to-face encounters became less common and were structured by competing class interests as much as by static conventions of social rank. Stuart Blumin tells us that in Philadelphia white-collar laborers—the clerks, business proprietors, and others of an emergent middle class—increasingly gathered into exclusive blocks beyond the means of most artisans or industrial workers. Manual workers, in turn, gathered onto streets of their own, and locations of manual work—factories and workshops—increasingly migrated away from locations of nonmanual work. Furthermore, an ornate architectural vocabulary of pillars, picture windows, elegant woodwork, and interior design developed to distinguish the professional or retail workplace from the place of material production. Cities that had been organized by the chance encounters of differently ranking individuals gradually reorganized along lines that emphasized horizontal class affiliation.[4]

The middle class achieved its cohesion from daily social practices other than work, of course. In Karen Halttunen's brilliant phrase, middle-class identity formed itself in an elaborately scripted "genteel performance" of dining, mourning, and visiting rituals that identified a family's taste, income, and capacity for social grace in the home. Moreover, as Mary Ryan and others have pointed out, the professionalization of the middle class to which Blumin and others have pointed was largely restricted to men. If the white-collar labor of men in the marketplace provided the prestige of a lucrative calling and the money to support the activities of the middle-class home, the actual making of that home came to rest squarely upon the women within it. Women of the emergent middle class increasingly abandoned the domestic production prominent during the republican years and took on the role of moral arbiter and guardian of the private, domestic domain. Bodily leisure and the abandonment of domestic arrangements of material production thus became a prime marker of middle-class prestige for men outside the home and for women within it.[5]

As Halttunen shows us, extreme anxieties accompanied the construction of middle-class professional and familial arrangements. If, for example, young men with ambitions to enter the middle-class were ideally defined by their professional success and women by their social finesse and spiritual custodianship of the family, middle-class culture also detailed pervasive threats to these idealized figures. A standard premonitory tale of middle-class advice literature showed men seeking their fortunes in the city only to be duped or seduced by confidence men who "compromised all the major elements of eighteenth-century republican ideology." Worse still, young men seeking places within the middle-class professions often seemed perilously close to con men themselves, to men on the make whose living came to them less through the virtues of productive labor and more through manipulations of truth and personality. In the same vein, the spiritual purity and cultivated manners of women always threatened to be understood as a form of rehearsed sincerity, as the art of "the painted woman . . . who poisoned polite society with deception and betrayal by dressing extravagantly and practicing the empty forms of false etiquette."[6]

Another sign of middle-class anxiety about its own emergence and separation from republican social structures is registered by the persistent invocation of the virtues of the yeoman farmer and independent artisan. Even among the staunchest advocates of industrialization and its accompanying social reordering, one could still routinely find valorizations and idealizations of manual work and its ideological virtues. Stuart Blumin demonstrates that virtually all political parties continued to valorize the independent manual laborer even as these parties came more and more to be dominated by white-collar workers and even as manual laborers were increasingly incorporated into industrial organizations of mass production.[7] Edward Everett, for example, whom Caroline Porter has insightfully pointed to as the quintessential political advocate of industrialization and its social reordering, could idealize the independent farmer in a very Jeffersonian mode: "The man who stands upon his own soil, who feels that by the laws of the land in which he lives, by the law of civilized nations, he is the rightful and exclusive owner of the land which he tills, is, by the constitution of our nature, under a wholesome influence, not easily imbibed from any other source."[8] When it came to craft laborers, speaking before the Massachusetts Charitable Mechanic Association in 1837, Everett exclaimed, "Mechanics of America! Respect your calling! respect yourselves! The cause of human improvement has no firmer or more powerful friends" (II, 255).[9]

It is both easy and accurate to say that such political rhetoric functioned somewhat instrumentally, as a way for those in or coming to power to placate and undermine any potential resistance from those increasingly dispossessed during the ongoing processes of industrialization. Craftworkers and even agricultural workers did typically lose their independence and often had their skills made obsolete within factories and emerging systems of "sweated" labor.[10] Rhetorically ennobling such workers may have obscured a harsher economic reality. My own sense, however, is that such rhetoric must be seen not only as a means of oppression but as a means of middle-class self-definition. For, to stay with the single example of Edward Everett, he repeatedly attempted to reconstruct the white-collar labor of the lawyer, the manager of capital, and the clerk in terms of the residual manual work that he idealized.

In one lovingly entitled speech, "Accumulation, Property, Capital, Credit," Everett found himself "at some loss to account for . . . the contrast in which capital has been placed with labor" because, as he said elsewhere, capital "was, itself, originally the work of men's hands" (II, 264, 293). The deployment of capital, as Everett imagined it, was itself something close to the materially productive work "necessary for the construction of a row-boat and an Indiaman, a pair of shoes and a railroad" (II, 283). Seemingly missing the point, when Everett delivered an address on the political feasibility of a national "Working-Men's Party" he assumed that its membership would be a "union of different kinds of workmen [including, for example, lawyers and merchants] in one harmonious society" (I, 291). Everett "endeavoured to show, in a plain manner, that there is a close and cordial union between the various pursuits and occupations" (I, 303). Not only the laborer, lawyer, and merchant, but artists, architects, poets, and surgeons ought to be part of any Working-Men's Party, thought Everett, because each of them, like the manual laborer, in some way used "the faculties of the intellectual and physical nature" (I, 298).

If such rhetoric were the primary focus of this chapter, numerous examples of similar speeches could be brought forth, but the incorporation of the manual into the self-identification of the middle-class worked itself out not only in verbal acts.[11] Rather, the transformation and appropriation of such work was one central achievement of the burgeoning and distinctly middle-class health reform movement. Health reformers were active in America before 1830, but only after the emergence of Sylvester Graham did hygienic systems multiply with almost frantic rapidity. The reformers—including, among many others, Graham, Edward Hitchcock, and William Alcott in the 1830s and 1840s and then, in addition, Catharine Beecher and Dioclesian Lewis in the 1840s, 1850s, and beyond—perceived a pervasive debility in America that crossed class boundaries but was particularly malignant within the urban middle class of sedentary male workers and supposedly leisured women. As correctives they presented a range of complicated programs emphasizing dietary abstemiousness, sensible dress, regular sleeping and waking hours, improved ventilation in the home, and, most crucially for my concerns, various forms of physical exercise. Exercise came to be envisioned among health reformers at this moment not only as physically therapeutic, but as a moral imperative, as a strenuous activity through which both the characters and bodies of the newly affluent middle class might be conditioned.[12]

The First [and only] *Annual Report of the Society for Promoting Manual Labor in Literary Institutions* (1833) begins to make clear the

ways in which antebellum health reform and sport movements re-
constituted manual labor. Spearheaded by Theodore Dwight Weld
(the author of the report) and Arthur and Lewis Tappan—all three
of whom devotedly followed Sylvester Graham's hygiene program
—the society set out to cure allegedly massive debility in the privileged and idle American student body.[13] After traveling for two
years, Weld compiled 120 pages of expert testimony documenting
the debility of the nation's university students, those, he points out,
studying to enter the already expanding middle-class professions.
The president of Columbian College in Washington, D.C., lamented
that "many of our young men fall victim to intense application, before they complete their studies! Others make wrecks of their con-
stitutions, and, after remaining upon the sick list a few years, and
performing half service, fall into premature graves" (19). Edward
Hitchcock, a widely read antebellum authority on physiology and
professor of geology and chemistry at Amherst College, had a similarly bleak outlook:

A large proportion of diligent, close students . . . have impaired health and
usefulness by a deficiency o[r] irregularity of exercise. Indeed, for several
years past, I have been in the habit of looking with a sort of surprise upon
any student whose countenance exhibited the rosy clearness and freshness
of health, and who had no detail of ailments to give. Among the valedic-
tory orators at our colleges whom I have happened to know, I think I do
not exaggerate when I say that one half of them have had their health so
much impaired, as to be compelled for years almost to suspend all efficient
study. Alas! not a few of them have sunk into an early grave. (19–20)

In response to this problem, the society planned and opened
"manual labor schools." The schools required what Weld called
periods of "moderate exercise"—three to four hours daily of manual
labor chopping wood, working in craft shops, or cultivating fields.
According to the society, such work had a "salutary and powerful" moral as well as hygienic influence (J. H. Coffin 58). The
manual labor school, said Weld, "WOULD TEND TO DO AWAY
WITH THOSE ABSURD DISTINCTIONS IN SOCIETY WHICH MAKE
THE OCCUPATION OF AN INDIVIDUAL THE STANDARD OF HIS
WORTH" (63).

The oddity of Weld's outrage in capital letters, the paradox in the entire project of the manual labor school as a means to preserve through ancillary work the health of university students, was that it reaffirmed as much as it "did away with" the distinctions Weld denounced. The logic behind the manual labor school, despite the society's condemnations of excessive study, carried throughout the implicit premise that manual labor—even up to four hours a day—ought to be, for scholars, an enabling rather than a primary or privileged activity. Manual labor most crucially allowed scholars to study without debility. The society, though it did acknowledge that the sale of goods produced by university students might make study more affordable, imagined manual labor not primarily as the necessary production of material goods for the subsistence or profit of the producer, but first and foremost as a form of exercise. On the one hand, the engagement of students and budding professionals (most notably ministers but others as well) in manual labor encouraged students to recognize the value of manual work and provided the corporal and moral benefits that health reform movements typically associated with such work. On the other hand, the manual labor school also served to articulate the social and economic separation of the students from the necessity of performing manual labor for any other than corporally and morally hygienic purposes.

This reconstruction of manual labor as middle-class exercise was not limited to Weld, but pervaded health reform literature. In his *American Modern Practice* (1826), James Thacer declared, "There is not one man in a hundred that exercises sufficiently in mercantile cities." According to John Betts, Thacer recommended, as if they were exchangeable, "horseback riding, walking, rope skipping, dancing, [and] the physical tasks of agriculture." [14] Sylvester Graham's *The Science of Human Life* (1839) was almost relentlessly nostalgic, looking to advocate what Stephen Nissenbaum has termed a "physiology of subsistence" by fighting back gourmandism, material indulgence, and other damaging social habits. [15] But, while doubtless obsessively concerned with luxurious diet, Graham also lamented that so many urban workers were "devoted to pursuits less favorable to health than the calling of the husbandman:

and a large majority of these pursuits are of a nature which does not admit of sufficient active, bodily exercise for health and comfort." [16] If the desk worker or manager could not exercise agriculturally, then Graham suggested that he might therapeutically substitute horse-back riding, sociable walks, or dancing.

Somewhat later in the period, Catharine Beecher, in her *Letters to the People on Health and Happiness* (1856), lamented that American adults and children were "train[ed] . . . to become feeble, sickly, and ugly." [17] She believed that "the labor appointed to man in cultivating the earth, in preparing its fruits, and in many mechanical pursuits, will be found to be that which exercises all the muscles of the body appropriately and healthfully" (88). Beecher thought that middle-class men were sickly, because each of them "who can do so, avoids these healthful pursuits as less honorable, and seeks in preference those that shut him up in study, office, or store to overwork his brain and leave his muscular system to run down for want of vigorous exercise and fresh air" (88). To remedy the problem of the debilitated paper pusher, to substitute for his divorce from manual labor, Beecher recommended walks, dancing, calisthenics, and the construction of a nineteenth-century version of the health club, complete with work-out machines and aerobic dancing. It would be, said Beecher,

a central site . . . on which should be erected a large and beautiful building—*A Temple of Health.* Around it should be every variety of pleasant walks . . . and other arrangements provided for outdoor sports and exercises in Winter. Within the building should be arranged a great variety of apparatus and accommodations for indoor amusements that *exercise the muscles*, and those which in most cases could be performed in *measures and to the sound of music.* (169)

Beecher and many others were not only concerned with protecting the health of physically idle middle-class men. Beecher believed that "a large portion of this nation, especially in the more wealthy classes," had drawn up "a plan for *destroying female health*" (7). While men endangered their well-being by avoiding "agricultural and mechanical pursuits," "almost every woman, who has it in her power, turns off the work that would make her and her daughters healthful, to hirelings, and takes sewing, reading, and other inactive pursuits as her exclusive portion" (88). For these allegedly leisured women, Beecher recommended dancing, calisthenics, horseback riding, walking, and backyard agriculture, all intermixed, one supposes, with occasional trips to the Temple of Health. Beecher also had one additional recommendation specific to women. She explained that "the labor appointed to women in the family state, involves just that variety of employment which, if wisely adjusted, would be exactly what is best calculated to develop every muscle most perfectly" (88).

This passage and others that insist on the homemaker's actual involvement in the physical chores and domestic production of the household suggest that Beecher's ideal homemaker does not correspond perfectly with the model of idle and materially nonproductive middle-class "true womanhood" postulated by Barbara Welter and others as emblematic of mid-nineteenth-century domesticity.[18] In fact, the passages I have cited from Beecher demonstrate a *fear* of idleness, a fear that middle-class women might become too far separated from the material work, the domestic labor and production that defined their familial role in an earlier generation. Accordingly, Beecher suggests that these women should perform domestic chores as exercise in much the same way that we have seen others recommend residual craft labor for the bureaucrat or manager.

Beecher's forms of male and female exercise, however, carry distinct and uneven gender implications. If the rhetoric of exercise that appropriated manual labor for an emergent middle class was operative for both men and women, it operated in rather different ways. The baking, sewing, and even cleaning performed by Beecher's homemaker were very much like the labor of the students at Weld's schools or the recreational farming mentioned by other reformers in that they were understood to satisfy most importantly spiritual or hygienic rather than economic needs. These domestic labors differed, though, from the kinds of work Weld recommended because they served not as a way of entering healthfully into the market or professions but as a means of caring for the family and preserving its health outside the market. If the performance of hygienic "work" helped to legitimize white-collar callings for men, the invocation of household labor as a therapeutic activity situated women more firmly within the domestic sphere.[19]

Many of the reformers I have mentioned to this point recommended the performance of actual work as exercise, but by the 1850s a notable shift had begun to emerge. Those most concerned about the idleness of the white-collar worker or middle-class women more and more came to emphasize sport as a substitute for physical work. Accordingly, Weld's movement for manual labor schools, already somewhat anachronistic in the 1830s, died out by the 1850s. At the same time, between 1820 and 1860, John Betts, Steven Riess, Melvin Adelman, and Guy Lewis tell us that American universities first built gymnasiums, introduced physical education classes, and even organized the first intercollegiate sports. According to his autobiography published serially in the *Atlantic*, George Windship, "The Roxbury Hercules," popularized weight training by lifting prodigious weights in public displays of strength. He inspired "lifting machines [to spring] up in parlors and offices and schools everywhere." Thomas Wentworth Higginson and the muscular Christianity movement lamented the weak constitution of young divines and other "professional or businessm[e]n." In "Saints, and Their Bodies" Higginson recommended that they grasp "the oar, the bat, or [once again as if interchangeably] the plough-handle." Ultimately, though, real strength would be measured "not . . . by sawing a cord of wood, but by an hour in the gymnasium or at cricket." Higginson, thus, very bluntly imagines manual labor as something for which middle-class sport should appropriately substitute.[20]

Even Catharine Beecher, whose work *A Treatise on Domestic Economy* (1842) so ardently advocated the actual performance of household chores as a moral imperative, became interested enough in exercise per se that in 1856 she published a monograph that brought her more into line with her contemporaries. Beecher's early *Treatise* does contain brief chapters "On Domestic Exercise" and "On Domestic Amusements" as well as recommendations for housework. Her *Physiology and Calisthenics for Schools and Families*, however, devotes itself almost exclusively to elaborate schematics of and recommendations for exercise that had little to do with actual work.[21]

Dioclesian Lewis provides one last example of the gradual transition from labor as exercise to exercise as labor's substitute. Like Catharine Beecher, Lewis was most concerned for the health of idle women in the home. Of all reformers in the period, Lewis designed the most elaborate workouts for women. He conducted, as far as I know, the nation's first sales campaign for workout gear that targeted middle-class women as much as or even more than men.[22] They enrolled in his Boston Normal Institute for Physical Education at a twenty-five percent discount and, accordingly, dominated the classes. Lewis emphasized that exercise, with the help of the right apparatus, could be performed in the home. He recommended the "Pangymnastikon," a complicated contraption of rings and stirrups: "When a lady is done with her morning cares, and would dress for dinner, she slips on her Zouave [the recommended workout costume] and stepping to the Pangymnastikon, devotes a few minutes to its exercise." Women, Lewis pointed out, could "obtain the Pangymnastikon at the factory in Boston, [where] Dr. Dio Lewis . . . has them so made that they will not give out at any point. . . . [H]andsomely finished and boxed and ready for shipment, the cost is $9, which is very cheap."[23]

Lewis's exercises, like those of the other reformers I have mentioned, did not so much eliminate the idea of manual labor from the consciousness of the white-collar man or the middle-class woman as they did shift the health and moral benefits once associated with such work to materially nonproductive activities emblematic of middle-class status. Self-declaring middle-class exercise, residual forms of more or less recreational labor, and spiritualized housework and domestic production became the means through which white-collar men and middle-class women could distinguish themselves from the working class even as they paradoxically claimed the moral, corporal, and spiritual benefits of increasingly transformed modes of physical "work."

Hawthorne's Residual Writing

In 1841 Nathaniel Hawthorne moved, if we use its full and original name, to the Brook Farm Institute for Agriculture and Education. Brook Farm, we know, was only one of many communal labor settlements in antebellum America, one part of a much broader utopian impulse that questioned the increasingly apparent class and labor divisions of emergent industrialization that I have been describing. Brook Farm, though it only later took on the explicit terms and more complex structure of the Fourierist phalanstery, was intended from its inception to establish a community in which each member contributed capital, labor, and intellectual talent to the common good. It included a school as well as a working farm and various craft shops. Those at the settlement were expected to move freely between the different types of work, but workers devoted exclusively to middle-class managerial and professional labors had no place at Brook Farm or in antebellum utopian communities of labor more broadly considered.[24]

When George Ripley, the founder of Brook Farm, wrote to Emerson he insisted that the community's primary "objects [were] to insure a more natural union between intellectual and manual labor than now exists; to combine the thinker and worker, as far as possible, in the same individual; to guarantee the highest mental freedom, by providing all with labor, adapted to their tastes and talents."[25] Brook Farm, Ripley and others believed, would eliminate distinctions of class and dignify manual labor by having the entire community participate in it. One oddity in Ripley's letter, however, is that much like the fitness rhetoric I have been discussing, it still imagines manual labor as a secondary or enabling activity, work less important in its own right than for the "mental freedom" it might provide. Even as Ripley and Brook Farm sought to dignify manual labor they continued to privilege the nonmanual. But if Brook Farm privileged nonmanual work, it was only a very particular type of it, intellectual work, not the work of bureaucrats, managers, clerks, or lawyers, and it sought to privilege this intellectual work (primarily writing) only within a smaller, separatist community.[26]

My point is that if Brook Farm sought to privilege intellectual work, particularly authorship, while claiming a basis for it in manual labor, it sought to do so by situating this intellectual work beyond the larger class and economic structures emerging in industrializing America. On the other hand, the fitness movements and political rhetoric I have been discussing functioned wholly within and only to legitimize and reinforce these larger structures, to emphasize the emergence and increasing prominence of the middle class during America's industrial expansion. The question at Brook Farm was not how one could legitimize middle-class status in a newly industrializing economy by establishing rhetorical ties to older traditions but, rather, a question of how intellectual work might be established outside the situation of this economy altogether. This alternative situation, this position outside the broader economy of antebellum America and its class divisions, was absolutely contingent upon the shared and literal performance of agricultural and artisanal labors. Brook Farm could only survive as long as it was economically viable in its own right, and this meant that manual labor in the community was not merely a form of exercise but a very real means of self-support.[27]

We know from Nathaniel Hawthorne's letters to his wife-to-be, Sophia Peabody, that he took up residence at Brook Farm at least partly to support the two of them after marriage. Hawthorne, at this point in his career, had met with absolutely no commercial success in the literary market and very frankly sought a means to become an adequate provider. Knowing this, reading letters in which Hawthorne complained bitterly about his labors at Brook Farm, and having reference to his less than flattering portrayal of a utopian community ten years later in *The Blithedale Romance*, critics have tended to assume that Hawthorne had absolutely no sympathy with any of the principles and ideals of the Brook Farm settlement. But, as Irving Howe pointed out decades ago, the motive of family support can, in and of itself, hardly be an adequate explanation for Hawthorne's commitment to the commune.[28] For Hawthorne not only lived almost a year at Brook Farm, he invested one thousand dollars in it, the larger part of a year's salary for his work in 1840 at the Boston Custom House. Moreover, though Hawthorne may have needed to support himself and his wife, residence in a utopian community could hardly be seen as the most obvious and practical choice for a thorough nonbeliever. Hawthorne, after all, was able and at least somewhat willing to take up more practical and certain modes of labor at other points in his career. He was in 1840 already working at the Boston Custom House; he would later work at the Salem Custom House.[29]

My sense is that while Hawthorne was clearly not in perfect sympathy with George Ripley on every ground, he was attracted to Brook Farm by the alternative economy of labor I have tried to describe above.[30] Hawthorne, after all, had failed more or less utterly in the larger economy of industrialization, had discovered by 1841 only that his authorial work gave him neither wealth nor status in it. Later, after the publication of *The Scarlet Letter*, Hawthorne would be able to claim some measure of commercial success and was very definitely established as one of America's literary lions. At the time of Brook Farm, however, even at the moment of writing "The Custom-House," Hawthorne had at best a cult following and no income from his literary work to speak of. Hawthorne's status as an unknown and a commercially unsuccessful writer is, in fact, one of the major topics of "The Custom-House."

Hawthorne, I am then suggesting, went to Brook Farm not only to support himself and his wife, but to situate himself in an economy that would reestablish a noncommercial basis for authorship by grounding it in support provided by labors of the hand.[31] One can, given Hawthorne's final disillusionment, too easily forget or ignore that observers of him at Brook Farm described Hawthorne as less cynical than his letters and journal appear. M. Gertrude Cutter, who arrived at Brook Farm after Hawthorne's departure, tells us that those who had known him remembered, "The idealistic phase of the Farm life [had] attracted [Hawthorne], and he fancied that his manual work might aid in the scheme of community life." George Bradford, who was at the commune with Hawthorne, tells us that Hawthorne "was attracted to the enterprise by the hope of finding some more satisfactory and congenial opportunity of living according to his tastes and views than in the common arrangements of society, and also of uniting successfully manual with intellectual work."[32]

My point is that Hawthorne's attraction to Brook Farm was not merely a matter of *practicality* (how could it have been?), but an attempt to imagine and experience the labor of authorship as a form of nonmanual labor situated rather differently from the managerial, clerical, and professional labors that fitness movements legitimated, a form of nonmanual labor truly (but finally disappointingly) aligned with and economically dependent upon the manual. The most insightful recent reader of antebellum literary attempts, including Hawthorne's, to negotiate between the manual and the mental is Nicholas Bromell. The "principal finding" of Bromell's important book is "that during the antebellum period work was understood primarily by way of a distinction between manual and mental labor, which in turn rested upon an assumed dichotomy of mind (and soul) and body." Bromell's final point, however, is not just that a mind-body dichotomy structured antebellum work, but also that within antebellum intellectual discourse, the mind was almost uniformly the privileged half of the dichotomy while the representation of labor and the body was elided.[33]

I think that Bromell exaggerates "manual labor's resistance to verbal representation" and "the relative invisibility of work in the literature of the so-called American Renaissance." Characters sweep, sew, saw, farm, and work in factories throughout mid-nineteenth-century writing, and this study should already have begun to make that apparent. Work is represented, in other words, but represented in ways that create for it particular ideological meanings that are not as easily schematized as the suggested erasure of the manual by a dominant middle class might imply.[34]

When, for example, Miles Coverdale in Hawthorne's *Blithedale* thinks, "Intellectual activity is incompatible with any large amount of bodily exercise," we need first to note that "exercise" and "work" have apparently become synonymous.[35] Furthermore, we need to distinguish between the type of bodily exertion that Hawthorne does and does not reject, that is, between the type of "exercise" that interferes with writing and the type that he hopes will enable it. Hawthorne, like Coverdale, might feel distaste for a "large amount" of bodily exercise without diminishing the centrality of all such exertion. For, as I have argued, and as his letters demonstrate, Hawthorne himself soured on Brook Farm not because he went to the community in absolutely no sympathy with its goals, nor because he was absolutely unwilling to "garden," but because he failed to understand and anticipate the extensive and even overwhelming commitment to manual labor that the Farm would require.

Where fitness movements and middle-class culture more broadly concerned used the manual as a secondary or enabling activity in a largely symbolic, figurative, and hygienic sense, Hawthorne (and others at Brook Farm) planned to perform manual labor as a primary means of economic support. Hawthorne, in other words, clearly failed to understand precisely what the logic of middle-class fitness makes so plain: manual labor serves effectively as an enabling condition of another form of nonmanual work only when that manual labor is more a pastime or figurative gesture, more an exercise or rhetorical invocation of the past than an absolute and continuously pressing necessity. The point is not so much that the body is lower than the mind in a fixed and oppositional dichotomy but, rather, that the properly class-defined exertion of the body is absolutely necessary to the mental well-being of the white-collar worker and author.

By the time of "The Custom-House" and the letter to Bridge cited at this chapter's beginning, Hawthorne had clearly learned his lesson from Brook Farm, clearly learned that while extended seashore walks and the "daily labor" of gardening for an hour or two might work to reinvigorate him for both his bureaucratic work and authorship, the back-breaking work of digging up potatoes as an economic necessity was to be avoided. Hawthorne's anxieties about his health as an intellectual worker and the means he imagines to ensure his bodily vigor have grown to be consistent with the logic of middle-class fitness in a way that his labors at Brook Farm were not, and they demonstrate an increasing accommodation to, not a rejection of, the importance of his physical being in class-specific terms.

One complication, however, in identifying Hawthorne wholly with the logic of the fitness movement in "The Custom-House" is that no sort of exercise can, for Hawthorne, ever legitimate or rehabilitate his middle-class bureaucratic work. Indeed, Michael Gilmore has persuasively called into question the utter complicity of Hawthorne in the making of the middle class so prominent in recent criticism. While critics such as T. Walter Herbert and Sacvan Bercovitch have emphasized Hawthorne's complicitous agency in the formation of middle-class ideology and social arrangements, Gilmore highlights Hawthorne's uneasiness with his own middle-class identity. Gilmore acknowledges that Hawthorne was "on the verge of redefining his social position as a member of the rising professional class," but he also underscores that Hawthorne saw "middle-class emergence [as] a fraught difficulty, not a matter for congratulation." [36] While I would argue (as Gilmore presumably would not) that Hawthorne's anxiety about middle-class work is exactly a part of what helped to define that class, we might see the disdain for white-collar occupations which Gilmore hints at in Hawthorne's description of work in the Custom House as "doing what really was no advantage nor delight to any human being" (109). Hawthorne understands the psychic poverty and physical debility that this bureaucratic headwork thrusts upon him, but he makes no claim, as did the fitness advocates, that a grounding in recreational labor or exercise might redeem him. Here we can see that if different forms of bodily exertion are differently privileged in Hawthorne's thinking, the same is true of different sorts of headwork. Hawthorne's work in the Custom House, far from having any connection to the prestige of middle-class labor, serves instead as the ultimate emblem of white-collar work fully separated from any kind of efficiency, value, or meaningfulness. It is managerial work (Hawthorne is, in his own words, the "chief executive officer") fully separated from any kind of usefulness or productivity. It is intellectual work depicted not only as nonproductive but as positively deleterious.

If the work of the Custom House is a form of intellectual work absolutely beyond rehabilitation, the work of writing is rather different, and we might see in this difference the precise terms in which

Hawthorne invoked the rhetorical models of the fitness movement even as he meaningfully shifted their emphasis. We might also see the extent to which manual work figures as absolutely central to the work of writing. For Hawthorne not only shows us that "bodily activity" fails to legitimize or connect his bureaucratic version of white-collar work to the ideologically familiar virtues of manual labor, he also attempts to imagine writing as a mode of artisanal labor thoroughly removed from the class and economic structures of emergent industrialization.

Though authorship itself is a form of middle-class, professional intellectual work, Hawthorne struggles to imagine it in terms very different from the work of the Custom House. Hawthorne does not want to think of writing as nonproductive work, nor does he wish to emphasize as central the commercial imperatives of it that have only been painful to him. "The Custom-House," rather, works to establish the unlikely possibility, the enabling fantasy, that writing has primarily to do with nostalgic versions of handiwork existing beyond the contingencies of monetary motivation and middle-class anxiety about nonproductivity and debility. Simply put, in "The Custom-House," Hawthorne attempts to separate the work of authorship from modes of monetarily motivated, materially nonproductive headwork by emphasizing writing's intimate connections to idealized modes of bodily work.

We have already seen Hawthorne undertake a similar effort to separate his intellectual work from commercial motivation when he moved to Brook Farm. Here Hawthorne literally took up manual work in the hope that it would enable him to write by uniting in an alternative economy the labor of the hand and the labor of the head. In "The Custom-House," however, Hawthorne creates this vision of authorship's affinity with the manual and separation from white-collar commerce and ill health not by literally taking up the plough, but by figuratively claiming an affinity between his writing and Hester Prynne's sewing. Once again, only now understanding the importance of rhetorical association rather than actual participation in bodily work, Hawthorne uses the manual not to justify his writing as part of the larger economy of antebellum America privileging commercial success and white-collar labor but, rather, to separate his writing from it.

It is, of course, fairly common to note that in his discovery of Hester's "A" Hawthorne discovers a figure for his own text, an intricate scarlet letter that is *The Scarlet Letter*. What ought to be emphasized in addition is that this figure is specifically a mediation between two particular and very different types of work. It is a way of selectively imagining the work of writing through the work of sewing, but also, of course, a way of imagining sewing as highly aestheticized, something like the intricate work of artistic authorship:

> But the object that most drew my attention, in the mysterious package was a certain affair of fine red cloth, much worn and faded. It had been wrought, it was easy to see, with wonderful skill of needlework; and the stitch (as I am assured by ladies conversant with such mysteries) gives evidence of a now forgotten art not to be recovered even by the process of picking out the threads. . . . It was the capital letter A. . . . Certainly there was some deep meaning in it, most worthy of interpretation, and which, as it were, streamed forth from the mystic symbol, subtly communicating itself to my sensibilities, but evading the analysis of my mind. (31)

When it comes time for Hawthorne to recover for authorship a figurative ground separating it from the quintessentially nonproductive work of the Custom House, he selects a mode of skilled artisanal production. It is not, after all, the work of lawyers, clerks, or salesmen, but the work of the seamstress, the art of materially and physically forming letters that figures authorial work.

We should also add, however, that Hester performs not merely the work of sewing, but a selected type of it. For historians have made plain that the moment at which Hawthorne wrote *The Scarlet Letter* is also the moment at which clothing began to be produced on an unprecedented scale within organizations of highly deskilled "sweated" labor. According to Sean Wilentz and others, in the years between 1825 and 1850 New York manufacturers started to produce ready-made clothing for local, Southern, and Western markets in ways that "metamorphosed . . . tailoring at every level of production," turning "ready-mades into one of the nation's largest local industries."[37] The grueling and increasingly deskilled work of the sweated outworker, dispossessed tailor, or, for that matter, any other type of purely utilitarian production is clearly not Hester Prynne's province, and just as clearly, invoking such work is not the way that Hawthorne, through the figuration of the "A," chose to separate authorial work from the bureaucratic nonproductivity of the Custom House.

Sewing, as Hester's "A" represents it, is skilled manual labor and material production and, accordingly, serves as a figure to quell Hawthorne's anxieties that authorship may be in any way related to work in the Custom House, the quintessential form of spiritually impoverished and physically damaging clerical labor. At the same time, Hester's "A" makes plain that to retrieve for authorship a status outside the meaningless and even damaging work of the Custom House, one need not go to the extremes of constructing literally an alternative economy grounded in manual labor; one need not go to the extremes of actually shoveling shit at Brook Farm. Rather, Hawthorne seems to hope, one can construct an image of authorship as inextricably tied to manual labor through the rhetorical means of metaphorical comparison.

What Hawthorne discovers in the "A," I am then suggesting, is a mode of uniting headwork and handwork that borrows from the techniques of association I have been attributing to the antebellum middle-class physical fitness movement. He discovers the connection between authorship and modes of material production increasingly outdated in the emerging class and economic structures of industrialization not by retrieving manual work as any kind of lived or economically essential reality, but by reclaiming the artisanal as something with a decidedly *figurative* or *rhetorical* weight in his life. He uses an idealized revaluation of manual work to justify and relieve his anxieties about a more primary mode of nonmanual, essentially middle-class work: authorship.

This is not to say, however, that Hawthorne's figuration of authorship in "The Custom-House" performed (any more than did his labor at Brook Farm) the same cultural work as antebellum fitness movements. The terms of comparison and borrowing need to be absolutely clear. Fitness advocates, as I have said, ultimately and persistently worked to validate precisely the structures and modes of headwork, the privileging of middle-class clerical, administrative, managerial, and professional work moving toward dominance in the industrial economy. Rather differently, Hawthorne's work at Brook Farm and his figurations of authorship in "The Custom-House" called into question the valuation of "nonproductive" work, and struggled to place authorship, whether literally in the utopian community or figuratively through associations with Hester's sewing, outside the dominant structures of labor and commerce that the fitness movement helped to legitimate.

Walden, Farming, and Authorship

On July 4, 1845, while Brook Farm continued to function without Nathaniel Hawthorne, Henry David Thoreau settled into his one-room cabin by Walden Pond. Thoreau, of course, had no patience for the communitarian impulse that had inspired collective labor at Brook Farm but, some years later, when he published *Walden*, Thoreau began by asserting a specific economic relation between his manual labors by the pond and writing: "When I wrote the following pages, or rather the bulk of them, I lived alone, in the woods, a mile from any neighbor, in a house which I had built myself, on the shore of Walden Pond, in Concord, Massachusetts, and earned my living by the labor of my hands only." [38] In the economy of *Walden*, Thoreau instantly suggests, manual labor serves as the material basis for writing. Only by providing for his material needs through his own hands, by departing from commercial structures of labor and exchange, did Thoreau establish the conditions of his authorial work. The fact that Thoreau did not actually write *Walden* during his stay by the pond, but only the journal entries from which it was later composed, serves to accent the desire he must have felt to construct the dependency of his writing on his physical labors.

We might well say of Thoreau, as we did of Hawthorne when he moved to Brook Farm, that the move to Walden worked toward constructing a version of authorship supported by increasingly residual modes of manual labor, because Thoreau's authorial work, like Hawthorne's in 1841, ultimately proved by any monetary measure to be a failure in the antebellum marketplace. My point is not, of course, that Thoreau moved to Walden or Hawthorne to Brook Farm only as a practical measure toward self-support but, rather, that in moving to Walden and Brook Farm these writers sought opportunities to think of and represent authorship through very particular mediations and associations. For Hawthorne, as I have mentioned, Brook Farm was largely a failure in this regard, but also a prerequisite to his later success in figuratively reconstructing authorial work as a type of manual labor that could leave behind the anxieties about the debility of the body and material nonproduction emblematized by his work in the Custom House. Hawthorne ultimately discovered that the act of writing could not take place and had little in common with the literal performance of arduous bodily toil, but he also learned that writing could be represented in purely rhetorical terms as an ideological and literary *mediation* of the manual and thus be valorized in ways inapplicable to white-collar work. Writing could be reconstructed as craftwork, but only when that craftwork was highly aestheticized, far from backbreaking, and conceived apart from the social and market realities structuring class, labor, and authorship in mid-nineteenth-century America. When it was, in other words, conceived through Hester's literary sewing as a form of healthful work opposed to his incapacitatingly useless and debilitating work as a surveyor.

For Henry David Thoreau the actual performance of manual labors, the work of house building, wood chopping, bean farming, and housekeeping turned out to be much more agreeable and much more full of rhetorical promise than they were for Hawthorne. After leaving Brook Farm, Hawthorne never used his work there as a positive figure for authorship and, even in the character of Miles Coverdale, was at pains to point out the antagonism between the two. Thoreau's *Walden*, on the other hand, looks backward with compulsive affection to his labors as figures for authorial work. The most famous of these figurations, of course, emerges from Thoreau's bean farming. Much as critics routinely recognize Hester's "A" as a figure for authorship, the trope of bean farming is generally recognized as having reference to Thoreau's writing even as the historical particularity of this farming often goes unexplored. Stanley Cavell tells us, for example, "Hoeing is identified not just with the content and effect of words; it is also an emblem of the physical act of writing." F. O. Matthiessen adds, "The depth to which [Thoreau's] ideals for fitness and beauty in writing were shaped, half consciously, by the modes of productive labor with which he was surrounded, or in fact by the work of his own hands in carpentry or pencil-making or gardening can be read in his instinctive analogies." For both Cavell and Matthiessen, farming has no specifically complex historical meaning. It merely and somewhat self-evidently makes reference to writing. A somewhat more historically influenced Nicholas Bromell adds that bean farming "enables Thoreau to figure his writing as an activity that complements, rather than stands over [and?] against, nature." For Bromell, bean farming and writing in Thoreau, as avowedly unnecessary and unimproving labors, resist the dominant "school of political economy that had established work as both the justification of private property . . . and as the creator of economic or exchange value."[39]

In one sense it is surely right to say that Thoreau uses agricultural labor to place his own authorial work outside the realm of dominant economic contingencies, but we also need to explore with some specificity the historical situation that made farming in particular an inviting vehicle for the refiguration of authorial work along these lines. Farming does not suggest "nature" in Thoreau as much as it does an idealized economic past. But it stands for this past in an exceedingly complicated way that insists on the past's figurative value in the present. Thoreau, in other words, invokes bean farming as a figure of authorial work in order, like Hawthorne, to enable a conception of writing grounded in the virtues of noncommercial, manual labor, precisely because the affirmation of the emergent mode of writing as commercialized headwork could only point to his debilitating failure. At the same time, as we know by now, to express anxiety about professionalized headwork by insisting on the necessary virtues of the manual and bodily hardly places Thoreau fully and completely outside the logic of white-collar or commercial ascendancy.

That the small-scale and independent farming Thoreau engages in was increasingly a residual labor in antebellum America is plainly a historical fact, one that Thoreau himself repeatedly recognizes in his observations of the commercial farms surrounding Concord:[40]

> Ancient poetry and mythology suggest, at least, that husbandry was once a sacred art; but it is pursued with irreverent haste and heedlessness by us, our object being to have large crops merely. We have no festival, nor procession, nor ceremony, not excepting cattle-shows and so-called Thanksgivings, by which the farmer expresses a sense of the sacredness of his calling. . . . By avarice and selfishness, and a grovelling habit, from which none of us is free, of regarding the soil as property, or the means of acquiring property chiefly, the landscape is deformed, husbandry is degraded with us, and the farmer leads the meanest of lives. (165)

It is precisely the outdatedness of Thoreau's own farming, its lack of commercial motivation, that he finally wants to emphasize. For though Thoreau goes to grossly exaggerated, even ironic, effort to tabulate his expenses and profits, it turns out in the end that he never worked primarily for money or even subsistence at all. Thoreau, it turns out, does not even like beans, refuses to eat them, makes by his own admission barely any money, and, in his words, comes to value the labor "only for the sake of tropes and expression, to serve [him] as a parable-maker one day" (162).

I have already suggested that the reconfiguration and appropriation of idealized but past or passing modes of manual labor could perform rather different sorts of cultural work. For fitness advocates, manual labor became a form of exercise that could legitimate the materially nonproductive labor of the emergent middle-class. For Hawthorne in "The Custom-House," Hester's craftwork sets his own authorship outside the bounds of anxieties about material nonproductivity in rhetorical terms, even as he rejects literal participation in manual labor and works instead at the Custom House, the quintessential home of the nonproductive bureaucrat and manager.

For Henry Thoreau manual labor seems, at first, to create a literal economy of support for authorial labor and a rhetorical figure for it. Indeed, my discussion of *Walden* has been significantly influenced by Michael Gilmore's suggestion that Thoreau's life at the pond is "inspired by agrarian ideals of the past." Thoreau settles at *Walden* to invoke the economic arrangements of an artisan and yeoman's republic, the self-sufficient subsistence idealized by Jefferson and others as an antidote to commercial life. The problem for Thoreau in Gilmore's reading, however, is that "in making a metaphor of those ideals, [his book] fails as a rejoinder to the [exchange ethos of the] nineteenth century." Gilmore's understanding of *Walden* seems to imply a kind of unequivocal intention to abdicate from the present in Thoreau. He claims that Thoreau moved to *Walden* with "political objectives," an "ambition to reform the polity," and that by participating himself in "the commodified thinking concealed in symbolization" Thoreau failed to do so.[41]

While Thoreau does invoke an idealized past, to understand *Walden* as a failure because it does not turn back the clock on the market ethos of the nineteenth century may be to misunderstand Thoreau's project. After all, unlike the Fourierists, Thoreau does not invite followers. Rather, from the very start of his book, Thoreau is more concerned with situating his aesthetic labor relative to contemporaneous modes of work and idealizations of the past than he is concerned or hopeful that he might actually cause idealized modes of residual labor to reemerge. The project of *Walden* is not to eliminate, in Gilmore's phrase, "the curse of trade," but to discover the figurative understanding that might enable his authorship within an economy that privileges trade.

The point, then, is not that Thoreau invokes the past as an alternative to, an abdication from, or even a reform of the present, but that he invokes the past precisely for its recuperative meaning *in* the present. Performing the self-consciously nostalgic and bodily work of subsistence while linking writing to it is not so much to oppose the implicitly acknowledged dominant valorization of the nonmanual and the commercial. Rather, it is a way, as we have seen throughout this chapter, of easing anxieties about and/or enabling particular forms of unprofitable or simply materially unproductive headwork. In Thoreau's case, it is a way to imagine an enabling figuration of authorship as grounded in bodily labor, in material production and economic self-sufficiency, even though authorship is not obviously or inherently grounded in any of these.

The figurative work of *Walden* as it emerges from the bean-field episode is not most importantly, as Thoreau seemed to promise at the outset, to present an economy in which manual labor supports authorial work but one in which distinctions between manual and authorial labor are mediated almost into nonexistence. Leo Marx describes "the literalness with which Thoreau approaches the simple life [of the pastoral genre]" and points out that bean farming "has a moral and spiritual as well as economic significance." [42] For Marx, there is no such thing as literal, but only literary labor when it comes to Thoreau's bean farming. The literal and literary are, in fact, so tangled together that the labor itself reads as if it were part of a pastoral prose poem.

Marx's ability to place Thoreau's "real work" within the bounds of literary convention emphasizes wonderfully the extent to which Thoreau's work always emphasizes its figurative, literary nature rather than any material production for actual exchange *or* subsistence. *Walden* presents an economy in which manual labor is transformed and carried into the realm of authorial work in order to legitimate the terms of the writing that Thoreau himself enacts. Bean farming, in the end, represents a model for authorial labor that insists upon the author's physical vitality and self-sufficiency, his moral, physical and spiritual health, all grounded in the bodily labors that figure writing.

Bean farming, then, shows us Thoreau using a recreational, avocational, or highly conventionalized performance of handwork to form a satisfactory and enabling vision of his intellectual work. By understanding his writing as he does, as connected to bodily exertion, Thoreau's labor takes on palatable meanings. The strategy, of course, is familiar, and it is useful to note the extent to which Thoreau seems to accept the rhetorical tactics of the emergent middle class even as he uses these tactics to position himself outside of it. [43] Whether one invoked manual labor as an exercise to quell anxieties about middle-class material nonproductivity or to separate authorship from such nonproductivity, one called on past or passing modes of labor increasingly separated from more dominant modes of commercial production, modes of labor that had rhetorical and symbolic value in the present precisely because they were no longer dominant.

This is not to say, however, that Thoreau's project of figuratively or rhetorically establishing the vitality and productivity of his labor merely repeated the logic of middle-class fitness. The fitness movement, as I have said, helped to legitimize commercial success and the privileged status of the white-collar worker by satisfying the culturally residual demand for bodily labor. The manual work invoked by Thoreau (and Hawthorne) serves to set authorship apart from these modes of middle-class work and bodily anxiety. For Hawthorne, this meant that authorship imagined through Hester's "A" was to be distinguished at once from utilitarian modes of bodily work and from the disabling headwork of the Custom House. For Thoreau, as we have already begun to understand, it meant that authorship as imagined through bean farming was to be distinguished from commercial agriculture or ice cutting but, as Thoreau's well-known parable of the Indian basketmaker makes plain, writing had also to be distinguished from the sort of commercially motivated headwork that lawyers might do:

Not long since, a strolling Indian went to sell baskets at the house of a well-known lawyer in my neighborhood. . . . Having seen his industrious white neighbor so well off, — that the lawyer had only to weave arguments, and by some magic wealth and standing followed, he had said to himself; I will go into business; I will weave baskets; it is a thing which I can do. . . . He had not discovered that it was necessary for him to make it worth the other's while to buy them. . . . I too had woven a kind of basket of a delicate texture, but I had not made it worth any one's while to buy them. Yet not the less, in my case, did I think it worth my while to weave them. (19)

The project of the Indian's basketweaving is set apart from the work of the lawyer primarily on two grounds. First, the lawyer "weaves" arguments, performs headwork, while the Indian weaves baskets, the work of material production. Second, the lawyer is commercially or economically successful in his enterprise while the Indian is not.

Thoreau's own "basket of a delicate texture" is a thinly veiled stand-in for *A Week on the Concord and Merrimack Rivers*, his book that had only recently failed miserably to sell. Thoreau, some critics assume, is claiming an almost complete affinity between himself and the Indian, between their shared failure in the marketplace.[44] Such a reading is initially attractive, but finally fails to acknowledge that the terms of comparison in this parable are not dual but three-way. Thoreau's "weaving" does not, after all, produce a basket, but "a kind of basket of a delicate texture," something far less obviously material or utilitarian in its nature. Furthermore, though the Indian is unsuccessful in the market, Thoreau imagines his labor wholly outside it: "Instead of studying how to make it worth men's while to buy my baskets, I studied rather how to avoid selling them" (19).

Thoreau's work of writing is not the work of the Indian any more than it is the work of the lawyer. Rather, it is an imagining of writing as occupying a mediated space, something which very clearly is not the commercially successful headwork of the lawyer but also something which is not concerned with the literal production or sale of material commodities, something which is not concerned with any lived or economically necessary version of manual *or* white-collar work. Thoreau's "baskets" are, instead, a form of mediated and aestheticized material production ("baskets of a delicate texture") or, alternatively, a form of almost materialized "argument." If only select forms of idealized manual work are able to salve the anxieties of both authorial and white-collar nonproductivity, in the worlds of Hawthorne and Thoreau it must also be true that only certain types of headwork—namely writing—seem to be redeemable at all.

Manly Professional Work

I have enlisted *Walden* and "The Custom-House" in my effort to bring forth a history of the figurative relationships among white-collar work, the transformation of physical labor into physical fitness, and the reconstruction of antebellum authorship because this history cannot be retrieved wholly outside the realm of literary understanding. It is less an accounting of social or political fact or truth than the history of figurative comprehension, a partial account of authorial and middle-class consciousness that can only be reached for by reading the works in which the figurations appear.

Though my discussion of antebellum authorship has been highly localized in its readings, limited largely to the work and careers of Hawthorne and Thoreau, it would not be difficult to find other authors reconstructing writing through increasingly residual labors in the antebellum years. Walt Whitman, for example, not only postured as "one of the roughs" within his poetry and in many of the photographs accompanying various editions of *Leaves of Grass*, he became deeply involved in the actual process of typesetting them—even as independent typesetters and typographical unions were increasingly displaced by the expansion and mechanization of the printing and publishing industries. For Whitman the work of typesetting was at once a past form of skilled manual labor and a form of labor that now had value for the achievement of his aesthetic ends. As in the case of Hawthorne and Thoreau, it would seem that Whitman undertook his "labor" and imagined himself as a "laborer" even as he distanced manual work from the realm of economic necessity and allied it instead with the work of aesthetic production.

If we keep in mind that the rhetorical relationships among white-collar work, fitness, and writing functioned in the authorial realm to create realizable, acceptable, and even *enabling* terms for entering into the authorial occupation for Hawthorne, Thoreau, and even Whitman, it becomes apparent that this history is more than merely rhetorical in its significance. Imagining authorship as a kind of mediated ground between the commercialized headwork of, to use Whitman's phrase, those "with dimes on the eyes" and the work of the republican yeoman or artisan enabled Thoreau, Hawthorne, and Whitman to function as they did in their authorial careers.[45] That is to say, it was partly by simultaneously imagining themselves outside the realm of the antebellum market signified by professional work even as they participated and sought a living in this market that Hawthorne, Thoreau, and Whitman produced the work they did—work that itself constructs this complicated market relation.

The idea that figurations of authorship through residual manual labors enabled a particular type of authorial work might be buttressed by the understanding that the attempt to mediate authorship in this way was largely limited to authors who, in David Leverenz's terms, imagined "a potentially hostile or indifferent audience . . .

preoccupied with competing for money and property." Leverenz argues that the writers of the traditional American Renaissance attempted to create alternative definitions of manhood to those founded on commercial success. One possible way of constructing authorship as manly work outside the commercial realm was to imagine it as a kind of work invoking the eighteenth-century valorization of the artisan.[46]

Authors who imagined their authorial careers along different lines and produced a rather different kind of writing tended much less often to invoke the artisanal as a metaphor for writing. We do not, for example, find such metaphors frequently operative in the women's sphere of sentimental fiction. Nina Baym's curt summary of the overplot structuring antebellum woman's fiction leads us toward the place of manual labor and its figurative associations in these novels. Baym persuasively claims that almost all popular woman's fiction of the period "chronicle[s] the 'trials and triumph' . . . of a heroine who, beset with hardships, finds within herself the qualities of intelligence, will, resourcefulness, and courage sufficient to overcome them."[47]

What Baym never points out is that the "trials" segment of these stories is very often signified and even dominated by the heroine's fall from a life of relative physical leisure to the grisly imperative of physical labor. We see this happen, for example, in Catharine Sedgewick's *New-England Tale* when Jane Elton's formerly wealthy but finally bankrupt father dies. Her mother soon follows him to the grave and, the sure sign of the commencement of her trials, Jane is forced to live with an aunt whose primary interest in the child is the distasteful chores she can foist upon her. In Fanny Fern's *Ruth Hall*, Ruth's wealthy husband dies, leaving her to cope with the necessity of taking in laundry and rubbing her hands raw while scrubbing the stairs of a boarding house in order to support herself and her child.

This pattern is repeated once more in Susan Warner's *The Wide, Wide World* when Ellen Montgomery, after the death of her mother, is forced into the disagreeable drudgery (not the consistently invigorating pleasure) of farm life with her Aunt Fortune. This novel features the antebellum period's most astounding rejection of the yeoman's labor as a figure for authorship. Though Ellen does finally come to enjoy particular aspects of the farm and household labor she performs while subject to the trials of Aunt Fortune's vicissitudes, her triumph at the novel's close resides largely in her removal from the necessity of performing such work.

Early in this story, in her last venture into public before dying, Mrs. Montgomery buys a portable mahogany writing desk for Ellen. This shopping trip is an elaborate celebration of purchasing pleasure. "It was," Warner tells us, "the first time [Ellen] had seen such a store." She and her mother spend five pages picking out luxuriously detailed items including "excellent ink powder," "letter paper, large and small," envelopes, note paper, a letter pager, pens, sealing wax, and so on.[48]

This early union of writing with the act of consuming, however, only foreshadows the concluding scene of the novel. Here, in a chapter that Warner did not publish in her lifetime, John Humphreys, the man whom Ellen has been destined to marry for most of the novel, gives to her a much more lavish and conspicuously valuable antique escritoire than the one her mother had provided, and Ellen is proportionately elated. Then, on looking through the writing desk, Ellen discovers that one of the drawers is stuffed with money. Far from an emblem of material or authorial production, the writing desk stands as testament to Ellen's power as an owner and consumer. Ellen need not produce a word at her escritoire for bills and coins to jump from the drawer and beg to be spent. Ellen's most appropriate activity at this desk is not writing books but signing checks. Rather than figuring writing through the productive and increasingly residual labors on Fortune's farm—labors that Ellen performs for hundreds of pages, but that are always at odds with her more cultivated middle-class sensibilities—Warner concludes by imagining the location of writing not as an open field, artisan's shop, or even a house in need of tidying, but as a treasure chest that funds Ellen's management of the household, a management that specifically precludes taking up her time with the "petty details" (582) and drudgery of household chores that she will delegate to the faithful servant Margery.

Jane Tompkins has noticed an antagonism between the spiritual and Christian values constantly invoked by *The Wide, Wide World* and the love of material objects that the novel's heroine persistently evidences. By the end of the novel what is most interesting about Ellen's absorption in objects of luxury is that they have been fully divorced from any imperative of labor. Unlike Fortune's farm where the labors for mere subsistence dominate life, at the Humphreys' house splendid objects—even money itself—magically appear to be enjoyed and spent. Ellen's fantasy is one in which the necessity of physical labor is simply eliminated.[49]

None of this is to say that Ellen is absolutely etherealized and entirely divorced from the realm of the body, even if she is divorced from the realm of physical work. Besides turning over the management of the household and a desk full of money to her, John Humphreys hopes to guarantee for Ellen "the highest perfection of body and mind." To do so he has "desired a friend . . . to send . . . out as good a riding horse for [Ellen] as can be had" (577). Ellen will not work with her body, but she must be sure to exercise.

In coming to adulthood during the final chapter of *The Wide, Wide World*, Ellen Montgomery telescopes the historical transformation from a form of women's economically imperative labor within a system of domestic production to a form of spiritually imperative household administration within a middle-class gender arrangement that replaces physical work with emblems of private leisure and consumption. The transition is so thorough, in fact, that a figuration of writing as the residual labors that Ellen leaves behind is utterly unthinkable in this novel. Housework becomes Margery's work, and cannot serve as a figure for writing, especially since writing itself is dislodged from its place of performance (the escritoire) by the activity of household management and consumption. In the end, *The Wide, Wide World* rejects not only physical labor and the figuration of writing through it, it seems to fantasize an ideal of luxury and leisure in which one need not write at all.

Warner's almost outlandish rejection of physical labors in favor of fantasies that imagine writing as, or even displace it with, a magically provided purchasing and managerial power, is extraordinary in the antebellum period, and must have something to do with her personal history. Warner spent her youngest years in a wealthy family that was driven into increasingly desperate economic circumstances after her father, a once prosperous lawyer, lost much of the family's money in the panic of 1837. As her biographers note, Warner moved from spending her leisure time studying languages and the piano to housekeeping and supporting her family through writing that was clearly a burden to her. Jane Tompkins emphasizes that the events of Warner's life may have fostered in her the fantasy of this final chapter, the fantasy that an appropriate and sufficiently wealthy man might rescue and release her from her labors and return her to the childhood she seems always to have missed.[50]

But Warner's fantasy of the removal from physical labor also drives home a broader point about the construction of antebellum authorship. Domestic novelists did not participate in the particular figuration of writing as a compensatory, healthful and bodily employment that I have attributed to Hawthorne and Thoreau, because they lacked the particular anxieties about emergent professional and vanishing republican manhood that these figurations conspicuously sought to soothe. While Catharine Beecher may have lamented the vanishing virtues of republican women who kept their own homes and made their own bread, she also acknowledged the lack of material necessity in the middle-class woman's acts of domestic production. Even more emphatically, domestic novels routinely and repeatedly identify substantial labor as a trial and celebrate their heroines' removal from it. Where exercise and figurations of physical work function to represent and enable the productivity and market activities of male professionals (including writers) in terms harkening back to the artisan and yeoman, the same figurations work simultaneously to situate middle-class women more and more fully within the realm of the home and the acts of spiritual custodianship and material consumption so strikingly imaged in Ellen Montgomery's nonwriting desk.

The idea of figuring one's work through the residual labors of the artisan's or yeoman's republic might also have been alien to women writers and enabling for the men of the American Renaissance for still another reason: the desire to understand one's work as in the tradition of the artisan or yeoman, in the tradition of idealized bodily work, vitality, and self-sufficiency has always been historically limited by gender. For, as Alice Kessler-Harris has noted, if early yeomen serve as cultural models of self-sufficiency, it is also true that colonies outlawed women's ownership of land, "recogniz[ing] that giving land to women undermined their dependent role." Kessler-Harris adds that the path of a seven-year apprenticeship to artisanal work was also "normally closed to women." Christine Stansell, Ava Baron, and Sean Wilentz have all shown that well into the nineteenth century the higher levels of artisanal privilege continued to be preserved as a largely male bastion, and David Leverenz has claimed precisely that the artisan paradigm of autonomous, vital, bodily self-sufficiency is "an ideology of manhood" inherited by antebellum writers from the colonial and republican periods. To idealize the bodily worker and identify one's own headwork with him in the terms that Thoreau and Hawthorne did, is to appropriate to oneself the virtue of the independent artisan or yeoman, a primarily masculine model of self-realization.[51]

The rhetorical history I have outlined, then, helped to enable the *actual*, lived practice of writing in particular, but not all, authorial careers. Furthermore, if this rhetoric had actual consequences in the authorial realm, it also had significance beyond the literary. The constructions concerning me suggest something about the way that middle-class professional identity was actually individually experienced. For the drive to transform labor into fitness shows us not what we are used to noting—that forms of leisure complemented forms of labor in an increasingly coherent middle class. Rather, it suggests that professional labors were, to some extent, *dependent* in the middle-class imagination upon the performance of particular sorts of leisure activities. In other words, if we can be relatively sure that the economic reorderings of the antebellum period gave birth to a class of white-collar workers, we can also be sure that fitness activities allowed for certain mediated understandings of white-collar work, the creation of particular paths of consciousness and activity that enabled, or at least eased, entry into nonmanual occupations.

Finally, then, what may be most interesting about the relations among white-collar work, fitness, and writing is that they show that the same matrix of figurative thinking and activities could be deployed in radically different ways to legitimate radically different careers. For if Hawthorne and Thoreau imagined themselves as "resistant" to, isolated from, or anxious about the dominant structures of class and labor cohering in antebellum America, they imagined themselves in this way partly by invoking differently inflected forms of the same rhetorical figures that helped that class to cohere. An essential problem for Hawthorne and Thoreau as well as for white-collar workers was the unfamiliarity of the newly emergent conditions of their labor. What their rhetorical strategies and literal activities suggest is that in constructing emergent forms of labor, nothing is more helpful than invocations of residual modes of ideologically valorized forms of work. Whether one moved to Brook Farm to enable writing or, much differently, worked out at the Temple of Health, one implicitly invoked a mediated version of the past to construct an acceptable present. Where Hawthorne and Thoreau took up the "work" of the farmer and artisan, first literally and then figuratively to enable their own work in an increasingly professionalized literary arena, white-collar workers took up the "work" of fitness to find a mediated, residual grounding for their new professional careers.

CHAPTER FOUR

Purloined Letters, Mechanical
Butterflies, and Watches in Girdles

Literary Property in
Mid-Nineteenth-Century America

When Minister D—— purloins the letter from the boudoir of an unnamed but worthy noblewoman, he does so without ever having read it. The minister's "lynx eye immediately perceives the paper," and he "recognizes the handwriting of the address," but the minister does not actually see the letter's contents. Though Minister D—— senses that the coercive value of the letter lies in its text, he also recognizes the letter in meticulously materialistic terms, terms further emphasized by his mode of theft. The minister steals the letter through an act of material exchange or substitution, by replacing the purloined letter with one similar in appearance to, however textually different from, the original.[1]

Even more than the minister, C. Auguste Dupin appropriates the letter valuable for its written content in highly, almost purely materialistic terms. From across the room Dupin focuses on the letter even more precisely than does the minister, as if catching it in the crosshairs of a bionic eye, and, like the minister, Dupin achieves his theft through an act of physical substitution without ever textually verifying or needing to verify his suppositions:

I kept my attention really riveted upon the letter. In this examination, I committed to memory its external appearance and arrangement in the rack;

and also fell, at length, upon a discovery which set at rest whatever trivial doubt I might have entertained. In scrutinizing the edges of the paper, I observed them to be more *chafed* than seemed necessary. They presented the *broken* appearance which is manifested when a stiff paper, having been once folded and pressed with a folder, is refolded in a reversed direction . . . This discovery was sufficient. (216)

Even the prefect of the Parisian police, although he has trouble recognizing the stolen letter under his nose, seems more sure of its physical traits than its written contents. While the prefect can summarize only in the vaguest terms the letter's message, he provides Dupin with "a minute account of the internal, and especially of the external, appearance of the missing document" (213). Indeed, one of the curiosities about this letter is that we can never be sure, with the logical but not necessary exception of Minister D—— after the theft, that anyone ever reads it. Even the lady, the rightful proprietor to whom it was addressed, is interrupted in the midst of her perusal.

Perhaps nothing in American literature has been more figurally belabored by psychoanalytic and grammatological critics than this stolen letter,[2] but I begin with it here for rather different reasons, because it seems to me that "The Purloined Letter" might reveal to us something about the cultural and social history, the cultural consciousness, of literary property in America. Edgar Allan Poe had something close to a personal obsession with questions of plagiarism and other forms of literary theft. Poe publicly accused many authors, including Hawthorne, Elizabeth Barrett Browning, and, most infamously, Longfellow, of plagiarism; on more than one occasion Poe was himself accused of it, and in response to one accusation, he filed a suit for libel. As the editor of *The Broadway Journal* in the mid-1840s, Poe stridently advocated the adoption of international copyright protection and strengthened enforcement of the existing legislation protecting domestically authored texts.[3]

My previous chapters have all explored ways in which antebellum authors sought to reconstruct their work as it moved from the realm of the avocational to the realm of the professional in an increasingly commercialized literary market and nation. Authors were, as I have argued, confronted with newly emerging market imperatives that changed the relationships of writers to their writing and audience. This historical moment left authorship (and other forms of labor) with unusually unstable meanings, fostering in authors the creation of definition through the most readily available medium, their own literary work. In antebellum authors' own texts, other forms of labor are made to resonate through analogy and metaphor with the work of authorship, providing each of them — but particularly the work of writing — the reconstructed cultural meanings that soothe particular anxieties growing out of both the literary expansion and larger commercial expansion of the United States.

Edgar Allan Poe's concern about the status of literary property was not at all unique or original in the mid-nineteenth century. Indeed, critics and historians often note the enormous growth of the literary marketplace in antebellum America and associate with it a newly emergent cultural understanding of literary property as a commercial commodity.[4] Where in 1800 publishing had, as a rule, been only marginally profitable and authorship even less so, by the mid-nineteenth century publishing had become a big business and authorship viable as a profitable profession. New techniques of production, strategies for promotion, networks of transportation, and the expansion of a literate middle class combined to create a literary market of unprecedented size and, accordingly, the potential for literary property to achieve an unprecedented commercial worth.

As William Charvat has pointed out, several copyright laws were passed prior to, even in anticipation of, this marketplace expansion and played a role in enabling it. Literary works needed to be recognized as ownable property before authorship could become profitable. Authors simply could not profit from their work as long as that work could be freely reproduced by those unwilling to pay for the rights to reproduction. The creation of the first copyright laws in the late 1700s, at least in theory, assured authors the right to gain recompense from their writing.[5]

But if the late-eighteenth century gave birth to copyright legislation in this country, it was only during the literary market's nineteenth-century expansion that copyright grew to be much more prominently a subject of debate in American culture. The first copyright laws introduced the concept of literary property to the United States, but the terms of this concept were still largely inchoate, still waiting to be formed in the crucible of public opinion, legislative debate, judicial review, and even in works of literature themselves. The emergence of the text as potentially more valuable than had previously been imagined spawned any number of competing constructions of literary property. What remains the bedrock case in American copyright jurisprudence, for example, *Wheaton v. Peters*, was heard by the Supreme Court in 1834, and *Wheaton* was followed by several other cases that served to clarify some of the finer points of copyright protection for domestically authored texts. In addition, a heated and extended congressional debate over international copyright legislation unfolded in the decades following the *Wheaton* decision and continued up to and then beyond 1891, when the United States, lagging decades behind most of Europe, finally adopted some form of international copyright protection.[6]

I want to explore in what follows not only the ways in which legislative and judicial powers created and defined literary property in terms of the copyright that protected its commercial value but also the ways in which certain antebellum literary texts and authors situated themselves relative to the copyright debate. My sense is that several antebellum works—I will be most concerned with Poe's "The Purloined Letter," Nathaniel Hawthorne's "The Artist of the Beautiful," and Fanny Fern's *Ruth Hall*—obliquely address and define literary property in ways only partially consistent with the definitions of it emerging from the courts and legislature. The various notions of literary possession and value operative in assorted cultural arenas should begin to suggest the enormously complex interplay, the wide variety of institutional and personal forces that came to focus in radically different and personal ways upon the same emergent cultural issue.

My purpose, then, is to bring to light some of the many definitions and institutions that worked simultaneously toward the cultural construction of literary property and, finally, to suggest some ways in which they might be said to have competed, interacted, and intersected. I will, however, present no supposedly "dominant" view of literary property, simply because this chapter seeks partly to establish that any such notion of dominance at this cultural moment must ignore the complexity and diversity of forces working to define a still amorphous and emergent cultural concept. Rather than emphasizing the dominance or hegemony of market or exchange values, this chapter will suggest that the multiple perspectives on literary property and the labor of writing through which such property came to exist established strict limits around the possibility of understanding the language of copyright and literary ownership as consistent with the language or ideology of a broadly conceived commodification. What does begin to emerge, however, is an almost remarkable resistance of the literary to such language. Indeed, by the end of this chapter, we will be able to note the extraordinary difficulty that courts, authors, and others had in defining the literary as a commodity like others, and will see instead that the logic of literary property created a historical position for literary work that is largely in conflict with the exchange or commodity consciousness of which critics typically make it a part.

Wheaton v. Peters

In recent years, many critics have suggested that literary property emerged in a kind of synecdochic relationship to a much broader and thoroughly hegemonic species of commodification during or just before industrializing periods in both Europe and the United States, and this argument in its tidiness has some intuitive appeal.[7] Mark Rose, for example, suggests that copyright found its philosophical and social grounding in the work of John Locke, in the belief that material property was a natural right, one prior to social organization, and that the worker had an inviolable right to accumulate wealth and property based on the labor he or she performed to alter or improve materials from their natural state. According to Rose, literary property as it came to be established in eighteenth-century England merely extended from this prototypically liberal and free-market-oriented right.

In its broadest form, however, Rose's argument reaches well beyond England, to what I take to be all of Western culture: "So long as society was and is organized around the principles of possessive individualism the notion that the author has the same kind of right in his work as any other laborer must and will recur." [8] The essential problem with this formulation for the American development of literary property lies in the historical fact that American copyright adjudication and legislation in the mid-nineteenth century consistently rejected arguments claiming that intellectual (usually literary) property could bear any strong analogy by its nature or in its claims of legal protection to material property. Simply put, nothing like a dominant view of literary property as "the same kind" of property as that produced by just "any other laborer" can realistically be said to have existed, and the antebellum courts routinely dismissed the notion that literary property had the protection afforded by Locke's notions of natural law or natural rights. [9]

In the landmark case *Wheaton v. Peters* the Supreme Court's majority specifically rejected any parallel between the ownership of material and literary property. *Wheaton v. Peters* unfolded after Henry Wheaton, the reporter of Supreme Court decisions from 1816 to 1827, filed suit for violation of his copyright against Richard Peters, who had taken over the job as court reporter and commenced publishing not only the opinions rendered during his tenure but, in condensed form, the reports and notes of all previously published Supreme Court decisions. Wheaton claimed that his work was protected from republication by both the copyright statutes operative at the time and by common or natural law. In his defense, Peters contended that no common-law copyright existed in the United States, that Wheaton had failed to fulfill the detailed requirements of the copyright statute and, therefore, that he lacked statutory protection as well.

The statute operative at the time mandated four steps for the procurement of a twenty-eight year copyright: "The depositing of a title of the work in the clerk's office of the district court, the publishing of the clerk's record in the book, public notice in the newspapers, and the depositing of the book with the Secretary of State." [10] Wheaton had performed indisputably only the first two (although he had sent eighty copies to the secretary of state for other purposes), and claimed that they alone were sufficient to establish his statutory copyright. The last two requirements, he claimed, were conditions subsequent to the official grant of copyright and, therefore, failure to perform them could not lead to forfeiture of the right.

Lyman Ray Patterson defines concisely the most important general issues on which the court rendered judgment: "There were two main points in the case: [First,], does an author have a common-law copyright in his work after publication? . . . The second main point of the case was the question whether the requirements of the Copyright Act for securing copyright had to be strictly complied with." [11] Considering the issue of common-law copyright after publication, Justice Smith Thompson, in his dissenting opinion, wrote:

> The great principle on which the author's right rests, is, that it is the fruit or production of his own labour, and which may, by the labour of the faculties of the mind, establish a right of property, as well as by the faculties of the body; and it is difficult to perceive any well founded objection to such a claim of right. It is founded upon the soundest principles of justice, equity and public policy. (670)

Through opaque grammar, Thompson claimed that the author ought to have a right in his property equivalent to the manual laborer's right in his. By invoking at different times in defense of copyright "natural justice," "common right," "common justice," and "moral rights," Thompson suggested that the protection of copyright had existence prior to and regardless of the statutory right, and that this natural right of literary ownership was strictly analogous to the well-established and natural rights of the manual worker to his material productions. Justice Thompson believed that copyright, like other property rights, ought to be recognized in perpetuity and without the necessity of fulfilling the bureaucratic obligations of the statute, because "every one should enjoy the reward of his labour. . . . [T]he author's copyright ought to be esteemed an invaluable right, established in sound reason and morality. . . . [E]very principle of justice, equity, morality, fitness, and sound policy concurs in protecting the literary labours of men to the same extent that property acquired by manual labour is protected" (672).

With his strong articulation of parallel rights in literary and material property created by mental and manual labor, Justice Thompson, together with Justice Henry Baldwin, found himself in the minority of a four-to-two decision with one abstention. Justice John McLean, writing for the majority in what he considered close reliance on the English precedent settled in *Donaldson v. Beckett* (1774), denied that any common-law or natural copyright in literary property existed after publication: "That an author, at common law, has a property in his manuscript, and may obtain redress against any one who deprives him of it, or by improperly obtaining a copy endeavours to realize a profit by its publication cannot be doubted; but this is a very different right from that which asserts a perpetual and exclusive property in the future publication of the work, after the author shall have published it to the world" (657).

McLean agreed with Justice Thompson that, as an *unpublished*, privately held material object of personal property, the manuscript was inviolable and that its expression could not be reproduced, unless, perhaps—the court made no judgment on this—by the tiniest chance, it was matched by someone ignorant of the original. As long as the author did not publish his work, it was, for all practical purposes, protected from unauthorized reproduction. But once a document was publicly offered, the author, in the logic of Justice McLean and the majority, lost all natural or common-law protection for "the ideas it contains, the instruction or entertainment it affords" (657). Justice McLean rejected any invocation of the common law as protection for published expression, because he believed that the author, in the "transfer of his manuscripts, or in the sale of his works, when first published" surrendered ownership and the exclusive right to reproduce his literary property (657). According to McLean, if common law were the author's only protection from unauthorized reproduction, then the author had no protection at all following publication. The publicly offered text became public property and, as far as natural or common law was concerned, could be copied with impunity by any member of the public.[12]

For Justice Thompson in dissent, the existence of common-law copyright made unnecessary the strict compliance with the bureaucratic details of the copyright statute, but the court's majority, in rejecting common-law copyright, found the fulfillment of every detail essential to any claim of statutory protection: "No one can deny when the legislature are about to vest an exclusive right in an author or an inventor, they have the power to prescribe the conditions on which such right will be enjoyed; and that no one can avail himself of such right who does not substantially comply with the requsitions of the law" (663–64). The full force of this sentence might be better understood if we substitute "meticulously" or "minutely" for "substantially." The court insisted that every condition mentioned in the statute had to be met for a work to receive statutory protection. It was not even clear to the court, as Wheaton argued, that sending eighty copies to the secretary of state for another purpose satisfied the requirement of sending one in explicit compliance with the statute. In a very strict construction, the majority saw all formalities as integral parts of the process by which an exclusive right to literary property was established.

What begins to emerge here is an extremely complicated historical moment in the construction of intellectual (particularly literary) property. Whether or not producers of literary property were seen to have something analogous to the strong and natural rights of ownership associated with material property depended very much on one's perspective. The court rejected such analogies by seeing copyright as purely statutory, highly restricted, specific, and limited in time. Justice Thompson, Justice Baldwin, and Henry Wheaton believed, by contrast, that this ruling abrogated or, in the words of Thompson, reduced to "empty sound" the idea of the author as the owner of intellectual property (677).

If there was a dominant opinion in the court—one backed by the force of political or institutional authority more than another—it would have to be that of the majority, an opinion suggesting not a consciousness of intellectual property as a type of commodity like any other, but great skepticism about such parallels.[13] At the same time, especially given the vote on the bench of four to two with one abstention, it would, I think, be foolish to assume that the majority opinion figuring intellectual property rights and ownership as relatively weak represented anything like a hegemonic consciousness or even a cultural consensus. The notion of what did and ought to define literary property, in other words, despite the court's finding, remained to be worked out more thoroughly in the cultural sphere, both in the courts and, as I want to suggest now, in other areas of influence, in editorials, stories, pamphlets, and legislative lobbying.

Poe's Polemics on Property and Plagiarism

If where one stood on the strength of literary property rights depended very much on who one was, it is still fair to say that the same set of intellectual uncertainties, the same dialectical conflicts between the material and the intellectual, the manual worker and the author, dominated many mid-nineteenth-century discussions explicitly devoted to copyright and literary property. Edgar Allan Poe, for example, probably never read the *Wheaton* opinions or even any of the copyright legislation passed in his lifetime but, insisting that American copyright protection was far too weak and that conventions of unauthorized and unpunished reproduction by piratical publishers infringed upon the property rights of authors, *The Broadway Journal*, which Poe edited, very definitely adopted the dialectical terms of the *Wheaton* debate by comparing the author to other, particularly manual, workers.

In "The Author's Tragedy, or The Perfidious Publisher," a piece published without attribution but very likely composed by Poe as editor, *The Broadway Journal*, echoing the Supreme Court's minority in *Wheaton*, lamented specifically the unfairness of the author's inability to claim the same rights to his product as the workman did to his. Scholarship has not explicitly recognized this sketch as coming from the pen of Poe, probably because the tone is highly didactic. Poe did, however, write many of the pieces that appeared without attribution in *The Broadway Journal*. The diction has moments of affinity with Poe's and, even more significantly, the story complements perfectly his editorializing on copyright. Finally, as we shall also see, the end of "The Perfidious Publisher" features a Poe-like moment of revivification. I believe that Poe probably did write this story, and that it has slipped through scholarly cracks, but even if he did not, as editor he clearly approved of and brought into print its views on the unjust appropriation of authors' literary property.[14]

In "The Perfidious Publisher" an author, Writefort, finds enormous difficulty bringing his *History of Pavonia* into print. Finally, a publisher brings it out "on the cheap and nasty plan . . . printed on dingy paper, stitched in a cover of dirty hue, and sold at retail for no more than a quarter of a dollar" (250). Writefort's dismay over these events leads to his death, and the author leaves behind a penniless widow and children.

After Writefort's death, however, another publisher pirates the cheap and nasty edition, and the widow discovers that "Mr. Bentley will publish early next month 'Writefort's History of Pavonia' in 3 vols. Octavo: price two guineas" (250). The widow realizes that "this advertisement would have saved my husband's life. But cannot I and my children reap some good from my husband's labors? Must Mr. Bentley fatten upon the toil of my dead husband and I gain nothing? O strange unequal world that secures to the meanest laborer, the mechanic, the merchant, the farmer, the fruits of their toil, the full extent of their possessions, but leaves the author destitute of protection" (251).

This lament is made beside the casket of the deceased Writefort, who, in the best style of Poe, responds by rising from the dead. He lifts the lid of the coffin, sitting up to exclaim, "An appeal like that, a wrong so gross, an inconsistency so strange, an evil so monstrous, a statement so startling could not fail to wake the dead. I am alive again. Dear wife and children dear, let those write books who will, henceforth I'll cobble shoes, and then I shall enjoy the fruits of my own labor" (251).

The moral of "The Perfidious Publisher" is not, of course, that authors ought to become cobblers, but that authors ought to enjoy the same rights to their property as cobblers do to theirs. "The Perfidious Publisher," like the analogies emphasized by Justice Thompson, insists that there ought to be a strict correspondence between material and intellectual property even though the two types of property were, as the majority opinion in *Wheaton* and the common practices of piratical publishers suggested, thought of by others in much different terms.

Poe became obsessive and almost delusional when observing the various ways in which the social disdain for strong rights of ownership to intellectual property manifested itself. In more restrained moments of outrage, *The Broadway Journal* merely objected that the lack of an international copyright agreement with Britain encouraged the inexpensive reprinting of English works to the exclusion of American writers. The United States, the argument went, could develop no literature of its own as long as publishers could reap greater profits by pirating foreign works than by paying Americans and American authors were denied the rightful ownership and rewards produced by their labor.

Part of Poe's argument for international copyright, then, was grounded in a belief that, like the creators of material property, authors ought to own and profit from the productions of their work. This argument also advocated literary nationalism, a desire for a uniquely American literature that could only emerge when writing became economically viable. "Without an international copyright law," Poe wrote in a letter, "American authors may as well cut their throats," because they could not possibly make a living.[15] Reprinting an essay by William Gilmore Simms, *The Broadway Journal* added that "the native author requires pay for his writings. . . . [T]he home market is required to do for him all it can by way of giving him compensation for his labor."[16] When recounting that the works of Charles Dickens had been reprinted with little money going to the author, *The Broadway Journal* wrote, "Knavery and swindling can descend no lower. But this is neither knavery nor swindling, but fair and legal trade . . . all for want of [an adequate] copyright law."[17] When arguing for the dependency of American literary development on international copyright and when objecting to the reprinting of American authors without payment, Poe stood within the mainstream of arguments that favored greater respect for literary property. He could find others whose views he might cite in his journal, and the logic connecting the work of the writer to the work of the tradesman in "The Perfidious Publisher" had, as we have seen, wide cultural expression.

The Broadway Journal grew more and more feverish, however, when it took up the subject of plagiarism. Poe, a kind of literary policeman possessed, scoured other journals and books for instances of what he called plagiarism only so that he could publish them in *The Broadway Journal*. Poe's outlandish policing of so-called plagiarists separates him from more typical advocates of copyright and points to an almost obsessional attitude about preserving the integrity and authenticity of literary property. One can hardly say precisely what constituted plagiarism in Poe's imagination, and he seemed often to find it where no conventional definition of the term would be applicable and where no other critic noticed it, even after the allegedly plagiarized passage was printed beside the supposed original.

In his frantic publishing to the world of perfidious plagiarists, Poe leveled against Henry Wadsworth Longfellow his most widely known and most highly theorized accusations.[18] Poe took up close to half of five separate issues of *The Broadway Journal* to make his position on Longfellow and plagiarism clear to skeptics, but his "definition of the grounds on which a charge of plagiarism may be based" remains frenzied and somewhat muddled. Poe comes to suggest that writers "assimilate" the writing of others, then forget they have done so. Later, an event triggers the recall of that earlier writing, but the author "feels it as *his own*" and in an act of "secondary origination" commits his or her thoughts to paper.[19] The precise terms of expression between the original and the secondary creation might be easily distinguished, but a charge of plagiarism will still be justified if one is able to point to something like what critics now call "literary influence." Indeed, this sort of plagiarism, says Poe, might occur by accident, and his argument suggests that it would require an elaborate interpretive argument even to make it noticeable, though it is also clear that the plagiarist remains culpable in Poe's eyes.

Some of Poe's many accusations of plagiarism clearly seem more valid than many others, and one does well to remember this. But it is also true that Poe had obviously become, in the words of Charles Frederick Briggs, his partner at *The Broadway Journal* and himself an advocate of strong copyright, "a monomaniac on the subject of plagiarism."[20] In the context of his and the broader culture's concerns over copyright, Poe's manic extension of "plagiarism" to cover any work that he could imagine to share the slightest similarity to any other seems most remarkable not because it led to many examples of well-researched violations of copyright or even creative dishonesty, but rather because it implicitly asserted enormously broad boundaries for the definition of literary possession. Any detectable (or even imagined?) similarity in the mind of a creative reader seems to be, at some level, a violation of literary property.

Poe's obsession with pointing out far-fetched plagiarisms and literary piracy, I am then suggesting, is his attempt to work through, insist upon, and extend—in the face of rather obvious social resistance—the sanctity of literary ownership. If, in other words, the majority opinion in *Wheaton*, the conventions of unpunished literary piracy, and the practice of plagiarism failed to recognize authors' rights in their property by permitting unjust appropriation of it, Poe's accusations work very much the other way, as efforts to extend the boundaries of literary proprietorship.

At some level, then, Poe seems to be hoping for and imagining literary property as protected by equal or perhaps even stronger strictures than those protecting material property, even though such strictures protecting literary works clearly did not exist. On the one hand, like the cobbler, the author ought to have the right to profit from his or her productions. On the other hand, the author's property ought to be even more sacred than the cobbler's, protected not just in itself, not even just from reproduction, but also acknowledged when any other work even remotely resembles it.

Purloined Letters

If we return now to "The Purloined Letter," the conflict between the practical state of literary property and Poe's personal desire to assert or imagine its inviolability becomes still more elaborate, still more dazzlingly worked through. I began this chapter by noting that C. Auguste Dupin enacts the letter's return in highly materialistic terms that largely ignore the literary content of the letter, even though that content might reasonably be thought of as the property that everyone wants to possess. Dupin acknowledges and retrieves first and foremost the meticulously observed piece of paper, and the text that it contains seems almost incidentally but unavoidably to be retrieved in the process.

Dupin, in other words, protects the letter from material theft, but he also retrieves it in the face of another, rather different threat to the integrity of the noblewoman's ownership. For, after obtaining the material letter, Minister D—— exercises his coercive power only through the threat of publication, the threat of the unauthorized reproduction, whether in oral or written form, of the letter for the Parisian royal court. My point is not that the letter will be bound, displayed, mass produced, or aggressively marketed for sale, but rather that this figuration of unauthorized publication suggests an entirely different economy of the literary than the one actually emerging at Poe's historical moment, the economy that made necessary the definition of literary possession and value in terms of copyright and the commercial rights to reproduce a given work.

The curiosity in the minister's threat is precisely that publication would destroy rather than enhance the value of the manuscript he holds. Were Minister D—— to bring forth the letter in any way, it would, after all, instantly lose all value to everyone concerned: the minister could no longer use it for blackmail; the lady would no longer be interested in paying for it; Dupin and the prefect would no longer have the possibility of claiming their substantial reward for its return. What needs to be understood about the dynamics of literary property in "The Purloined Letter" is precisely that monetary value and literary possession are conceived of strictly in terms of material possession of the original document—not the intangible right to copy. For the minister to blackmail the lady, it is less crucial for him to know what the letter says and thus be able to reproduce its text, than it is for him to possess the actual letter. Assuming the minister has read the letter, Dupin's retrieval, after all, does nothing to eliminate his knowledge of what it contains. Still, blackmail seems to be impossible without the original document but also impossible were that document to be multiplied. Furthermore, it seems apparent that even the lady herself, the recipient of the *billet doux,* values not so much the text of the letter but the possession of the actual, physical manuscript. In the puzzling logic of "The Purloined Letter," it is only by stopping publication (or in the case of Minister D—— by threatening but not actually undertaking it) that the value of the letter can be established or preserved.

I am fully aware that my understanding of "The Purloined Letter" depends on our willingness to believe that Poe might have subconsciously (I do not claim any intentionality) used the purloined letter as a figurative vehicle to work through his own compulsive (and the more broadly cultural) debates on the subject of literary property. Such a reading does not, however, depend on understanding the purloined letter as having reference only or specifically to conventionally literary or artistic texts. In his editorializing on plagiarism and copyright, Poe was most concerned to protect the rights of literary authors, but as *Wheaton* might already have suggested, judicial and legislative wrangling over literary property emerged not only, not even primarily, with specific reference to the conventionally "literary."

In fact, another early and important copyright case adjudicated in the federal courts, *Folsom v. Marsh*, was heard in 1841, only three years before the publication of Poe's story, and it debated very exactly the definition of literary property with specific reference to personal letters. The opinion in this case was authored by Justice Joseph Story, who later served on the Supreme Court and became America's preeminent judicial authority on copyright at mid-century, the justice who most often authored the opinions pertaining to matters of literary property. *Folsom* involved specifically the rights to print the personal and official correspondence of George Washington, but Justice Story seized the opportunity to ponder and define the much broader topic of literary property in letters. In the words of Story: "I hold that the author of any letter or letters, (and his representatives,) whether they are literary compositions, or familiar letters, or letters of business, possess the sole and exclusive copyright therein; and that no persons, neither those to whom they are addressed, nor other persons, have any right or authority to publish the same upon their own account, or for their own benefit."[21] Justice Story ruled, in what might still seem to us counterintuitive logic, that while the recipient of a letter gained the right to own the single physical copy in his possession, the author of the letter (or his representatives) maintained all significant rights to its reproduction and publication. Whether or not letters were literary, they firmly embodied literary property and *Folsom* makes even more clear than *Wheaton* that in the eyes of America's judiciary, literary and material ownership of a text were fully separable from, rather than analogous to, one another.[22]

This sort of split between purely literary and material property rights was endemic to the logic of copyright, inherent in any discussion of literary possession that imagined value in terms of reproducibility rather than material possession, and it is precisely the sort of split that "The Purloined Letter" will not acknowledge. "The Purloined Letter" insists on a consonance between, an inseparability of, literary property and its original embodiment. When the author of the letter sends it to the lady, he surrenders the letter fully to her, and his rights simply are not at issue in the story; when Minister D—— steals the material letter without ever reading it, he also inextricably steals the text of the letter; when Dupin retrieves the letter, this simultaneous transfer of material and literary value shows itself yet again. In fact, if the repeated substitution of look-alikes for the original in this story shows us anything, it may be that copies are never pure, are never substitutes, are never property worth holding, and that copyright is, therefore, only the right to produce the valueless imitation.[23]

Why would Poe, a crusader for copyright, turn around in "The Purloined Letter" and imagine a thoroughly fetishized original, an economy that seems to obviate the necessity of the copyright protection that he persistently lobbied for? We must, after all, acknowledge that Poe repeatedly recognized the value and marketability of copies, the worth in reproduction that copyright presumed, even if "The Purloined Letter" denies the possibility of such value. Technologies of reproduction and printing exploded during Poe's lifetime, as the steam press, stereotyping, and more efficient divisions of labor in ever larger printing establishments facilitated literary reproduction in greater and greater quantity. John Tebbel and other historians of print and publishing describe the second quarter of the nineteenth century as the period that revolutionized the production of books in America.[24] Moreover, Poe was himself far from ignorant of the emergent technologies and demands for literary reproduction. In one essay, for example, he heralded the technique of "anastatic printing," a kind of etching process that Poe believed would "revolutionize the world" by making possible the stereotyping of any image "with absolute accuracy, in five minutes." The quickly made stereotype plate could then produce "absolute facsimiles of the original printed page . . . *ad libitum.*" He then pointed out very directly that such new technologies of reproduction "will not only not obviate the necessity of copyright laws . . . but will render this necessity more imperative and apparent."[25]

We can see, then, that on the one hand Poe clearly positioned himself as an advocate of the unprecedented potentialities of literary reproduction opening up in his lifetime, but he was also, more than any author of his period, obsessed with the image and meaning, the value and significance, of the unique and handwritten letter and document. Poe's stories are riddled with words, hieroglyphs, cryptographs, and ciphers that declare themselves to be the product of the hand, manuscript figures that define themselves as such. Besides the purloined letter that so concerns those in the Parisian court, another of Poe's stories, "The Gold-Bug," features a "parchment" with "characters rudely traced," a long catalogue of mysterious symbols situated between "a death's-head and a goat." "The Narrative of A. Gordon Pym," of course, concludes with a lengthy explication of a hieroglyphic text of mysterious "Ethiopian Characters." Furthermore, Poe had a seeming obsession with chirography, the study of handwriting, and published in *Graham's Magazine* in the early 1840s a lengthy series of articles that printed the signatures of dozens of well-known antebellum personages and then claimed to analyze the personalities behind the autographs.[26]

John Irwin and Shawn Rosenheim have both suggested that Poe's interest in the hieroglyph was grounded in a desire to imagine a semiotic purity, an Adamic form of unfallen language in which the written figure might be reassociated with its referent in a kind of one-to-one correspondence between signifier and signified.[27] This seems to me exactly correct, but what needs to be acknowledged is that the obsession with the hieroglyph is not only Poe's working through of the abstract process of linguistic signification wholly apart from his cultural situation, it is also his way of imagining the purest and most deeply signifying form of literary production as manual writing at the moment when the possibilities of mechanistic reproduction so dramatically expanded. Handwritten hieroglyphs not only are pure in their referentiality as Poe imagines them, they are also in the nature of their origins very much at odds with literary mass production, with the notion that value might be judged by the multiplication of impersonally produced signs or texts rather than by the singular purity and meaning that can be discerned only in and through the analysis of the handwritten (or drawn) page.

We ought then to recognize that the fetishization of the original, of the mysterious and deeply meaning manuscript, is not at all inconsistent or unusual within Poe's literary work on the whole, and the essential problem must be to understand how this emphasis on the value and power of the singular or manually produced text could be reconciled with his advocacy of copyright, an advocacy that by its very nature recognized and embraced the value of mechanically reproduced textual property.

The oddity is that in the logic of those advocating common-law copyright through the insistence on parallels between the material production of the laborer and the literary production of the author, Poe's emphasis on the inviolable manuscript was the ultimate extension of, rather than a divergence from, arguments for copyright. Furthermore, it seems to me that any argument hoping to conflate material and literary property could only reasonably be made as Poe makes it in "The Purloined Letter," in literary or figurative rather than more directly expository terms. For, speaking as directly as possible, it simply made no sense to say that literary property was identical to the goods produced by materially productive laborers. The very creation of a specialized category of intellectual property through copyright suggested that texts were a different kind of property than material goods. No matter how strongly one made explicit arguments in favor of copyright based on an analogy between material and literary production, the very practical necessity of copyright undermined the analogy invoked to justify it.

The conflict between attempting to insist that literary property was like material property but, at the same time, that copyright was necessary to protect it explodes throughout Justice Thompson's dissenting opinion in *Wheaton*, an opinion, as I have said, that insists on the author's and laborer's analogous, common-law rights. When Thompson finally surrenders such analogies, when he moves away from the realm of the clearly figurative, the contradictions in his logic break free: "Though the nature of literary property is peculiar, it is not the less real and valuable. If labour and effort in producing what before was not possessed or known will give title, then the literary man has title, perfect and absolute, and should have his reward" (691). Literary property is just like any other material property in the second sentence, but in the first it is "peculiar." It is peculiar, of course, precisely because it is *unlike* these other types of property in its immateriality. Literary property may be "real" as Justice Thompson claims but, as he also suggests, it is not real in the same immediate and tangible sense that material property is.

"The Purloined Letter," I am finally suggesting, allowed Poe to construct what could not logically be imagined in any other than a figurative way: the complete union of literary and material possession and transferability. Such an imagining was neither inconsistent with Poe's general valuation of the manuscript, nor with his specific advocacy of copyright. Rather, it demonstrates, and even takes to its most extreme conclusion, the possibility that the literary should be protected as or more strongly than the material. It does so by articulating what makes only figurative but not legalistic sense in the world of antebellum legislation and adjudication. The textual should be protected as strongly as the material because, as "The Purloined Letter" imagines it, the two cannot be separated.

International Copyright

The debate over international copyright, like the debate over domestic legislation, originated prior to the mid-nineteenth century, but it was only in the 1840s, with Charles Dickens's celebrated tour of the United States in support of the cause, that international copyright became a conspicuous subject of public debate. Throughout the 1840s, 1850s, 1860s, and beyond, copyright associations formed, disbanded, and formed again under the direction of prominent authors such as William Cullen Bryant and publishers such as George Palmer Putnam. Poe joined a New York international copyright association while Bryant was president in 1843. Most of these associations sought to lobby Congress on the issue of international copyright.[28]

The rhetoric of the arguments for and against international copyright echoed the dialectics of the debate in *Wheaton*, the continuous references to parallels and disjunctions between the author and the manual laborer, between literary and material property. In 1844, for example, Nahum Capen, a Boston publisher, spent the better part of his testimony before Congress insisting that if the craftsman had a right to his property then the author ought to have the same right: "Why a carpenter should be entitled to a perpetual occupancy of a house which he has erected by his own hands . . . and *an author* be refused the perpetual right of controlling his own productions . . . is certainly a question involving not only much mystery but evident absurdity."[29] William Cullen Bryant also imagined the author as a kind of craftsman: "[The author] enters a great forest of ideas, which is common ground, hews down trees, shapes them into articles of furniture, or builds a house with them, and he who takes from him that furniture is a thief, and he who breaks into that house is a burglar."[30]

By the late 1840s the two major opponents of international copyright legislation emerged as Henry C. Carey and the publishing house of Harper & Brothers. Those arguing against the strong and perpetual rights of the author (whether domestically or internationally) insisted not only that the literary and the material were different types of property but also insisted on the educational and cultural benefits of cheap access to books. By reprinting or appropriating books, publishers had to pay authors little or nothing, and those opposed to copyright argued that to grant an author a monopolistic right to the publication of his work would lead necessarily to inflated book prices.

Harper & Brothers became America's largest publisher mostly on the strength of inexpensive reprints of British works, and from early on had their business interests very intimately tied to the laxity of international copyright legislation. In the 1840s, however, when it became apparent to the Harpers that no major publisher would profit as long as magazines and other publishing houses continued to pirate literature and cut prices, their firm joined very tentatively and ambivalently in the cause of international copyright. When the profitability of their business depended on it, in other words, the Harpers temporarily pushed aside arguments about the incompatibility of strong copyright laws and the affordability of books, insisting instead that publishers and authors could not survive without some legal guarantees against unauthorized republication.

At the same time, however, the Harpers, as both manufacturers and publishers, generally advocated copyright only for foreign works manufactured in this country. Accordingly, when presented with forms of legislation emphasizing the protection of authorial rather than publishers' and manufacturers' rights, the Harpers could retreat into their old arguments. As late as 1872, for example, the Harpers all but doomed any international copyright agreement with Great Britain by asserting to Congress that "any measure of international copyright was objectionable because it would add to the price of books, and thus interfere with the education of the people." [31]

Though also from a publishing family, Henry Carey left the business in 1835 and seems to have based his objections to strong copyright protection much more in political or rational principle than did the Harpers.[32] Carey never abandoned his objections to copyright. After printing one edition of his *Letters on International Copyright* in 1853, he printed a second in 1868 and throughout the mid-nineteenth century he remained the most strident opponent of

the various copyright associations. Besides advocating the benefits
of public access to literary works, Carey relentlessly attacked the
kind of metaphors that I have cited above, insisting that the manual
worker and the author, material and literary property, had relatively
little in common.

Carey believed that the author and craftsman worked in fundamentally different media with fundamentally different implications
for the ownership of their products. He insisted that the author's
ideas were public property and that the craftworker's raw materials
were personal property. Accordingly, said Carey, an object made of
ideas belonging to the public should rightfully revert to that public
while an object made of personal property belonged to its maker:

> The question is often asked: why should a man not have the same claim
> to the perpetual enjoyment of his book that his neighbor has in regard to
> the house he has built? The answer is, that the rights of the parties are en-
> tirely different. The man who builds a house quarries the stone and makes
> the bricks of which it is composed, or he pays another for doing it for him.
> When finished, his house is all, materials and workmanship, his own. The
> man who makes a book uses the common property of mankind, and all he
> furnishes is the workmanship. Society permits him to use its property, but
> it is on condition that, after a certain time [the period of statutory copy-
> right?] the whole shall become part of the common stock.[33]

The right of the public to a book as Carey represented it was
the right to the raw materials, the ideas that composed it. Those
opposing Carey seemed at once to agree and disagree with him on
the public's ownership of ideas. As I have already suggested, those
supporting copyright tended in their metaphors of manual labor to
imply that the author, like the craftworker, worked in theoretically
ownable materials similar to leather for shoes or wood for houses.
At the same time, however, many of these metaphors and arguments
in support of copyright were less concerned with claiming the right
to the raw material of ideas and more concerned with claiming that
the author's final product, like the craftworker's, became ownable
property by virtue of the labor of transformation and composition. In other words, the real interest for most of those advocating
stronger copyright legislation was not in who owned the materials

or unexpressed ideas, but in who owned the product after labor. In the passage cited above, for example, Bryant's "forest of ideas" is "common ground" transformed into personal property by authorial work.[34]

Carey, however, in order to undermine arguments for copyright based on craft labor seemed to argue that ideas were never transformed or discovered but merely appropriated, stolen, or rearranged. Authors were

> in the condition of a man who had entered a large garden and collected a variety of the most beautiful flowers growing therein, of which he had made a fine bouquet. The owner of the garden would naturally say to him: "The flowers are mine but the arrangement is yours. You cannot keep the bouquet, but you may smell it, or show it for your own profit for an hour or two, but then it must come to me." (12–13)

In the cases of both those arguing for and against strong copyright, the ownership of unexpressed ideas was not primarily at issue. Rather, the question was who owned and had the rights to reproduce a particular and fully realized literary expression. To Bryant and others emphasizing the legitimacy of craft metaphors for authorship, the author, by virtue of transforming the raw materials of his ideas, came to own his text; to Carey, who attacked the legitimacy of such metaphors, the author was more a flower picker, one who appropriated and rearranged ideas while doing insufficient labor to make them his own for any but the briefest period of protection.

This continuing concern over the ownership of rights to copy a fully realized expression demonstrates again that discussions of copyright tended to define literary property primarily in terms of its value as a reproducible commodity in the literary marketplace. Both those arguing for and against copyright were unconcerned with protecting the ownership of unexpressed literary ideas, ideas that had not yet been fully realized and thus had no way of being brought before the market. Rather, unrealized ideas, the so-called raw materials of authorship, were assumed by those on both sides of the copyright debate to exist in the public domain.

Mechanical Butterflies

Nathaniel Hawthorne, unlike Poe, seems to have been remarkably unconcerned with the subject of literary property. He published nothing on copyright and his letters and journals, as far as I know, make no direct reference to the subject. But if Hawthorne paid little attention to the strident voices debating the issue of commercial rights to reproduction, he was not fully without a sense of literature's commodity value. Any number of personal letters negotiating sales prices, contracts, and deadlines might be invoked to demonstrate Hawthorne's consciousness of the literary as a commercial property, and several critics have convincingly pointed out that Hawthorne himself was deeply involved in his own market-oriented promotion.[35]

It would, in fact, be fair to say of Hawthorne's literary career, even more than Poe's, that it spanned and developed within the context of the literary market's expansion. The audience for literature existed on a fairly wide scale in the 1840s, the primary decade of Poe's literary activity, and various periodicals such as *Graham's Magazine* (which Poe edited for a time) and particular authors (usually English) already had a fairly wide circulation.

It was in the 1850s, however, that the American-authored bestseller emerged on an unprecedented scale, and it is more than merely historical coincidence that the biggest bestseller of them all, Harriet Beecher Stowe's *Uncle Tom's Cabin*, became in 1853 the first particularly literary text to require adjudication of its ownership.[36] *Uncle Tom's Cabin* sold hundreds of thousands of copies, by some accounts more than a million, and this popularity must have inspired one F. W. Thomas to believe that a German translation published for immigrants in the United States could be profitably marketed. In fact, Stowe's attorney, S. C. Perkins, pointed out that the rights of copyright as they pertained to translations of American works published in America had never been an issue before the courts, in part because no previous work had achieved a popularity so great as to make the domestically published translation potentially profitable.[37]

Stowe sued Thomas claiming that the translation violated her copyright, but the courts, still hesitant to see any kind of strongly defended property in literary ownership, insisted that translations were original works in their own right and, therefore, that copyright statutes provided no protection against them. Once again, in another very strict construction, the rights of literary ownership and the sense of the text as an ownable commodity were drastically circumscribed when they might equally well have been strengthened by the courts.

Within the broader cultural context I have been discussing we might very well ask how Hawthorne could possibly have avoided the discussion of literary property. For, as I have been trying to make clear, the copyright debate, like the expansion of literary marketing, was hardly a local phenomenon, hardly a cause taken up only or in isolation by authors as different as Edgar Allan Poe and Harriet Beecher Stowe. The issue of literary property was addressed by judges, legislators, political scientists, publishers, and other literary professionals of every stripe. Even Hawthorne's most intimate professional acquaintances, from Herman Melville to his publisher James T. Fields, found themselves intimately involved in the debates on literary property.[38]

Given this environment, for Hawthorne to have ignored the subject of literary rights would have required a kind of superhuman act of individual transcendence and assertion of personality to overcome not only the broadly cultural but his highly personal and professional surroundings. Rather than suggesting that Hawthorne existed wholly apart from this pervasive cultural and particularly literary concern, I suggest that the subject of literary property was driven underground but is nonetheless addressed within his work.

"The Artist of the Beautiful" provides the most enlightening example of the way in which Hawthorne reacted to the logic of copyright in figurative and oblique terms. For if Owen Warland's butterfly resists commercialization, if it is a very thinly veiled discussion of the artist's (and implicitly the author's) triumph over materialism, the butterfly is also, inevitably, a kind of artistic property. The ideas of intellectual property operative in "Artist," however, diverge strongly from those supporting or attacking the establishment of intellectual property through copyright. Far from concerning itself with rights to copy, "Artist" seems to suggest that the most important terms of ownership and literary value lie not in a materially realized production or manifestation, but in the intangible and unmarketable appreciation of one's own work that copyright neglects to privilege, or even rejects, as a thing of value.

Owen Warland's butterfly seems not fully to belong to any generic category of art, though the analogies attempting to situate it are plentiful. The butterfly is not a text in any conventional sense of the word, though it is repeatedly likened to one, to poetry most often. "Artist" also compares the butterfly to a painting, but the butterfly is not a painting either. What is, however, clear from the start is that Hawthorne imagines in this butterfly a very particular type of property, one with very notable and unavoidable references to the aesthetic.

The other notable fact about Warland's butterfly is that in its original form it is not material property at all but an idea. That is to say, the original of the butterfly is not the butterfly, but Warland's conception of it. Over and over we are told that the process of making the butterfly is not the process of creation, but of "re-creating" an idea that already exists. But as this story also tells us, such re-creation, such copying, is extraordinarily difficult, and for most of the story Warland's butterfly remains "a dimmer and fainter beauty imperfectly copied from the richness of [his] visions."[39]

The difficulty in copying this butterfly begins to suggest where the real location of value and ownership lies in Hawthorne's conception of intellectual property. I have said above that copyright debates, in their emphasis on commercial value, concerned themselves only with the protection and reproduction of materially realized and potentially salable expression, but Hawthorne seems to be fantasizing a protection that runs considerably deeper than anything that the logic of copyright might encompass. In "Artist" not only is the butterfly unreproducible, the idea of the butterfly cannot even be enduringly copied, commodified, or published. While a work in progress, the butterfly is repeatedly touched and damaged or destroyed by onlookers. Annie Hovendon, the woman whom

Warland admires but loses to Danforth, crushes it accidentally; Danforth threatens to do the same deliberately; and even Warland himself accidentally destroys it. Then, finally, when the butterfly is completed and presented to the public, when Warland has finally copied his idea with an adequate measure of accuracy, he takes it to the Danforth household where the blacksmith's brutal child almost instantly demolishes it, leaving only "a small heap of glittering fragments" (475).

We might thus begin to say that "Artist" reinscribes the economy of publication that Poe imagined in "The Purloined Letter," only it does so in more violent and dramatically literalized terms. In "The Purloined Letter" the act of bringing one's property before the public eye leads not to the commercial enhancement but to the destruction of value in the letter; in "Artist," this threat in public exposure becomes figured not so much as the destruction of value but quite directly and unavoidably as the actual destruction of Warland's artistic property itself. To bring the butterfly into public is to have the butterfly destroyed as an object worth owning.

To stop at this point, however, would be to stop only midway on the path to understanding the nature of artistic property in "Artist," because any parallel between the purloined letter and the butterfly must ultimately strain under the obvious fact that the letter and the butterfly are very different sorts of commodities as the stories conceive them. As I have said above, Poe's letter has no obvious or necessary relation to the artistic. It addresses the issue of literary property not so much through any emphasis on aesthetic or spiritual grounds, but rather by associating literary property with its physical manifestation. The letter participates fully, even exaggeratedly, in the logic of common-law copyright that attempted to define literary ownership in highly materialistic terms.

"The Artist of the Beautiful," on the other hand, imagines a type of artistic ownership that is unassailable even after its physical manifestation is destroyed, because the most important element of the property, the original and immaterial idea, stands ontologically in the possession of the artist. Warland watches Danforth's child crush the mechanical butterfly, but afterwards, far from lament, he "looks placidly at what seemed the ruin of his life's labor, and which yet was no ruin. He had caught a far other butterfly than this. When the artist rose high enough to achieve the beautiful, the symbol by which he made it perceptible to mortal senses became of little value in his eyes while his spirit possessed itself of the enjoyment of the reality" (475).

The particular property imagined in "Artist" differs partly from that of the letter precisely in that the material embodiment, even the singular and unreproducible material original, is very nearly worthless. What is at stake in "Artist" is not so much the insistence on the parallels between material and literary property, a kind of extension of the reasoning behind common-law copyright, but the imagining of an ontological artistic copyright. The right to reproduction, to copy and profit from an artistic idea, can rest only with the artist because only the artist has access and an adequate spiritual capacity to realize the vision of his uncommon and materially evanescent or even unrealizable idea.

Such a relocation of literary possession fully away from material expression must lead, of course, to a complete rejection of the importance of market or monetary value, the sort of worth that copyright, with its emphasis on the rights to a reproducible manuscript, emphasized. In the logic of "Artist," onlookers are welcome to possess, or even to destroy and mutilate, the material manifestation of a work, but they will never be able to reproduce it or ruin its artistic value, because meaningful "possession" and productive capacity reside only in the artist's hands and mind and are, safely prized and kept from view, fully unassailable.

Watches in Girdles

As I have been trying to understand these two stories they present two radically different figurations of literary property. Poe insists on the exaggeration of common-law copyright while Hawthorne attempts to carve out a wholly different, ontological kind of protection against reproduction, a conception of artistic ownership and possession fully removed from the commercial concerns that the copyright debate emblematized. Neither finds copyright, with its fundamental emphasis on a statutorily limited right to reproduce, a wholly adequate (or wholly commodifying) means of defining property. For Poe in "The Purloined Letter," an original is an original, and duplicates, while they might be produced, lack inherent value. The distinction between the right to own a physical object and the right to reproduce that object insisted upon by the logic of copyright is figuratively undermined in Poe's story. Here the value of literary property, like the value of material possessions, exists only in the ownership of the object itself. For Hawthorne, the very notion of copyright fails to understand the nature of origination. In "Artist" copyright is simply unnecessary, because the only property worth protecting is the idea or thought behind a creation, and that idea or thought never finds perfect public expression in material form. If Justice McLean, writing for the majority in *Wheaton*, argues that writers have a natural, inviolable, and perpetual right to an unpublished manuscript that was forfeited by the act of publication, Hawthorne fantasizes a type of literary property where publication is irrelevant to ownership.

These competing constructions matter because they demonstrate on a small scale the possible ways in which literary property might have been imagined. We might, in other words, point to the complexity presented by these stories and authors, not to mention the courts that repeatedly saw literary property as very weakly and only statutorily held, and know that recent critics have participated in a rush to hegemonic commodification where the understanding of literary property is concerned. Literary property simply was not, even in an age of rapidly expanding urban industrial capitalism and possessive individualism, hegemonically understood to be a natural, inalienable, or self-evident possession of the writer or anybody else. Furthermore, even when institutions of social power recognized such property, they explicitly separated the ownership of material objects from the ownership of the right to reproduce a particular expression.

My understanding of these stories and their alternatives to the *Wheaton* decision begs an obvious question: to what extent could submerged literary figurations have had any meaningful social effect when established institutions of legal power refused to see copyright either as the kind of common-law protection or ontological fact of artistic endeavor that Poe and Hawthorne respectively imagined? The first answer may be that standing alone such figurations had little or no consequence. One must, after all, realistically recognize that the day-to-day economics of monetary reward and the professional viability of authorship and publishing depended less on literary representation and more on the property laws and market dynamics operative at the time. Moreover, it may be said that literary representations have only limited powers of social self-implementation fully independent from the institutions that govern literary production or profitability. The final bit of evidence suggesting that such figurations carry little force may be the ever-increasing clarity and power of copyright laws. More and more, copyright has throughout the last century become the prevailing way of thinking about the author's right to his or her property.

At the same time, however, one would be foolish to dismiss wholly the ability of literary representations to reflect and influence the culture and society of which they are a part. Furthermore, the fact that these stories not only came into print but have become more or less canonical works suggests that their figurations do not and did not exist wholly apart from institutions of literary production, that their figurations of literary value and property have worked themselves into the American consciousness through literary institutions as tremendously powerful alternatives to a purely statutory and legislatively limited copyright. If we see "The Purloined Letter" and "Artist" in this light, then the question of which figurations or representations of literary property were and are dominant in American culture depends almost wholly on which elements of the culture one chooses to emphasize. A somewhat less tidy but critically more sophisticated understanding of literary property's genesis will recognize the variety of its representations without necessarily or unjustifiably privileging any one.

Though I have emphasized ways in which particular literary texts and judicial plaintiffs seemed to find different bases for defining literary ownership and value than did the courts and legislature, other texts might be said to have an understanding and appreciation of literary property that more closely approximates the terms of copyright as the legal system defined them in the mid-nineteenth century. Fanny Fern's *Ruth Hall*, for example, does not so much interrogate as celebrate and accept as sufficiently powerful the extant conception of copyright and literary property.

Most recent critics of *Ruth Hall* have concentrated on explaining this novel's subversion of conventional or dominant modes of middle-class womanhood and woman's fiction. Nina Baym, Susan Harris, and Joyce Warren all recognize a double-voiced quality in the novel, a simultaneous embrace of and attack on sentimental ideology and its narrative forms.[40] In its early chapters, as Ruth comes of age and marries, the novel features deeply conventional representations of Ruth as a submissive, silent, dependent, and worshipful wife and mother. Her marriage to Harry Hall stands in pointed contrast to the marriage of Harry's parents. The elder Halls intrude overbearingly upon the model of sentimental marriage lived by Ruth and her husband by emphasizing outdated forms of severe Calvinist religiosity, frugality, and practicality at the expense of domesticity's kinder Christianity and material comforts. Ruth's mother-in-law puts it this way to Ruth: "As to the silk stockings you were married in, of course you will never be so extravagant as to wear them again" (20). Where Harry commutes to and from the city each day to earn his living as a businessman, his father is a severe and backward country doctor who works out of the home practicing conspicuously primitive forms of medicine.

The early chapters of *Ruth Hall* fashion moments of normative domestic womanhood by contrasting Ruth and Harry's marriage to older models of wedlock. These chapters heighten Ruth's gendered authority in the realms of the home and of sentiment and Harry's authority in the realm of urban commerce. In these early pages, Ruth's place within the sentimental ethos of womanhood is powerfully suggested by her capacity to give birth (with the physical process—including the nine months of pregnancy—completely eliminated from the text) and by her emotional identification with all things "womanly": "Hark! to that tiny wail! Ruth knows that most blessed of all hours. Ruth is a *mother!* Joy to thee, Ruth! Another outlet for thy womanly heart; a mirror, in which thy smiles and tears shall be reflected back; a fair page, on which thou, God-commissioned, mayst write what thou wilt; a heart that will throb back to thine, love for love."[41]

In these early chapters, especially when passages such as the one above are placed within the body of Fern's work, *Ruth Hall* approaches an over-the-top ironization of domestic idealizations even as it invokes them. In Lauren Berlant's view, Fern typically uses this turn toward "stereotypicality" or "female genericization" to enforce "the distance between domestic ideology and everyday experience."[42] This embrace of domesticity slides even more fully toward a lampooning of it, toward an inevitable conflict between the idealized vision of silent, private, and dependent womanhood and Ruth's actual experience as she faces an increasingly imperative need to provide for herself and her children. After Ruth's husband dies, she finds herself without any money and even without the support of her own and her husband's relatives. Thrust into the need to support herself, Ruth is removed from the domestic world of the early chapters. She takes up various forms of drudgery such as laundry and scrubbing in boarding houses to provide for herself and her children before she considers the possibility of writing for a living.

From the moment authorship emerges as a possibility in *Ruth Hall*, Ruth imagines it as a necessary means of economic support, a way to provide for herself and her family. In *Ruth Hall*, to have the satisfaction of the literary idea without the profitable sales it might bring is to have relatively little. Over and over this novel insists that Ruth writes in order to support herself and her family, and they cannot eat texts. Ruth writes, "because it will be bread for my children"; she "scribble[s] on, thinking only of bread for her children"; she responds to an admirer that her "articles were written for bread and butter" (130, 133, 136). This is not, of course, the logic of Owen Warland, in which the idea is privileged for its own sake.

Similarly, to possess a manuscript only in its original and material form—a concept of property privileged in "The Purloined

Letter"—is to have relatively little. Rather, the manuscript requires a publisher to establish its value. The first questions that enter Ruth's mind upon beginning to write are about how her work will be reproduced and disseminated: "She would begin [to write] that very night; but where to make a beginning? who would publish her articles? how much would they pay her? to whom should she apply first?" (115). From the very moment that Ruth conceives of writing, she understands literary value and property as existing almost exclusively in reproduction and circulation, an understanding at the heart of the notion of literary property protected and defined by statutory copyright.

If critics have been right to emphasize that *Ruth Hall* seems very much at odds with middle-class conventions of womanhood in its representation of a woman's professional and economic evolution toward independence and in its ironizing of sentimental language, it is also true that this novel's idea of authorship and its motivations is far from radical or dissident on all fronts. Ruth participates fully in and even celebrates the conventional logic of copyright and the commercially determined value of literary property that it implies. The entire narrative of Ruth's professional triumph is fully grounded in her ability to adjust and adapt to a commercialized and fully professionalized conception of the literary in which her understanding of copyright plays a central role. While Ruth's professionalization of herself may appear to be a subversive act in purely gendered terms, her story also works almost transparently as a celebration and reinforcement of the increasingly dominant conception of the literary valuation and professionalization implicit in copyright.

Ruth's enthusiastic participation in the logic of copyright develops throughout her story. She receives almost nothing for her first contributions to a magazine called "The Standard," and these articles, according to the accepted practices that angered Poe, are widely reprinted in other publications that pay Ruth absolutely nothing. When John Walter, editor of the "Household Messenger," takes an interest in Ruth, however, the value of her articles starts to grow. Now we discover that "there are so many ready to write (poor fools!) for the honor and glory of the thing, and there are so many ready to take advantage of this fact, and withhold from needy talent the moral right to a deserved remuneration" (141).

Walter, after introducing the language of the author's moral right to make money from the publication of her work, offers to pay Ruth well for the *exclusive* right to publish her pieces. By his enforcement of that exclusive right, Walter directly introduces Ruth to something that she seems to have felt intuitively all along: a notion of literary ownership and value constituted by the right to reproduce it commercially. Walter introduces Ruth to the joys of copyright, a statutory protection that, almost as much as Walter himself, becomes Ruth Hall's hero.

Indeed, this novel virtually rewrites the conventional love plot of sentimental fiction, in which the heroine finds an appropriate, often protective, prosperous, and emotionally supportive husband to wed, as a falling-in-love with the power and virtue of copyright protection. The statute itself seems to offer Ruth Hall the financial and familial security usually associated with a male figure. Susan Harris has implicitly noted this romance of professional success in her observations that the voice in this novel is "at least as business oriented as it is parental" and that as her career develops Ruth becomes "far more interested in business power than in love power."[43] As evidence that this is a novel that at least partially substitutes a romance of professional achievement for a sexual or romantic one, Harris points to Ruth's incredibly steep learning curve as she maneuvers through the hazards of the publishing industry finally cutting out a privileged and protected domain. John Walter clearly stands at the sidelines watching rather than orchestrating or enabling Ruth's rise.

Almost all of Ruth's turns toward good fortune, toward the security and independence from unreliable husbands and malicious family members, occur when her copyright is at stake. Her publishing arrangement with Walter signals one early step toward economic independence (even as it is almost incidentally her first step toward love), but Ruth's professional evolution culminates in the decision she must make between selling her copyright for a fixed sum of eight hundred dollars to a firm that wants to publish her book or keeping that copyright and claiming royalties. The decision is somewhat agonizing:

> Ruth glanced round her miserable, dark room . . . ; $800 *copyright money!* it *was* a temptation; but supposing her book should prove a hit? and bring double, treble, fourfold that sum, to go into her publisher's pockets instead of hers? how provoking! Ruth straightened up, and putting on a very reso-lute air, said, "No, gentlemen, I will *not* sell you my copyright; these autho-graph letters, and all the other letters of friendship, love, and business, I am constantly receiving from strangers, are so many proofs that I have won the public ear. No, I will not sell my copyright." . . . But then caution whispered, what if her book should *not* sell? "Oh, pshaw," said Ruth, "it *shall!*" (153)

The most agonizing, conflicted, and important decision Ruth has to make in this novel is not about marriage, it is about copyright. Ruth chooses to maintain her copyright—what this novel under-stands as the full and adequate ownership of her property—and through this copyright becomes a woman of independent means be-yond the power of exploitative publishers, family, and any others who might show her disrespect. The decision is radically dissident in its gender implications, in its assumption that women might have professional or commercial interests of their own. But the decision is also radically conventional and even unimaginative in its under-standing of literary value that seems to have no existence beyond the commercial terms of copyright. Ruth's final sense of security is de-rived through a departure from gender conventions as well as con-ventions of domestic fiction; but it is a departure that fully grounds her conception of authorship in and celebrates the convention of copyright as the determinant of literary value and property.

Part of *Ruth Hall*'s celebration of monetary independence gained through copyright surely derives from Fanny Fern's lived position in the literary market. All readers of the novel agree that it is highly autobiographical. Fern, like Ruth, suffered the death of a husband (she was also divorced from another); Fern, like Ruth, was rejected by her family, suffered a period of trial, then sought to make a living through her writing, and succeeded marvelously in doing so.

Even in particular details, Fern rose to success and relative wealth very much along the lines of her heroine. She made a significant amount of money when Robert Bonner, the publisher of the *New York Ledger*, took the then unorthodox step of buying from her the exclusive right to publish a weekly column. Unique among antebellum publishers, Bonner promoted his weekly by paying authors unprecedented sums for copyrighted pieces and stories, then advertising that he had done so, that readers could find popular authors exclusively in the *New York Ledger*.[44] Above each of Fanny Fern's columns, one finds, as required by statute, official notice of copyright held in Bonner's name. Even for Bonner, this practice seems to have been exceptional. The notices typically appear only above the feature story on the cover page and over Fern's column. One suspects that Bonner would have advertised his copyright in this way, even if the statute had not absolutely required the notification. Bonner's strategy of exclusivity, his privileging and deployment of copyright, worked to make money for everyone, as the *New York Ledger* became one of the most widely circulated weeklies of its day.

In *Ruth Hall*, Ruth seems to be awakened to the meaning of property in copyright by John Walter, but in real life Fern came to this awareness well before meeting Bonner. In 1853, two years before she signed her contract with the *New York Ledger*, Fern (like Ruth) had to make the decision between selling the copyright to or keeping the royalties from her first collection of articles. Her publisher, J. C. Derby, offered Fern ten cents a copy or one thousand dollars to buy the copyright. As Ruth does in the novel, Fern chose the royalties. In less than a year she earned almost ten thousand dollars from the book.

It would be fair to say, then, that through 1855, copyright functioned as a kind of hero in both Fern's novel and her life by guaranteeing both her and her heroine an otherwise unattainable wealth and independence while protecting them from exploitation. Fern's literary life and her depiction of it in *Ruth Hall* feature an unabashed celebration of the literary as property created by a statute sufficiently strong to protect the writer's economic interests. But if our sense that Fern sought no understanding of the nature of literary property beyond the statutory were still incomplete, if we needed more evidence that for Fern the value of her books lay in the copyrights held, we need look no further than a prenuptial agreement signed with her third and last husband, James Parton, before their marriage in January of 1856:

Whereas the said Sara [Fern's given name] has and ownes certain property consisting of funds invested and to be invested, Stock in Bank or corporate institutions, the Copyright of and to Books & Publications, Contracts and other effects and interests . . . Sara shall have, hold, possess, own, manage, use, control, and enjoy her said property, and each and every part and parcel thereof, and the income, profits, interest, dividends, and payments accruing or to accrue.[45]

This agreement gives Fern complete control of her assets after marriage and emphasizes the importance of financial independence to her. It also highlights, of course, the nature and the terms of possession of literary property through the economically valuable right to reproduce it.

But this agreement tempts one to note a potential problem in Fern's way of thinking about her literary property too. Though Fern's lawyers clearly wrote the agreement, it might suggest the willingness of their client to equate the possession of literary property through copyright with the possession of money, stocks, contracts, and "other effects and interests." In short, this agreement seems to imply at some level that the ownership of literary property through copyright is very much like the ownership of all other kinds of property. In Fanny Fern's mind, and perhaps in the minds of her lawyers at the moment of writing, literary property stands undifferentiated from other possessions.

It makes some sense that Fern would have thought this way. Copyright law had served her very well, and *Ruth Hall* suggests that through 1855 Fern had absolutely no sense of the weaknesses in copyright's statutory protection. Even a year and a half later, in July of 1856, Fern's confidence in the value of copyright, in a protection of her literary property as strong as the protection of her material property, was reaffirmed. In a *Ledger* column from August of that year, Fern tells the true story of a man named William Fleming who attempted to publish a cookbook in Philadelphia under the name of Fanny Fern. Fern suggests that the book is "an attempted imitation of her style; that it is ungrammatical; vulgar, and somewhat obscene." She insists that Fanny Fern is her nom de plume and, in the kind of figuration familiar to us by now, she adds that "no one has any more right to appropriate it than to take the watch from my girdle." Fern argues that she has a right to her pen name, that this name ought to be rightfully and naturally protected as strongly as her material property.[46]

We have seen the essential problem with this mode of thinking: such parallel rights, such arguments for equal strength of ownership, simply are not acknowledged by the antebellum court in any consistent way. The remarkable thing about Fern's case, though, is that the court found in her favor. The United States District Court at Philadelphia issued an injunction prohibiting Fleming from using the name Fanny Fern, and Fern's August 2, 1856, column rings a jubilant note of triumph and renewed confidence in the potency, the absoluteness, of ownership granted by copyright. "What is the use of laws if they were not made for my use?" asks Fern. She goes on to affirm specifically the meaning of her victory to her readers: "Know, henceforth, that Violet Velver, is as much your name, (for purposes of copyright and other rights,) as Julia Parker, if you choose to make it so." The remarkable point, given the nature of antebellum jurisprudence, is that Fanny Fern could prevent someone from adopting her pen name. The case must have evidenced what her life and writing had led her to think all along: property in the literary was as secure and very much like the watch in her girdle.[47]

A little more than a year later, however, Fern's romance with existing copyright protection and her understanding of the literary as a commodity like any other ended. On November 28, 1857, she took up the subject of international copyright.[48] Prior to the publication of this column, I know of no writing that demonstrates Fern's critical awareness of the relatively weak protection of literary property afforded by antebellum copyright. Here, however, she stands outraged, as if she has just discovered the weakness in what she had once valued for its strength. It could be that her husband, James Parton, awakened Fern to the lack of international copyright, or at least to her lack of ardent advocacy of it. Parton had written in the *New York Tribune* as early as 1853 to advocate the adoption of an international copyright agreement with Great Britain. He later served as the secretary of an international copyright association headquartered in New York. In 1867, he wrote a lengthy article in *The Atlantic* expressing his outrage at international literary piracy. In 1869, as an official representative of the copyright association, he traveled to Washington, D.C., with his wife to lobby the president on the matter of copyright.[49]

Whether Fern awakened on her own or because of Parton, her sense that she held her literary property as securely as her other effects has obviously waned in this column. Fern, who had prospered through copyright laws and celebrated their capacity to preserve her name for her exclusive use, no longer has the sense that her literary property is adequately defined or protected by existing statutes:

Two of my books translated into German. It's all very well to talk about the "compliment," and the "honor," and all that sort of thing—that sounds very well—but I'm not going, in these "Panic" times, to thank anybody for putting their forefinger and thumb into my pocket, and helping themselves, because they make me a graceful bow while they are doing it. Why don't they do the handsome thing by authors? Yes—why don't we have an international copyright law? I'm getting interested in the subject.[50]

Fern discovered in 1857 what Wheaton learned in 1832, what Stowe learned in 1853 (when translations of *Uncle Tom's Cabin* were not found to be a copyright infringement), and what Poe objected to throughout the mid-1840s at *The Broadway Journal*: prevailing interpretations simply did not understand literary property to have the same kind of protection as material possessions such as watches or money (whichever is being picked from Fern's pocket in the passage above). Fern complains that she knows of eleven editions of her books published in England for which she has not received a cent. "Just as well might you refuse to pay your landlord his rent," she says, as deny writers money for the reproduction of their property. It is, she says elsewhere in this very brief column, "the unprincipled principle of the thing—it is the cool impudence of it—it's the idea that what's yours *isn't* yours. That a rasping nutmeg-grater can be secured by a patent and a rasping book can't. I won't stand it." [51]

Fern's romance with the power of copyright laws has clearly come to an end. The precise logic that she invokes elsewhere—that literary property protected by copyright is like other forms of property—comes undone in this column. Goods in pockets cannot be stolen; tenants cannot live in houses without paying rent; nutmeg grinders are protected from piracy. Literary property, on the other hand, can be and is appropriated with impunity by foreign publishers.

Fern does not respond to this awakening by conjuring up systems that value or create literary proprietorship on other terms. She does not, in other words, respond as Poe and Hawthorne did. Rather, Fern simply pledges herself to the enactment of international copyright agreements:

I'll take a hat, and go round and collect the "ayes" and "no-es." I'll draw up a petition, and get more signatures to it than I ever had enemies, and that's pledging myself for considerable. I'll go to Washington—I'll bother [President] Buchanan within an inch of his bachelor life—I'll waylay him in the White-House, and I'll beset him in his "Kitchen Cabinet," as they call it. . . . I'll not only "continually come," but I'll never go. [52]

Fern does not seek an alternative to copyright, but seeks instead the intensification of it. But the point to which Fern would like to push copyright in figurative terms is the point at which copyright ceases to exist as copyright at all. In other words, Fern is caught in the same vise as all of those who, like Justice Smith Thompson, want to argue metaphorically that literary property is just like other forms of property even as they insist simultaneously that it requires the unique legal protection that copyright provides.

Fern shows us that even a literary figure absolutely committed to the commodification of the literary, a figure insistent that her productions are "just like" other forms of exchangeable property, ultimately confronts a social reality in which her understandings are misunderstandings—in which "what's yours *isn't* yours." My point is not the ideologically naive one that literary property has an inherent, mystical, ontological, or transcendent position beyond the bounds of economic or legal contingencies. Rather, I insist that these contingencies positioned literary labor almost by necessity at the margins, or even outside the bounds of broadly conceived ideologies of possessive individualism and commodified exchange. For we have repeatedly seen here the extreme difficulty, perhaps the impossibility, of maintaining an idea that the literary is a commodity just like any other, or that the author's labor is commodified like other labors precisely within the logic of social and legal arrangements during the antebellum years. This historical ordering—not primarily the transcendent capacities of individual writers—made the partial or entire absorption of authorship into dominant valorizations of commercial worth, property, and exchange altogether unlikely. Rather, literary property during the antebellum years shows itself to be a unique sort of possession if it is possessed at all, a property with a commodity status that must always be debated (and undermined) rather than assumed within the given structures of power—even when, as in the case of Fanny Fern, the union of the literary with other salable commodities is a consummation devoutly to be wished.

Afterword

The Harpers' Horse

By the end of the 1850s, the Harper brothers of New York owned the largest and most profitable of all American publishing houses. More than any other publishers, the Harpers stood at the center of a dispute over how and even whether authors ought to be able to make a living from their work. To some, the Harpers were a potent force in the creation of the authorial profession. With their channels of advertisement and distribution, they could foster the careers of chosen writers and the cause of American literature as a whole. Horace Greeley wrote, "The Harpers have probably done more for the advancement of literary taste and the advantage of native authorship than all other publishers. Their treatment of authors has always been liberal and generous, and we have never heard a complaint uttered against them. On the contrary, we hear them highly commended by all men of letters who have any dealings with them." [1]

But if Greeley eulogized the supposedly liberal pay and promotion of American authors provided by the Harpers, others were less complimentary. The Harpers built their business largely by reprinting entire series of British works while paying relatively little for them. Where several other publishers, most notably George Putnam, worked actively to bring American writers into print and pay them meaningful fees for their work, the Harpers seem to have been far more interested in maximizing their profits. Indeed, where *Putnam's Monthly Magazine* devoted itself almost exclusively to printing native authors, *Harper's New Monthly Magazine*, the best-selling monthly of the 1850s, typically included more reprinted English material than anything else. George R. Graham, the publisher of *Graham's Magazine*, went so far as to describe *Harper's* as "a good foreign magazine." It was partly by clipping articles from elsewhere that the Harpers were able to make good on their promise to provide "more reading matter (144 two-column pages) and at a lower price (twenty-five cents a copy) than any other magazine." One writer, driven to distraction by the Harpers' unwillingness to pay, took to parading in front of the publishing house with a large sign saying, "One of Harper's authors. I am starving."[2]

The Harpers had rationalized the publishing business for maximum profit and production as no other publisher had. They not only marketed books and magazines but also manufactured them. As late as 1833, the Harpers (like most other printers in the United States) did not even own a fully automated press. In this year, however, they introduced a steam press to their business and retired to pasture the faithful horse that had powered their publishing for years. The horse had lived in the firm's cellar "harnessed to a beam which drove a perpendicular shaft" from seven in the morning to six at night with one hour for lunch at noon. When first trotting into the meadow, the Harpers' horse seemed ready to appreciate his golden years of pastoral luxury. He "rolled over in the grass [and] rushed about the meadow," luxuriating in the new surroundings. After a few days, however, the horse came slowly out of its shed in response to the seven o'clock whistle of a nearby factory. It walked "to the center of the pasture where there was a solitary tree, [and] around this tree the horse traveled, round and round . . . until twelve o'clock sounded." The horse took a one-hour lunch break. At the one o'clock whistle, the horse returned to orbit the tree until six o'clock.[3]

The horse and the Harpers point to the commercialization of literary production and its participation in a larger rationalization of labor in an emergent industrial capitalist economy. When the horse goes to his pastoral retreat—what might be his version of Walden Pond—he takes with him his role as a fully disciplined but alienated laborer within a much larger system of production. The Harpers' horse stands as a completely formed fantasy of what managers and owners might like to see in their operatives, and the Harpers probably understood many authors in something like the terms they understood their horse: as parts of a literary machine designed for production and profit.

But if the Harpers' horse stands as a somewhat whimsical emblem of the expansion of the publishing business, of the rationalization of authorship, it also remains inadequate as a figure for authorship. The horse, after all, has none of the conflicted consciousness or anxiety about its work that this study has articulated. Antebellum authorship was a tremendously unstable, fluid, half-formed, and multiply signified idea. Figurations organized the meaning of authorship and its position relative to other labors during a period of industrial capitalist expansion. What makes the period's figurations of authorial work remarkable, however, is not that they constitute a fully closed or perfectly formed understanding of what literary production was, but that they constantly undergo a process of formation.

Understanding antebellum authorship as a form of work engaged in its own discursive positioning relative to other modes of work allows us to organize our idea of mid-nineteenth-century literature in new ways. Authorship appears as a type of labor that is always struggling to find its position and meaning relative to other forms of work, even as the meaning of these other labors may also be somewhat unstable and constructed within antebellum discourse. The figurations brought forth here point decisively to the idea that authorship must be understood and examined as it generally has not been. It must be interrogated not as a product of a purely literary or intellectual history conventionally conceived, but within a broader history emphasizing varied and conflicting cultural paradigms embodied by particular forms of labor. Only in this way can we begin to grasp the complexities and anxieties about class status, gender, and the place of an "artistic" self-identity that accompanied the emergence of authorship as a profession within an incipiently industrial capitalist economy.

But if this study argues by example for a new perspective on authorial history achievable only through an increased emphasis on the material conditions and discursive paradigmatics of work, it also uses this perspective to reorganize on new grounds "types" of antebellum authors and the texts they produce. Which authors share concerns about and conceptions of their work's position at this time? I suggest that this question can be answered only partly by our familiar divisions of authorial work along the lines of gender and genre. To answer it more fully requires that we position authors as they position themselves, as figures not wholly defined by gender or genre but as writers who deploy notions of gender and genre within a complicated cultural system of labor to create multifaceted constructions of authorial practice. Hawthorne, Jacobs, and Stowe all shared anxieties that they were becoming "slaves" to the literary market, though these anxieties were inflected by particularly gendered, economic (and in this case racial) understandings. Melville and numerous domestic authors depicted women's writing as a form of economic compulsion, though Melville wedded this apparently gendered conception to a class-based depiction of literary mass production. Edgar Allan Poe and Fanny Fern both wanted to believe that the work of writing was like the work of tradespeople who created material property in which they had a generally acknowledged natural right, but both also were forced to acknowledge that literary and material property were not quite the same thing.

These, of course, are some of the isolated examples of constructions of authorial labor that I presented in the preceding pages. Taken together, they tell us that by centering our understanding of authorial work on writing's position relative to other simultaneously constructed forms of labor, we will find many unfamiliar concerns affecting the ordering of antebellum authorship. The point is not, of course, to embrace the unfamiliar merely because it is so, but to recover the sometimes surprising, often conflicting, history of figuration that helped to place antebellum authorship within an interlocking system of labor, economic, and gender difference. In our resituation of authorship with respect to other sorts of labor, we undoubtedly lose some comfortable coherences in our ideas about antebellum literary work. Lines that have sometimes seemed almost impassable—for example the boundary between the romantic and the sentimental—become blurred when we understand that writers in both modes often shared differently inflected versions of similar figurative strategies. This is not to make the outrageous claim that all forms of authorship were identical or that authors understood them to be so. Indeed, as I have evidenced, similar figurations could be used precisely to insist on radical differentiation as much as on shared identity among various kinds of authorial endeavor. I do, however, want to emphasize that concerns and figurations often shared by antebellum writers as they created their middle-class profession have often been obscured by the structures of authorship that we have recently imposed. If we are willing to undertake a significant redrawing of authorial borders in our attempt to recover antebellum authorship's figurative history, the substantial reward will be not only revitalized readings of particular texts but also a revitalized understanding of the culture that helped to produce them.

Reference Matter

Notes

Introduction

1. Hawthorne, *Letters*, Vol. 15, 138–39.
2. Baym, *Hawthorne's Career*, 15–20. Baym reads only naive enthusiasm in Hawthorne's earliest authorial aspirations. She claims that he enjoyed popular books, believed he could write them, and had no "understanding [of] the precarious economic situation" of writers and publishers (17). I think this misses the misgivings implicit in Hawthorne's self-presentation.
3. Hawthorne, *The Scarlet Letter*, 10.
4. Ibid., 26–27.
5. Charvat, 5–48, 168–89, 283–316. For a still more dedicatedly materialist account of the changing terms of antebellum authorship see Zboray. He questions some of the particularities of Charvat's argument, but not the most central points about authorship's reorganization at a time of literary expansion.
6. Davidson, 38–54; Baym, *Novels*, 174–78; Baym, *Fiction*, 17; Douglas, 9–13; Buell, 63.
7. Williams, *Culture and Society*, 37–39.
8. Ibid., 42.
9. Buell, 69.
10. Hawthorne, *The Marble Faun*, 10.
11. Kelley, 285–315. On the emergence of a particularly female mode of literary professionalism also see Coultrap-McQuin, 1–26.
12. Gilmore, 8, 13; Michaels, 20.
13. Nicholas Bromell, *Sweat*, 179, also see 'Introduction.'
14. Ibid., 241.
15. Weinstein, 5, 32–52.
16. Ibid., 13, 38.
17. Brown, 5–7.
18. Ibid., 5.

Chapter One

1. Matthiessen, 173.

2. Harding, 16-17, 56, 157-59.

3. Ibid., 57, 157-59. Emerson, *Journals*, Vol. 6, 496.

4. Thoreau won various awards from mechanics' associations for his pencils and Harding says they "had become the best on the market" (159). Thoreau's trip to New York is mentioned by Harding (254). Emerson's letter is in a relatively rare pamphlet, *Thoreau's Pencils*.

5. This tenet underlies most labor history on the period. See, for example, Wilentz, 107-40; Laurie, 37-42; Gutman, *Work*, 32-40; Ware, xiii-xiv; Prude, ix.

6. Charvat, 68.

7. Buell, 57; Williams, *Sociology*, 44-54.

8. Cott, 1; Smith-Rosenberg, "The Female World of Love and Ritual" in *Disorderly Conduct*, 53-76.

9. Tompkins, 124-147.

10. Baym, 13, 17.

11. S. Harris, 21.

12. Kelley, 28; Coultrap-McQuin, 20.

13. Fetterley, 601-602.

14. Ibid., 607. Fetterley's position as an advocate of celebratory appraisals of gender-distinct literary work is most apparent in her critique of *The Culture of Sentiment*, ed. Samuels. Fetterley applauds the anthology's "seriousness of attention and engagement" (607), but dislikes what she insists is an exaggerated emphasis on the "essentially negative assessments" of sentimentality as a culture privileging the middle class while subjugating others. In *The Culture of Sentiment* see particularly Wexler, "Tender Violence."

15. For an article that sounds many of the same notes as Fetterley's see Showalter, 126.

16. Wexler, 28-36; Lang, "Class," 129.

17. Baron, 16.

18. Scott, 39. Scott is "troubled . . . by the exclusive fixation on questions of the individual subject and by the tendency to reify subjectively originating antagonism between males and females as the central fact of gender."

19. Hawthorne's letter to William D. Ticknor is in *Letters*, Vol. 17, 304. Melville's assessment of *Pierre* appears in a letter to his publisher, Richard Bentley, in *Letters*, 150. Jehlen mentions Melville's inability, whether he willed it or not, to write a novel in the domestic mode (593). Rogin describes parts of *Pierre* as "a mocking celebration of domesticity" (168).

20. Wilentz, 108, 129–32. For other works on the move of artisanal toward industrial labor see Laurie, Gutman, Prude, and Ware.

21. This tendency to exaggerate the historical similarities between industrial and authorial work penetrates many works that recognize the simultaneity of industrialization and the literary market's expansion. See particularly Douglas (81–84) and Gilmore. The introduction to Gilmore's book is dominated by the language and idea of literary proletarianization: "Publishing had become an industry, and the writer a producer of commodities for the literary marketplace" (4). For more on the historical problems of imagining the literary market in terms correspondent to the broader commercial expansion of the antebellum period see Chapter 4.

22. On the role of domestic fiction in the formation of middle-class gender conventions see, among others, Kelley, Tompkins, Coultrap-McQuin, Douglas. For a historian's discussion of the "angel in the house," the mother at the center of domestic family structures, see Ryan, 155–65.

23. Denning, 85–118.

24. Ibid., 18. Denning cites several passages in evidence of his claim that cheap fiction came to be seen as industrial production. Many of them fall between 1860 and 1870, but the most remarkable, from Edward Bok, appeared later, in 1892: "Of course we all know that all kinds of factories exist in New York, but until last week I never knew that the great metropolis boasted of such a thing as a real and fully equipped literary factory" (17). For other treatments and mention of the phrase "fiction factory," see Bold, 29–46, and Q. Reynolds. Bold is primarily concerned with later westerns. Reynolds addresses some of the earlier dime novels of the mid-1850s, but does not trace this fiction as far back as Denning does, to the 1840s and Lippard.

25. Denning, 17–27, 85–118.

26. On the conditions of authorship faced by domestic authors see Kelley and Geary. On the conditions faced by Hawthorne and Melville, a good source remains Charvat.

27. Hawthorne to William Ticknor on January 19, 1855 in *Letters*, Vol. 17, 304.

28. Williams, *Culture and Society*, 297–300; *Keywords*, 192–97.

29. Jefferson, 217. One could find a virtually endless number of citations that used "mob" to condemn the cultural tastes and behavior of specifically working-class groups throughout the mid-to-late nineteenth century. To name but one more example, Henry Lee Higginson, when donating $100,000 to Harvard, had in mind the preservation of a very obviously class-based cultural standard: "Educate and save ourselves and our families and our money from mobs!" in L. Levine, 205.

30. On the fame that accompanied the literary domestics see Kelley. For some sales figures and details about the emergent art of advertising see Geary.

31. Fisher, "Pins," 43–44. Fisher points out that since the industrial revolution Western society has tended to identify the art object in terms of nonutilitarian craft labor while opposing it to industrial production. He insightfully sees Hannah Arendt as representative of this cultural vision, while pointing out that it is an inadequate scheme for defining the artistic object. I tend to agree with Fisher about this inadequacy, but that does not change the cultural force called into play when such terms are invoked.

32. This way of thinking underlies much recent cultural criticism and evolves primarily from the various works of Michel Foucault. I find Foucault's clearest general articulation of the function of discursive power in "Two Lectures" in *Power/Knowledge*, 78–109.

33. Blewett, 37–38.

34. Dublin, *Women*, 76–79, 123–30. Other important discussions of Lowell appear in Kessler-Harris, P. Foner, and Eisler. Edward Everett delivered one of the most articulate and thorough addresses on the virtues of Lowell and its promises of paternal protection, "Fourth of July at Lowell, 1830," in *Orations*: "It would seem that the industrial system of Europe required for its administration an amount of suffering, depravity, and brutalism which formed one of the great scandals of the age. . . . But you will all bear me witness, that I do not speak the words of adulation when I say, that for physical comfort, moral conduct, general intelligence, and all the qualities of social character which make up an enlightened New England community, Lowell might safely enter into a comparison with any town or city in the land" (63).

35. For one example of such a story see "Abby's Year in Lowell," *Offering*, 1 (1841): 1–8.

36. *Offering*, 1 (1840): 25–26. Full text in P. Foner, 37.

37. Harriet Farley, "Letters From Susan," *Offering* 4 (1844): 145–48. Full text in Eisler, 47.

38. Dublin, *Farm to Factory*, 28; *Women at Work*, 41–48.

39. Elizabeth to Sarah Hodgdon on March 29, 1840. The letters exchanged by Sarah Hodgdon and her family are in Dublin, *Farm to Factory*.

40. Quoted in Dublin, *Women at Work*, 125.

41. Quoted in Gutman, *Work*, 28.

42. Quoted in Dublin, *Women at Work*, 124; Harriet Farley, "Editorial: The Ten Hour Movement," *Offering* (1845): 96. Full text in Eisler, 203.

43. Quoted in P. Foner, 61. Foner's book reprints this piece and most of the exchange between Harriet Farley and Sarah Bagley (57–96).

44. It is no accident that once this vision of labor at Lowell became impossible to maintain, the percentage of native New Englanders working there began a rapid decline. By the mid-1850s, Lowell increasingly employed not women from the countryside but immigrant labor. Lowell, in short, once it could no longer understand itself in paternalistic terms as protecting and promoting domestic womanhood, lost women devoted to this sense of themselves.

45. Hawthorne, *The Scarlet Letter*, 82. Further page references to this text are made parenthetically.

46. Hawthorne, "The Artist of the Beautiful," in *Mosses*, 450. All quotations from "The Artist of the Beautiful" and "Drowne's Wooden Image" are from this edition. Page numbers are cited parenthetically in the text.

47. Bromell, *Sweat*, 103; Bell, 39. Bell locates the mystical inspiration of these artist figures with respect to romantic aesthetics. Though Bromell emphasizes the materiality of the body rather than an infusion of the spirit as the source of the artist's inspiration, his reading seems only to substitute the mystery of physical attraction for the mystery of romantic inspiration.

48. Wilentz, 134.

49. Schivelbusch, 14. Schivelbusch does not speak directly of the literary or of craft work but is brilliant in describing the ways that industrialization resituated preindustrial modes of practical travel as nostalgic forms of recreation. The railroad meant that the "final fate of carriage-riding, the traditional mode of travel, was to become the amateur sport of the privileged classes. In everyday existence, the new technology took over."

50. Brodhead, *School*, 56–57.

51. Wallace, 210. Wallace's work is a very timely corrective to the deluge of recent criticism that sees Hawthorne as purely antagonistic to all models of female authorship. His thorough research into Hawthorne's journals and letters uncovers the ambivalence about and partial identification with women writers as various as Julia Ward Howe, Fanny Fern, and Margaret Fuller. Other critics have also noted the penetration of domesticity's themes, especially the idealization of domestic privacy, into Hawthorne's work. See particularly Brown, 69–81. For one example of a critic who sees Hawthorne as purely antagonistic when it comes to female authorship see Tompkins, 7.

52. Melville mentions his visit to a paper mill when writing Evert A. Duyckinck on Feb. 12, 1851. His journals detail a visit to the temple in London Dec. 20–22, 1849. For scholarly relations of these visits to the paired stories see Robert S. Forsythe, "Tagahonic," in *Saturday Review of Literature* 8 (September 19, 1931): 140; Elliott, 55–58; Leyda in Melville, *Complete Stories*, 466.

53. Renker, 123–50. The possibility that Melville may have beaten his wife is far from new. See Kring and Carey.

54. Rogin, 205–208.

55. Young, 125.

56. Coultrap-McQuin, xvii, 37.

57. Melville, *Letters* (July 15, 1846), 39.

58. *Letters* (May 1, 1850), 106.

59. *Letters* (June [1?], 1851), 128.

60. *Letters* (September [12?], 1851), 138.

61. Dimock, 7–8, 31; Anderson, 3; Leverenz, 97.

62. Miller, 5, 284. I am grateful to John McWilliams for pointing to Irving as the preeminent figure of anglophile gentility in writing that Melville depicts in "Paradise."

63. Irving, 9–10.

64. Melville, *Piazza Tales*, 322. Further page references to this text are made parenthetically.

65. Miller's in-depth account of Young America and Melville's place in it covers two lengthy chapters (9–118).

66. Sealts, *Pursuing Melville*, 155–70.

67. Ibid., 158–67.

68. Wiegman, 736, 738; Franklin, 55. The quotation is Wiegman's apt summary of Franklin on this topic.

69. Martin, 11, 70. Martin takes, on the whole, a considerably more optimistic view of homosocial bonds in Melville, claiming that they question normative patriarchal privilege and thereby have "feminist goals" and affirm "the values of nonaggressive male-bonded couples." Even Martin, however, recognizes the "implicit misogyny" of "Paradise" (105).

70. I know of no account of "Paradise" that emphasizes the almost parodically class-bound literary habits of the lawyers, though Sealts comes close. Rogin also seems to see the lawyers' habits of gourmandism and consumption as parodies of nonproductive, middle-class activity in general (201–202).

71. I hope I have been clear in saying that Melville's models for authorship were continuously shifting and evolving throughout his career; by saying that he here imagines authorship in particular ways does not exclude the possibility that he imagined it in other ways at other times. I have suggested some of these alternatives in my notes to Jehlen, Brodhead, Dimock, Miller, and Sealts.

72. Wiegman and Rogin both point to the transformation and co-opting of feminine reproduction by modes of industrial production in this story.

73. Kelley, 138. For more on the image of forced and reluctant labor in the dynamics of literary domesticity see Brodhead, "Veiled Ladies," 273–94.

74. Quoted in Coultrap-McQuin, 56.

75. All of these quotations appear in Kelley, 150–52. Also see Foster, 23–24.

76. Locke, Vol. 1, 121.

77. Ibid., 125.

78. "Afterword" in *Offering* 1 (1841): 376. The phrase also appears in a poem in the *Offering* 2 (1842): 40.

79. Louisa Currier, "The Western Antiquities," in *Offering* 1 (1841): 45–47. Reprinted in Eisler, 123–24. Lydia S. Hall, "The Funeral of Harrison" in *Offering* 1 (1841): 84–85.

80. Quoted in Robinson, 111.

81. "Afterword" in *Offering* 1 (1841): iv, 376.

82. Ibid., 377–78.

83. Ibid., 376.

Chapter Two

1. The best source of information on the Fruit Festival is the September 29, 1855, issue of *American Publishers' Circular*. Fields's poem appears there (74); also see "Authors Among Fruits," *New York Daily Times* (September 28, 1855): 1; "Publishers and Authors Feast," *New York Herald* (September 28, 1855): 8; French, 357–67.

2. After bringing out new editions of the author's work, Fields himself helped to organize Dickens's 1867 tour. Tebbel, Vol. 1, 403.

3. On P. T. Barnum's place in the history of promotion see N. Harris, *Humbug*; on Calvinism's shifts and Beecher's calculated appeal to the middle class see Clark and Hibben; Sinclair Lewis's scathing introduction to Hibben claims that "[Beecher] was a combination of St. Augustine, Barnum, and John Barrymore. He differed from the Reverend Elmer Gantry chiefly in having once, pretty well along in young manhood, read a book" (vii); on the changes in political campaigning that emerged with Jackson see Pessen, 155–56; and for an examination of public space and celebrity in the postbellum period see Fisher.

4. Besides Charvat's, some of the more significant works include Douglas, Gilmore, and Wilson.

5. On the formation of communities through reading see particularly Zboray, 78–82.

6. Braudy, 494. Braudy's enormous book spends over 200 pages detail-

ing what he calls "the democratization of fame." On the renaissance theater, see 319.

7. I hope that I am sufficiently clear in my implications that the Fruit Festival presents itself readily as the progenitor of contemporary television programs that invite us to share a staged version of closeness to figures we know only through the anonymous mass media. My insights here are indebted to the two best books I know of on celebrity and its history. On photography see Braudy, 494. Schickel's wonderfully dire contemplation of the false intimacy twentieth-century audiences feel with their celebrities demonstrates some historical unawareness by insisting that celebrity emerged only in the twentieth century, with movies and TV. Also see Gamson.

8. The most helpful works in forming my sense of the history of abolitionism have been those of Walters, Bormann, E. Foner, and Kraditor.

9. All of the above passages are quoted in E. Foner, 41–48. Whether or not the plantations and slave labor were in reality economically efficient and productive remains an issue of historical debate. See Fogel and Engerman, Gutman, and Genovese.

10. Quoted in E. Foner, 30. Walters points out that various abolitionists had varying degrees of sympathy for impoverished workers but he ultimately concludes that abolitionist concerns for the working class existed "only on a superficial level" (118). E. Foner claims that Republicans such as Horace Greeley may have been capable of sympathizing with urban industrial workers, but failed to recognize labor as a class, emphasizing instead the common interests of the capitalist and worker, the worker's possibility of moving West to escape poverty, and more generally the openness of opportunity for economic independence in the expanding North (18–29).

11. Michaels and Brown present intriguing discussions of the Southern economy as reinscribing the free-market ideologies of the North. Moreover, my sense that slavery might serve to suggest forms of cultural labor, particularly writing, owes a debt to Michaels's discussions of authorship. It seems to me, however, that both Michaels and Brown fail to acknowledge, and even tend to eliminate artificially, the force of free-labor rhetoric by flattening the differences between the exchange of goods and the exchange of people, between what, in the idealization of the Republicans, distinguished the free from the slave economy (Michaels, 109; Brown, 29–34).

12. Detailed scenes of torture and irrational murder, rape, and so forth exist most famously in Frederick Douglass's narrative (1845) and in Weld, 57–94—a gruesome and thorough compilation. Chapter 9 of Jacobs's *Incidents* also provides such a list at a time (1861) contemporaneous with the appeal of Republican free-labor rhetoric. I discuss this work in some depth later in the chapter. Also see Stowe, *Key.*

13. Child, 23–24.

14. Stowe, *Uncle Tom's Cabin*, 478. Further page references to this text are made parenthetically.

15. Wexler, 9–15. Also see Douglas and Tompkins.

16. Cott, 63–100; Kelley, 246–49, n. 3; Boydston, Kelley, and Margolis, *The Limits of Sisterhood*, 47–48. In her impressive new biography of Stowe, Hedrick is the latest critic to emphasize the conflicts between domestic and public, literary life for Stowe. Hedrick quotes from Stowe writing to her husband: "Our children are just coming to the age when everything depends on my efforts. They are delicate in health, and nervous and excitable, and need a mother's whole attention. Can I lawfully divide my attention by literary efforts?" (139). The persistent answer to Stowe's apparently rhetorical question was "yes." But, as the question itself suggests, she could only divide her attention by understanding her authorial self to be somewhat in conflict with her maternal and wifely self.

17. Wardley, 205.

18. Ibid., 204.

19. Two essays that have helped me to see the metaphorical link between Eva and the slaves through their physical vulnerability are Sanchez-Eppler, 28–59, and Romero, 715–34. Sanchez-Eppler says relatively little about *Uncle Tom's Cabin* in particular but explores very subtly the various ways in which abolitionist-feminists tended to align the slave's physical predicament with their own oppression in the North. Romero discusses Stowe's ideas of bodily economy and suggests that Eva demonstrates the tendency of patriarchal society to consume recklessly the bodies of white women and slaves (722–23).

20. On the sensation of the sentimental or domestic authors see Kelley, Douglas, and Geary, 365–93.

21. Forrest Wilson, 363, 377, 379.

22. Hedrick, 239. On the whole, Hedrick presents Stowe as somewhat less internally conflicted about publicity than does Kelley. In Hedrick, Stowe's adoption of true womanhood often comes across as something of a guise or a strategy to palliate a public rather than as something internally felt. Still, Hedrick would without a doubt acknowledge that Stowe had throughout her authorial life anxieties about public appearance. For Hedrick's discussion of the trip to London see 233–48.

23. Bercovitch, "Hawthorne's," 50; Arac, 253. Michaels suggests that another work of Hawthorne's, *The House of the Seven Gables*, was entangled with ideas about slave labor in the antebellum period (87–112). Bercovitch and Arac read *The Scarlet Letter* as an oblique articulation of political faith in, respectively, compromise and inaction. But if Hawthorne rejected the

aggressive agitation of the abolitionists, I will suggest, he nonetheless borrowed from their categorizations of labor. It is, after all, worth remembering, as Bercovitch and Arac do, that Hawthorne had no real affection for slavery, only distaste for radicalism.

24. Bronstein, 194. Michael Rogin brought this very helpful essay to my attention.

25. Branding seems to have taken place in no context other than slavery. Whipping, as Melville's *White-Jacket* makes plain, was not an uncommon disciplinary practice on board naval ships, but, as Rogin argues, it was precisely the identification of sailors with slaves through the lash that gave Melville's antiwhipping campaign its most powerful effect (90).

26. Hawthorne, *The Scarlet Letter*, 49. Further page references to this text are made parenthetically.

27. Weld reprints advertisements for a number of slaves marked and identified by whipping stripes as well as letters: M, E, JM, G, T, and A (77–80). "Runaway a negro Mary, has a small scar over her eye, a *good many teeth missing*, the letter A. *is branded on her cheek and forehead*" (78).

28. Brodhead, "Sparing the Rod" 67–96. Brodhead's essay is devoted primarily to more popular antebellum fiction, but he does suggest briefly that Dimmesdale's self-inflicted corporal punishments exist as part of the larger cultural expression and extension of the antebellum subject's interiorization of psychological discipline. Dimmesdale "regenerates . . . as inward impulses external discipline's traditional corrective tools" (79). This is very close to the point that I am trying to make, but I think it suggests that in some ways Dimmesdale fails to participate completely in the cultural move away from corporal to interiorized discipline. Dimmesdale does not juxtapose at all neatly the public and corporal with the private and psychological. Rather, Dimmesdale shows us a character who brings the public desire for corporal punishment very literally into his psychological and private world. Unlike the domestic novels and advice books that Brodhead discusses in depth, Dimmesdale suggests the extension of precisely public modes of corporal (rather than psychological) punishment into the private realm.

29. Berlant, 126.

30. Gilmore, 95.

31. Hawthorne, *Blithedale*, 5. Brown, 115; also see Brodhead, "Veiled Ladies," 273–294.

32. Willis, *passim*.

33. Barnum, 214.

34. Irwin reads brilliantly the parallels between Hawthorne's and Dimmesdale's modes of veiled self-presentation. My own sense, however,

is that Dimmesdale ultimately demonstrates not this ideal, semi-concealed state, but the impossibility of maintaining it (115).

35. Stepto, 20–26.

36. Carby, 48. For a critic who very puzzlingly insists on the happy ending of *Incidents* see Blassingame, 373.

37. Andrews, 6–7; Smith, 93. Also see Baker. All of these writers emphasize the success of slave narratives in resisting what Smith calls "the gaze of embodiment." My argument will be that this kind of reenslavement, this overexposure of the self, is exactly what Jacobs experiences and writes about, not what she resists or avoids.

38. The degree of Child's editorial assistance in the writing of *Incidents* has long been a subject of debate. As recently as fifteen years ago most critics assumed the narrative to be ghost-written by Child (see, for example, Blassingame). More recently Yellin has uncovered evidence that Child's part in the narrative was relatively minor. More recently still, Mills has argued that Child brought *Incidents* into line with Northern women's expected representations of motherhood and a policy of nonviolent resistance to slavery. Mills, while respecting the work of Yellin, insists more strongly than she that "Child's editorial lens . . . had a consequential effect upon the structure of the slave narrative" (255–56). I have relied for most textual information and Jacobs's personal correspondence on Yellin's edition of *Incidents*. All quotations from *Incidents* are from this edition. Pages are cited parenthetically.

39. See, for example, Fox-Genovese, 170; Carby, 54; Yellin, *Women*, 94.

40. Carby, 50–55. Yellin, "Texts and Contexts," 267; Yellin, *Women and Sisters*, 78; Fox-Genovese, 169–72. Also see Sale, 695–97, 707–710. Sale is more concerned with Jacobs's attempts to subvert dominant male understandings of African American racial difference than she is concerned with Jacobs's relation to domesticity.

41. Though Berlant is less than sensitive to the specific historical contingencies that surround the testimony of women as various as Harriet Jacobs, Frances E. W. Harper, and Anita Hill, she is surely right to note that acts of testimony against sexual abuse by these women are seldom effective in creating real reform. This is, I think, a helpful corrective to the more optimistic readings of Jacobs (such as Carby's) that seem to see something inherently empowering and liberating in the act of Jacobs's self-revelation. Lauren Berlant, "The Queen," 552.

42. Jacobs to Amy Post, 232.   43. Yellin, xxiv–xxv.

44. Jacobs to Amy Post, 232.   45. King, 222.

Chapter Three

1. Hawthorne, Vol. 16, 312.

2. Hawthorne, *The Scarlet Letter*, 34–35. Further page references to this text are made parenthetically.

3. Wilentz, 94. The literature on the republican idealization of the independent and materially productive yeoman and artisan is enormous. Other helpful works include Wood, Pocock, Nash, and Appleby.

4. Blumin, 83–107, 163–78.   5. Halttunen, 93; Ryan, 165–79.

6. Halttunen, xiv–xv, 9.   7. Blumin, 108–38.

8. Everett, Vol. 1 of 2, 496. Subsequent references are to these texts with volume and page number in parentheses.

9. Porter, 69–79.

10. On the emergence of "sweated" labor prior to 1850, particularly in the production of clothing, shoes, and furniture, see Wilentz (119–29) and Laurie (37–42).

11. Though labor-union and working-class rhetoric are not my primary concerns, it should be noted that they too idealized the craftsman for rather different purposes. The point of working-class rhetoric, of course, was not to define the middle class as having any affinity with the virtues of labor or material production but, rather, to define clerks, lawyers, capitalists, and so forth, as "nonproductive" workers who had destroyed the independence and rightful monetary rewards of the artisan. The literature on the deskilling of the artisan and the working-class rhetoric that accompanied it is voluminous. See, for example, Wilentz; Herbert Gutman, *Work*; and Ware.

12. The best general discussions about the emergent middle-class health anxieties are Whorton, Nissenbaum, and Burbick. Peter Levine emphasizes that antebellum sport served to foster entrepreneurial competitiveness while establishing the rules of conduct by which competition should take place both on and off the field (625). The idea that sport functioned within rapidly expanding antebellum cities as a means for the middle class to define itself echoes throughout scholarly writing on sports history. See Adelman and Riess.

13. Weld, *First Annual Report*. Further citations refer to this text. Page numbers are in parentheses.

14. Betts, 140.

15. Nissenbaum, 3–24.

16. Graham, Vol. 2, 656.

17. Catharine Beecher, *Letters*, 8. Further page references to this text are made parenthetically.

18. Welter, 372–92. For another account of domesticity with only somewhat less emphasis on the idleness of the middle-class woman see Cott. Other critics have argued persuasively that increased wealth and social standing have no direct connection to idleness or leisure, that domestic work is transformed into the labor of maintaining the middle-class home rather than eliminated by prosperity. See Boydston, *Home and Work*, 120–41; and Cowan.

19. One of the most dramatic illustrations of the spiritually rather than materially necessary labor of domestic production appears in Beecher's prescription for homemade bread. Beecher acknowledges that servants might make bread, or that bread might be bought, but that in either of these cases the bread will not nourish the body and soul as would bread from the mother's hands (*Receipt Book*, 227–30). Graham, as Nissenbaum points out, had recommended homemade bread for similar reasons thirty years earlier (5–9). For more on the therapeutic value of housework and exercise in Beecher's work see her *Treatise*.

20. G. Lewis, 222–29; for Betts, Riess, and Adelman see my citations above. Windship is quoted in Whorton 274–75. Higginson, 585.

21. For an excellent biography of Beecher see Sklar, esp. 214–16. Sklar emphasizes Beecher's prescribed antidote for invalidism as "proper physiological knowledge, healthy diet, exercise, and, above all, some kind of worthy and engaging labor" (215). I am less sure than Sklar that the prioritizing of labor remains consistent throughout Beecher's work, though Sklar clearly captures the proper elements of Beecher's hygienic prescriptions.

22. For an excellent discussion of women's exercise movements and advocates in the period and the suggestion that the rigor of them stands opposed to "The Cult of True Womanhood" see Cogan, 29–61. My own sense is that these exercises are at once opposed in their physical demands to the idea of middle-class leisure, but, at the same time, in the particular forms of exertion they recommend, emblematic of that leisure.

23. D. Lewis's pricing policy is mentioned by Whorton (276). His advocacy and advertisement of the Pangymnastikon appear in D. Lewis, 171, 256.

24. The most complete history of Brook Farm itself is in Curtis. Works devoted in part to utopian communities of labor and other sorts as responses to the dislocations of industrialization are numerous. See, for example, Holloway, Fellman, and Guarneri.

25. Quoted in Myerson, ix.

26. On the impulse to dignify manual work while still privileging the intellectual at Brook Farm see also Elizabeth Palmer Peabody's description

of the community originally printed in *The Dial*. Peabody suggests that "all labor is sacred," but also points out that "as the labor becomes merely bodily, it is a greater sacrifice to the individual laborer, to give his time to it; because time is desirable for the cultivation of the intellect." Peabody's essay is reprinted in Myerson 11–23. The passage cited appears on p. 13.

27. That agricultural and artisanal production at Brook Farm were remarkably inefficient is indicated by the fact that the settlement was constantly in debt and, it would seem, operating at a loss, even with the income provided by tuition for the school. This does not mean, however, that the hope of supporting the farm through agricultural and artisanal production did not exist, but that, in the end, not only the passing of the Fourierist fad but the economic straits of the community caused it to disband. When the new phalanstery building burnt down in 1846, the Brook Farmers simply did not have the means to build another.

28. Howe, 165.

29. Curtis emphasizes Hawthorne's "hope that membership in Brook Farm would provide the means of supporting a wife" (54). In perhaps the strangest explanation of Hawthorne's move to Brook Farm, E. Miller suggests that Hawthorne invested the money and took up residence for the opportunity to be "a voyeur, as it were," of intellectuals and idealists with whom he had no shared belief. Alternatively, but equally improbably, Miller suggests that Hawthorne moved to Brook Farm in order to *delay* his marriage, even though he claimed to be searching for the means to support it. Miller also suggests that Hawthorne invested 1,500 dollars in the community rather than the 1,000 dollars that most biographers and critics cite (189).

30. Hawthorne's attitude toward Ripley and the Brook Farm project, as well as the evolving disenchantment, are summed up by Hawthorne himself in a letter of July 18, 1841. After describing his doubts about Brook Farm working as planned because a shortage of capital had made the necessity and amount of labor greater than he had expected, Hawthorne goes on: "[Mr. Ripley] perceives, or imagines, a more intimate connection between our present farming operations and our ultimate enterprise than is visible to my perceptions. But as I said before the two things are sufficiently connected to make me desirous of giving my best efforts to the promotion of the former. . . . Nevertheless, we did, several days since, (he and myself I mean) have a conversation on this subject; and he is now fully possessed of my feelings in respect to personal labor" (*Letters*, Vol. 15, 553).

31. The biography most in sympathy with my view of Hawthorne's attraction to Brook Farm is Mellow, esp. at 179. Mellow acknowledges that

Hawthorne hoped Brook Farm would be a decent place for him and Sophia to live, but also that Hawthorne hoped to "labor and write [at Brook Farm]; he would no longer be dependent on the whims of publishers and the public. With considerably more optimism than the chary Emerson, Hawthorne invested 1,000 dollars of his Custom House savings."

32. Both Cutter's and Bradford's remarks are reprinted in Myerson's collection of first-hand accounts (201, 295).

33. Bromell, *Sweat*, 7.

34. Ibid., 4, 34. Elsewhere Bromell adds that "work takes place everywhere yet appears to find cultural representation almost nowhere" (2).

35. Hawthorne, *Blithedale*, 66.

36. Gilmore, "Hawthorne," 234, 235. Gilmore's essay seems to be written primarily as a corrective to Bercovitch and Herbert. Bercovitch, *The Office*, xiii–xiv; Herbert, xvi–xvii. Also see Pfister.

37. Wilentz (120–21), also Stansell (106–19).

38. Thoreau, *Walden*, 3. Further references are to this edition. Further page references to this text are made parenthetically.

39. Cavell, 25; Matthiessen, 173; Bromell, 217, 221.

40. The best account of agriculture's evolution toward larger commercial farms and other elements of its history is Danhoff.

41. Michael Gilmore, *American Romanticism*, 35, 40, 51.

42. Marx, 244, 256.

43. Neufeldt's *The Economist* does an outstanding job of showing the ways that Thoreau's thought process is caught up in the dominant language of commerce and manners in his time even as he attempts to distance himself ironically from them (168–79). Neufeldt is more concerned with Thoreau's complicated position on the value of enterprising individualism than he is with Thoreau's figuration of his writing in other modes of work.

44. Gilmore, *American Romanticism*, 50; Neufeldt, 55.

45. Whitman, 112.

46. Leverenz, 15, 80–84.

47. Baym, *Woman's Fiction*, 22.

48. Warner, 32–36. Further page references to this text are made parenthetically.

49. Tompkins, Afterword in Warner, 600; Bromell understands Ellen Montgomery to have a much stronger attachment to the physical labors of keeping house. While I agree with him that this novel lovingly concentrates on material surfaces in ways that are at odds with its message of valuing the spiritual, it seems mistaken to see in Ellen's adoration of objects any fondness for the process of producing them.

50. Tompkins, Afterword in Warner, 601-602; Foster, 23-24.

51. Kessler-Harris, 11, 13; Stansell, 15; Wilentz 61-103; Ava Baron, 47-69; Leverenz, 78. Wilentz's chapter has little to say about women but its almost exclusive emphasis on men in the trades makes the point. Baron's essay tells us that adult male printers reacted to the introduction of poorly apprenticed, less skilled boys into their craft by worrying about, in one of the printer's own words, "the ruination of manhood" (61).

Chapter Four

1. Poe, "The Purloined Letter," *The Complete Tales*, 210. Further page references to this text are made parenthetically.

2. For a collection of essays see Muller and Richardson.

3. The best biographical account of the charges and countercharges of plagiarism surrounding Poe throughout his career appears in Moss, who also mentions Poe's advocacy of stronger copyright laws. On the complicated meaning and place of plagiarism in Poe's literary practice see Rachman.

4. The foundational work on the expansion of the market, the professionalization of the author, and the commodification of the literary is Charvat's *Profession of Authorship*. Douglas and Gilmore among others have, with some problems that I will discuss shortly, taken up Charvat's concern with the growth of the literary market by placing it within the broader terms of America's industrialization and the more general alienation, commercialization, and commodification of labor. Tebbel has written the most thorough history of publishing in America.

5. Charvat, 5-7.

6. All references to the *Wheaton* decision are to *Wheaton v. Peters* in *Reports of the Supreme Court*, ed. Richard Peters, Vol. 8, 591-699 (Philadelphia: Desilver, Jun, and Thomas, 1834). Page numbers are cited parenthetically. A chronological table of significant English and American copyright laws, acts, and adjudication can be found in Bowker, 653-75. In the fifty years between this country's first copyright laws and *Wheaton*, no significant cases on copyright were heard by any court in this country. In the twenty years following *Wheaton*, at least five other notable cases came before the circuit and supreme courts. For the general legal history of copyright I have relied on Patterson.

7. This assumption is fundamental, if unstated, in Douglas's important study of the expanding literary market and literary culture in the nineteenth century. The brand of literary commodification that Douglas is so

concerned with describing emerges almost completely as part of, even as representative of, industrialization's larger trends toward unprecedented commercialism. Gilmore's *American Romanticism* suggests somewhat less subtly that the economic forces of emergent industrial capitalism came to be embodied in the expanding, increasingly profit-oriented, professionalized, and alienated literary market.

8. Rose, 70.

9. Davidson also exaggerates the parallels between textual and other commodities, not to mention the parallels between these other commodities themselves: "Once the product of the author's mind passes from idea to artifact and takes its form in the printed page, it necessarily becomes somebody's property and, as such, is subject to the same kinds of market conditions that govern the distribution of hogs or hog shares, patent medicines or blue-chip stocks, or any other commodity" (83). These very heterogenous commodities are subject to the "same kind of market conditions" only in the broadest possible terms, and I will be arguing throughout that the idea of literary property as it developed in the nineteenth century reflected a consciousness of differences between, for example, the market conditions for hogs and those for literature.

10. Patterson, 209.

11. Ibid., 208.

12. *A Plea for Authors and the Rights of Literary Property* (1838), a pamphlet attributed to Washington Irving or Grenville A. Sackett, emphasizes the extent to which the *Wheaton* decision codified legal distinctions rather than parallels between literary and other types of property. The pamphlet argues against *Wheaton* precisely by insisting that literary property is just like corporeal property, that authors, for example, should no more be thought to surrender their rights by publication than owners of horses should be thought to surrender theirs by bringing the animals into public. The pamphlet, of course, by insisting on such analogies draws our attention to the different market conditions of horses and books. In one case the horse, the material property, is valued; in the other it is not the book but the right to reproduce it that is most important.

13. The weakness of American copyright protection relative to laws protecting material property can be emphasized by comparing the findings of *Wheaton* to those in *Donaldson*, the court's declared English precedent. In *Donaldson*, the courts did not deny that common-law copyright had existed, but only claimed that it had been superseded by the Statute of Anne, England's first copyright law, passed in 1709. Furthermore, the English courts seemed to believe that the primary purpose of copyright statutes was only

to limit ownership in perpetuity. Accordingly, copyright was more or less guaranteed for the statutory period by a common-law right whether or not the author fulfilled every bureaucratic requirement. It seems impossible to say whether McLean and the majority misread the judgments rendered in *Donaldson* or only saw them as a precedent insofar as it suited them to do so. Kaplan describes the implications of these differences: "American law . . . started from the same baseline as the English, but with us there was added an insistence on punctilios which has continued, with occasional displays almost of savagery in forfeiting copyrights, down to recent days" (26–27).

14. "The Author's Tragedy, or The Perfidious Publisher," *The Broadway Journal* 1 (April 14, 1845): 250–51. Further page references to this text are made parenthetically. In its (literally) day-by-day account of Poe's life, Thomas and Jackson's *The Poe Log* contains the most thorough research on the exact contributions of Poe to *The Broadway Journal*. The book makes no mention of "The Author's Tragedy," but notes that three and a half years later (September [21?], 1848), Poe gave Sarah Helen Whitman "a complete set of *The Broadway Journal*. In her presence he [went] through the two bound volumes and initial[ed] the more important of his unsigned contributions with a penciled 'P' " (755–56). Thomas and Jackson's qualified "more important" leaves the door open to a minor story such as the one I attribute to Poe.

15. Poe, *Letters*, 210.

16. *The Broadway Journal* (Aug. 16, 1845): 94.

17. *The Broadway Journal* (Feb. 1, 1845): 77.

18. Moss discusses the specific charges and countercharges that grew out of Poe's accusation of Longfellow (137–81).

19. *The Broadway Journal* (April 15, 1845): 211–21.

20. Charles Frederick Briggs to James Russell Lowell, New York, March 8, 1845, quoted in Silverman, 252.

21. *Folsom v. Marsh, The Federal Cases Argued in Circuit and District Courts*, Vol. 9, 346 (St. Paul: West Publishing, 1895).

22. As for the specific case at hand, Story ruled that the inheritors of Washington's private correspondence had inherited with it the literary rights to publish these letters. Accordingly, Folsom, the original publisher of the correspondence, won his suit against Marsh, who had reprinted Washington's letters largely on the claim that letters, as "non-literary" documents, could not be limited by restrictions applicable to "literary" property. Marsh, in other words, simply did not understand that "literary" in this sense referred not to artistic or intellectual achievement but generically to what Justice Story calls "the thoughts and language of the writer reduced to written characters" (346).

23. The subject of duplication in "The Purloined Letter" is, of course, often discussed, but usually only by noting the ways in which characters, most notably Dupin and Minister D——, double one another. Critics also routinely point out that the letter is duplicated in the substitutions of it, but generally fail to note that the *incompleteness* of this duplication, the fact that it is only the *appearance* of duplication, is what so strongly emphasizes the value of the fetishized original itself. Jacques Derrida, for example, in his own doubling-back language, seems to suggest that the frantic doubling in this story undermines the very notion of an original. Derrida describes "The Purloined Letter" as being carried "off infinitely far away in a labyrinth of doubles without originals, of facsimile without an authentic" (109).

24. Tebbel describes "the technological explosion in printing . . . from 1825 to 1850" (I, 257–62). Also see Lehmann-Haupt, 58–83.

25. Poe, "Anastatic Printing," 163–64.

26. Poe, *Complete Tales and Poems*, 63, 882–83. The first of Poe's essays on autographs was "A Chapter on Autography," *Graham's Magazine* 19 (1841): 224.

27. Rosenheim, 378; Irwin, 61.

28. For a concise history of these associations see Putnam, *Question*, 40–64. Like his father before him, Putnam was deeply involved in the agitation for an international copyright law and his writings are an invaluable source for understanding the procopyright position.

29. "Memorial of Nahum Capen," 3.

30. *International Copyright Meeting*, 14.

31. Quoted in Putnam, *Question*, 386. In *The House of Harper*, an authorized history of the publishing firm, Exman charitably describes the Harper brothers as taking "a median position" between those opposed to and those advocating copyright. He points to Fletcher Harper's membership in a copyright organization in the 1840s. The Harpers, however, were conspicuously absent from or in conflict with almost every major procopyright organization throughout the 1850s and 1860s.

32. H. Carey was the son of Matthew Carey, one of the founders of Carey and Lee, America's largest publishing firm in the first quarter of the nineteenth century. He was made a partner in the firm in 1814 and served as the head of Carey, Lee & Carey before leaving and becoming a widely read political economist.

33. H. Carey, 20. Further page references to this text are made parenthetically.

34. Also see Francis Leiber's address made during the same 1868 meeting at which Bryant spoke: "We do not claim any property in ideas, any more than Beethoven claimed property in the tones he indicated . . . but he justly

claimed by natural right the ownership of his symphonies, and, therefore, the exclusive right of multiplying them by signs and on material" (*International Copyright Meeting*, 22).

35. On Hawthorne's promotion as a literary figure and his own activity in it see Brodhead, *School*, 48–66. As one example of Hawthorne's very thorough commercial understanding of his own work in his correspondence see his letter to Rufus Griswold on Dec. 15, 1851, *Letters*, Vol. 16, 518–19: "I have by me a story which I wrote just before leaving Lenox, and which I thought of sending to Dr. Bailey of the National Era who has offered me $100 . . . but . . . will send it to the International, should you wish it at the price above-mentioned. The story would make between twenty and thirty pages in Ticknor's editions of my books—hardly long enough to be broken into two articles for your magazine; but you might suit yourself on that point. I cannot afford it for less than $100, and would not write another for the same price."

36. On the emergence of the bestseller in the modern sense of the term and the accompanying techniques of promotion the best work is Geary. Wallace, Brodhead ("Veiled Ladies"), and Tompkins situate Hawthorne relative to the emergence of the bestseller on a new scale, as I do in Chapter 1. Douglas (121–65) and Kelley have made plain that the best-selling domestic novels of this period emerged to satisfy the particular cultural needs and self-image of an emergent, literate middle class.

37. *Stowe v. Thomas, The Federal Cases Argued in Circuit and District Courts*, Vol. 23, 201 (St. Paul: West Publishing, 1896).

38. Fields and Melville both advocated the cause of copyright. Indeed, in the late 1840s and early 1850s Melville intimately associated himself with a literary group in New York that took the name "Young America." Headed by Duyckinck and Matthews, this group, and Matthews in particular, were very early and very strident advocates of a strong international copyright law that might assure both American and English authors of the profitability of their work. On Young America and the advocacy of copyright see P. Miller. For an example of Matthews's advocacy of copyright see an article published in *Graham's* under Poe's editorship: "An Appeal to American Authors and the American Press in Behalf of an International Copyright," *Graham's Magazine* 21 (1842): 121–24. Several of Melville's letters address the subject of copyright. See for example, one written to his English publisher, Richard Bentley, on July 20, 1851 (*Letters*, 133–34).

39. Hawthorne, *Mosses*, 458. Further references to "Artist" are to this edition with page numbers included in my text.

40. The most sophisticated reading of the self-conflicted and ironic lan-

guage of the novel is in Harris. Warren and Baym emphasize more fully the novel's deviation from standard domestic plots that achieve closure through ideal marriages. Harris, 115–20; Joyce Warren, 130–35; Baym, *Woman's Fiction*, 252–53.

41. Fern, *Ruth Hall*, 24. Further page references to this text are made parenthetically.

42. Berlant, "The Female Woman," 438, 440, 444.

43. Harris, 124.

44. On Bonner, Fern, and the *New York Ledger*, see Warren, 143–49.

45. Quoted in Warren, 153.

46. *New York Ledger* (Aug. 2, 1856): 4. Fern seems to be quoting the judge in the case as he recapitulates her argument.

47. Ibid.

48. Fern, "International Copyright," 4.

49. Flower, 108–11; Parton, "International Copyright," 430–51. Parton's contribution to the debate is consistent with many others.

50. Fern, "International Copyright," 4.

51. Ibid.

52. Ibid.

Afterword

1. Quoted in Exman, *The Brothers Harper*, 119.

2. Exman, *The House of Harper*, 70–72.

3. Ibid., 13–14.

Works Cited

Primary Sources

Barnum, P. T. *Barnum's Own Story*. Ed. Waldo R. Browne, 1927; rpt. Gloucester, Mass.: Peter Smith, 1972.

Beecher, Catharine. *Letters to the People on Health and Happiness*. New York: Harper Bros., 1856.

———. *Miss Beecher's Domestic Receipt Book*. New York: Harper Bros., 1846.

———. *A Treatise on Domestic Economy*. Rev. ed. Boston: Thomas H. Webb, 1842.

The Broadway Journal 1-2 (1844-45).

Carey, Henry. *Letters on International Copyright*. Philadelphia: A. Hart, late Carey and Hart, 1853.

Child, Lydia Maria. *An Appeal in Favor of that Class of Americans Called Africans*. Boston: Allen and Ticknor, 1833.

Cummins, Maria S. *The Lamplighter*. Ed. Nina Baym. New Brunswick: Rutgers University Press, 1988.

Davis, Rebecca Harding. *Life in the Iron Mills*. New York: Feminist Press, 1972.

Emerson, Ralph Waldo. *Journals*. 20 vols. Boston: Houghton Mifflin, 1909-14.

———. *Thoreau's Pencils*. Cambridge, Mass.: Harvard University Press, 1944.

Everett, Edward. *Orations and Speeches on Various Occasions*. Vol. I. Boston: Charles C. Little, 1850; Vol. II. Boston: Little, Brown, 1860.

Fern, Fanny. "A Premonitory Squib Before Independence." *New York Ledger* (2 August 1856): 4.

———. "International Copyright." *New York Ledger* (28 November 1857): 4.

————. *Ruth Hall and Other Writings*. New Brunswick: Rutgers University Press, 1986.

Graham, Sylvester. *Lectures on the Science of Human Life*. Boston: Marsh, Capen, Lyon, and Webb, 1839.

Hawthorne, Nathaniel. *The Blithedale Romance*. Centenary ed. Columbus: Ohio State University Press, 1964.

————. *The Complete Novels and Selected Tales*. New York: Modern Library, 1965.

————. *The Letters of Nathaniel Hawthorne*. Centenary ed. Vols. 15–17. Columbus: Ohio State University Press, 1984.

————. *The Marble Faun*. Centenary ed. Columbus: Ohio State University Press, 1968.

————. *Mosses From an Old Manse*. Centenary ed. Columbus: Ohio State University Press, 1974.

————. *The Scarlet Letter*. Centenary ed. Columbus: Ohio State University Press, 1962.

Higginson, Thomas Wentworth. "Saints, and their Bodies." *The Atlantic* 1 (1858): 582–95.

International Copyright Meeting of Authors and Publishers. New York: International Copyright Association, 1868.

[Irving, Washington or Grenville A. Sackett?]. *A Plea for Authors and the Rights of Literary Property*. New York: Adlard and Saunders, 1838.

Irving, Washington. *The Sketchbook of Geoffrey Crayon, gent.* London: C. S. Van Winkle, 1819.

Jacobs, Harriet. *Incidents in the Life of a Slave Girl*. Ed. Lydia Maria Child (1861) and Jean Fagan Yellin. Cambridge, Mass.: Harvard University Press, 1987.

Jefferson, Thomas. *Notes on the State of Virginia*. In *The Portable Thomas Jefferson*. Ed. Merrill D. Peterson. New York: Penguin, 1975.

King, Stephen. *Misery*. New York: Signet, 1988.

Lewis, Dioclesian. *The New Gymnastics for Men, Women, and Children*. Boston: Ticknor and Fields, 1862.

Lippard, George. *The Quaker City; or, the Monks of Monk Hall: A Romance of Philadelphia Life, Mystery, and Crime*. Philadelphia: Published by the author, 1845.

Locke, John. *An Essay Concerning Human Understanding*. Ed. Alexander Campbell Fraser. New York: Dover, 1959.

Lowell Offering. Vols. 1–5. Lowell, Mass.: Powers and Bagley (1840–45).

Matthews, Cornelius. "An Appeal to American Authors and the American Press in Behalf of International Copyright." *Graham's Magazine* 21 (1842): 121–24.

Melville, Herman. *The Complete Stories of Herman Melville.* Ed. Jay Leyda. New York: Random House, 1949.

——. *The Journals of Herman Melville.* Ed. Howard Horsford. Evanston and Chicago: Newberry Library and Northwestern University Press, 1989.

——. *The Letters of Herman Melville.* Ed. Merrell R. Davis and William H. Gilman. New Haven: Yale University Press, 1960.

——. *The Piazza Tales and Other Prose Pieces, 1839–1860.* Evanston and Chicago: Northwestern University Press and Newberry Library, 1987.

——. *Typee.* Evanston: Northwestern University Press and Newberry Library, 1968.

"Memorial of Nahum Capen." Document 61, 28th Congress, 1844.

Myerson, Joel, ed. *The Brook Farm Book: A Collection of First-Hand Accounts of the Community.* New York: Garland, 1987.

Parton, James. "International Copyright." *The Atlantic* 10 (1867): 430–51.

Poe, Edgar Allan. "Anastatic Printing." *The Complete Works of Edgar Allan Poe,* 163–64. New York: G. P. Putnam's Sons, 1902.

——. "A Chapter on Autography." *Graham's Magazine* 19 (1841): 224.

——. *The Complete Tales and Poems.* New York: Modern Library, 1965.

[——?] "The Author's Tragedy; or, The Perfidious Publisher." *The Broadway Journal* 1 (14 April 1845): 250–51.

Putnam, George Haven. "An International Copyright Will Not Increase the Price of Books." *Dissertations on English Language and Literature.* Vol. 14. Buchdruckerei von Heinrich John, 1903.

——. *The Question of Copyright.* 2d ed. New York: G. P. Putnam's Sons, 1896.

Sedgwick, Catharine Maria. *A New-England Tale.* Bliss and White, 1822.

Stowe, Harriet Beecher. *The Key to Uncle Tom's Cabin.* Boston: John P. Jewett, 1853.

——. *Uncle Tom's Cabin.* Ed. Ann Douglas. New York: Penguin, 1981.

Thoreau, Henry David. *Walden and Civil Disobedience.* New York: Penguin, 1983.

——. *Journal.* Ed. John C. Broderick. Princeton: Princeton University Press, 1981.

Warner, Susan. *The Wide, Wide World.* New York: Feminist Press, 1987.

Weld, Theodore Dwight. *American Slavery as It Is.* 1839; rpt. New York: Arno Press, 1968.

——. *First Annual Report of the Society for Promoting Manual Labor in Literary Institutions.* New York: S. W. Benedict, 1833.

Whitman, Walt. *The Complete Poems.* New York: Penguin, 1987.

Willis, N[athaniel] Parker. *Memoranda of the Life of Jenny Lind*. Philadelphia: Robert E. Peterson, 1851.

Secondary Sources

Adelman, Melvin L. *A Sporting Time: New York City and the Rise of Modern Athletics, 1820–1870*. Urbana: University of Illinois Press, 1986.

Anderson, Quentin. *The Imperial Self: An Essay in American Literary and Cultural History*. New York: Knopf, 1971.

Andrews, William. *To Tell a Free Story: The First Century of Afro-American Autobiography, 1760–1865*. Urbana: University of Illinois Press, 1986.

Appleby, Joyce. *Capitalism and a New Social Order: The Republican Vision of the 1790s*. New York: New York University Press, 1984.

Arac, Jonathan. "The Politics of *The Scarlet Letter*." *Ideology and Classic American Literature*. Eds. Sacvan Bercovitch and Myra Jehlen. Cambridge, England: Cambridge University Press, 1986.

Baker, Houston. "Autobiographical Acts and the Voice of the Southern Slave." *The Slave's Narrative*. Ed. Charles T. Davis and Henry Louis Gates, Jr. New York: Oxford University Press, 1985.

Baron, Ava, ed. *Work Engendered: Toward a New History of American Labor*. Ithaca: Cornell University Press, 1991.

Baym, Nina. *Novels, Readers, and Reviewers: Responses to Fiction in Antebellum America*. Ithaca: Cornell University Press, 1984.

———. *The Shape of Hawthorne's Career*. Ithaca: Cornell University Press, 1976.

———. *Woman's Fiction: A Guide to Novels by and about Women in America, 1820–1870*. Ithaca: Cornell University Press, 1978.

Bell, Millicent. *Hawthorne's View of the Artist*. New York: State University of New York, 1962.

Bercovitch, Sacvan. "Hawthorne's A-Morality of Compromise." *The New American Studies: Essays From "Representations"*. Ed. Philip Fisher. Berkeley: University of California, 1991.

———. *The Office of the Scarlet Letter*. Baltimore: Johns Hopkins University Press, 1991.

Berlant, Lauren. *The Anatomy of National Fantasy: Hawthorne, Utopia, and Everyday Life*. University of Chicago Press, 1991.

———. "The Female Woman: Fanny Fern and the Form of Sentiment." *ALH* 3 (1991): 29–454.

———. "The Queen of America Goes to Washington City: Harriet Jacobs, Frances Harper, Anita Hill." *American Literature* 65 (1993): 549–74.

Betts, John. "American Medical Thought on Exercise as the Road to Health, 1820-60." *Bulletin of the History of Medicine* 45 (1971): 138-52.

Blassingame, John. *The Slave Community: Plantation Life in the Antebellum South*, 2d ed. New York: Oxford University Press, 1979.

Bledstein, Burton. *The Culture of Professionalism: The Middle Class and the Development of Higher Education.* New York: W. W. Norton, 1976.

Blewett, Mary. "The Sexual Division of Labor and the Artisan Tradition in Early Industrial Capitalism: The Case of New England Shoemaking, 1780-1860." In *'To Toil the Livelong Day': America's Women at Work, 1780-1980.* Eds. Carol Groneman and Mary Beth Norton. Ithaca: Cornell University Press, 1987.

Blumin, Stuart. *The Emergence of the Middle Class: Social Experience in the American City, 1760-1900.* Cambridge, England: Cambridge University Press, 1989.

Bold, Christine. "The Voice of the Fiction Factory in Dime and Pulp Westerns." *Journal of American Studies* 17 (1983): 29-46.

Bormann, Ernest, ed. *Forerunners of Black Power: The Rhetoric of Abolition.* Englewood Cliffs, N.J.: Prentice-Hall, 1971.

Bowker, Richard Rogers. *Copyright: Its History and Its Law.* Boston: Houghton Mifflin, 1912.

Boydston, Jeanne. *Home and Work: Housework, Wages, and the Ideology of Labor in the Early Republic.* New York: Oxford University Press, 1990.

Boydston, Jeanne, Mary Kelley, and Ann Margolis. *The Limits of Sisterhood.* Chapel Hill: University of North Carolina Press, 1988.

Braudy, Leo. *The Frenzy of Renown: Fame and Its History.* New York: Oxford University Press, 1986.

Brodhead, Richard. *Cultures of Letters: Scenes of Reading and Writing in Nineteenth-Century America.* Chicago: University of Chicago Press, 1993.

———. "Sparing the Rod: Discipline and Fiction in Antebellum America." *Representations* 21 (1988): 67-96.

———. *The School of Hawthorne.* New York: Oxford University Press, 1986.

———. "Veiled Ladies: Toward a History of Antebellum Entertainment." *ALH* 1 (1989): 273-94.

Bromell, Nicholas. *By the Sweat of the Brow: Literature and Labor in Antebellum America.* Chicago: University of Chicago Press, 1993.

———. " 'The Bloody Hand' of Labor: Work, Class, and Gender in Three Stories by Hawthorne." *American Quarterly* 42 (1990): 542-64.

Bronstein, Zelda. "The Parabolic Ploys of *The Scarlet Letter*." *American Quarterly* 39 (1987): 193-210.

Brown, Gillian. *Domestic Individualism: Imagining Self in Nineteenth-Century America.* Berkeley: University of California Press, 1990.

Buell, Lawrence. *New-England Literary Culture from Revolution through Renaissance.* Cambridge, England: Cambridge University Press, 1986.

Burbick, Joan. *Healing the Republic: The Language of Health and the Culture of Nationalism.* Cambridge, England: Cambridge University Press, 1994.

Cameron, Sharon. *The Corporeal Self: Allegories of the Body in Melville and Hawthorne.* Baltimore: Johns Hopkins University Press, 1986.

Canby, Henry Seidel. *Thoreau.* Boston: Houghton Mifflin, 1939.

Carby, Hazel. *Reconstructing Womanhood: The Emergence of the Afro-American Woman Novelist.* New York: Oxford University Press, 1987.

Cavell, Stanley. *The Senses of Walden.* New York: Viking Press, 1974.

Charvat, William. *The Profession of Authorship in America, 1800–1870.* Ed. Matthew J. Bruccolli. Columbus: Ohio State University Press, 1968.

Clark, Clifford. *Henry Ward Beecher: Spokesman for a Middle-Class America.* Urbana: University of Illinois, 1978.

Cogan, Frances. *All American Girl: The Ideal of Real Womanhood in Mid-Nineteenth Century America.* Athens: University of Georgia, 1989.

Cott, Nancy. *The Bonds of Womanhood: "Woman's Sphere" in New England, 1780–1835.* New Haven: Yale University Press, 1977.

Coultrap-McQuin, Susan. *Doing Literary Business: American Women Writers in the Nineteenth Century.* Chapel Hill: University of North Carolina Press, 1990.

Cowan, Ruth Schwarz. *More Work for Mother: The Ironies of Household Technology from the Open Hearth to the Microwave.* New York: Basic Books, 1983.

Curtis, Edith Roelker. *A Season in Utopia: The Story of Brook Farm.* New York: Russell and Russell, 1961.

Danhoff, Clarence. *Change in Agriculture: The Northern United States, 1820–1870.* Cambridge, Mass.: Harvard University Press, 1969.

Davidson, Cathy. *Revolution and the Word: The Rise of the Novel in America.* New York: Oxford University Press, 1986.

Denning, Michael. *Mechanic Accents: Dime Novels and Working-Class Culture in America.* New York: Verso, 1987.

Derrida, Jacques, "The Purveyor of Truth." Trans. William Domingo, et al. *Yale French Studies* 52 (1975): 31–114.

Dimock, Wai-chee. *Empire for Liberty: Melville and the Poetics of Individualism.* Princeton: Princeton University Press, 1989.

Douglas, Ann. *The Feminization of American Culture.* 1977; rpt. New York: Doubleday, 1988.

Dublin, Thomas. *Farm to Factory: Women's Letters, 1830-1860.* New York: Columbia University Press, 1981.

———. *Women at Work: The Transformation of Work and Community in Lowell, Massachusetts, 1826-1860.* New York: Columbia University Press, 1979.

Eisler, Benita, ed. *The Lowell Offering: Writings of New England Mill Women (1840-1845).* Philadelphia: Lippincot, 1977.

Elliot, Harrison. "A Century Ago an Eminent Author Looked Upon Paper and Papermaking." *Paper Maker* 21 (1952): 55-58.

Exman, Eugene. *The Brothers Harper.* New York: Harper & Row, 1965.

———. *The House of Harper: A Century of Publishing in Franklin Square.* New York: Harper & Row, 1967.

Fellman, Michael. *The Unbounded Frame: Freedom and Community in Nineteenth-Century American Utopianism.* Westport, Conn.: Greenwood Press, 1973.

Fetterley, Judith. "Nineteenth-Century American Women Writers and the Politics of Recovery." *ALH* 6 (1994): 600-611.

Fisher, Philip. "Appearing and Disappearing in Public: Social Space in Late-Nineteenth Century Literature and Culture." In *Reconstructing American Literary History.* Ed. Sacvan Bercovitch. Cambridge, Mass.: Harvard University Press, 1986.

———. "Pins, A Table, Works of Art." *Representations* 1 (1983): 43-58.

Flower, Milton. *James Parton: The Father of Modern Biography.* Durham: Duke University Press, 1951.

Fogel, Robert, and Stanley Engerman. *Time on the Cross: The Economics of American Negro Slavery.* Boston: Little, Brown, 1974.

Foner, Eric. *Free Soil, Free Labor, Free Men.* New York: Oxford University Press, 1970.

Foner, Philip, ed. *The Factory Girls: A Collection of Writings on Life and Struggles in the New England Factories of the 1840s.* Urbana: University of Illinois Press, 1977.

Foster, Edward Halsey. *Susan and Anna Warner.* Boston: Twayne Publishers, 1978.

Foucault, Michel. *Discipline and Punish: The Birth of the Prison.* Trans. Alan Sheridan. New York: Vintage, 1979.

———. *Power / Knowledge: Selected Interviews and Other Writings, 1972-1977.* Trans. Colin Gordon. New York: Pantheon, 1977.

———. *The Birth of the Clinic: An Archaeology of Medical Perception.* Trans. A. M. Sheridan Smith. New York: Pantheon, 1973.

Fox-Genovese, Elizabeth. "To Write Myself: The Autobiographies of Afro-

American Women." *Feminist Issues in Literary Scholarship*. Ed. Shari Benstock. Bloomington: University of Indiana Press, 1988.

Franklin, Bruce. *The Victim as Criminal and Artist: Literature from the American Prison*. New York: Oxford University Press, 1978.

French, Warren. " 'Honor to Genius': The Complimentary Fruit and Flower Festival to Authors, 1855." *The New York Historical Society Quarterly* 39 (1955): 357–67.

Gamson, Joshua. *Claims to Fame: Celebrity in Contemporary America*. Berkeley: University of California Press, 1994.

Geary, Susan. "The Domestic Novel as a Commercial Commodity." *PBSA* 70 (1976): 365–95.

Genovese, Eugene. *The Political Economy of Slavery*. New York: Pantheon, 1965.

Gilmore, Michael. *American Romanticism and the Marketplace*. Chicago: University of Chicago, 1985.

———. "Hawthorne and the Making of the Middle Class." *Rethinking Class: Literary Studies and Social Formations*. Ed. Wai-chee Dimock and Michael Gilmore. New York: Columbia University Press, 1994: 215–38.

Guarneri, Carl. *The Utopian Alternative: Fourierism in Nineteenth-Century America*. Ithaca: Cornell University Press, 1991.

Gutman, Herbert. *Slavery and the Numbers Game: A Critique of "Time on the Cross"*. Urbana: University of Illinois Press, 1975.

———. *Work, Culture, and Society in Industrializing America*. New York: Knopf, 1976.

Halttunen, Karen. *Confidence Men and Painted Women: A Study of Middle-Class Culture in America, 1830–79*. New Haven: Yale University Press, 1982.

Harding, Walter. *The Days of Henry Thoreau*. 1962; rpt. Princeton: Princeton University Press, 1982.

Harris, Neil. *Humbug: The Art of P. T. Barnum*. Boston: Little, Brown, 1973.

Harris, Susan. *Nineteenth-Century American Women's Novels: Interpretative Strategies*. Cambridge, England: Cambridge University Press, 1990.

Hedrick, Joan. *Harriet Beecher Stowe: A Life*. New York: Oxford University Press, 1994.

Herbert, T. Walter. *Dearest Beloved: The Hawthornes and the Making of the Middle-Class Family*. Berkeley: University of California Press, 1993.

Hibben, Paxton. *Henry Ward Beecher: An American Portrait*. New York: The Press of the Readers Club, 1942.

Holloway, Mark. *Heavens on Earth: Utopian Communities in America, 1680–1880*. New York: Dover, 1966.

Howe, Irving. *Politics and the Novel*. New York: Horizon Books, 1957.

Irwin, John. *American Hieroglyphics: The Symbol of the Egyptian Hieroglyphics in the American Renaissance*. New Haven: Yale University Press, 1980.

Jehlen, Myra. "Archimedes and the Paradox of Feminist Criticism." *Signs* 6 (1981): 575–601.

Kaplan, Benjamin. *An Unhurried View of Copyright*. New York: Columbia University Press, 1967.

Karcher, Carolyn. *Shadow Over the Promised Land: Slavery, Race, and Violence in Melville's America*. Baton Rouge: Louisiana State University Press, 1980.

Kelley, Mary. *Private Woman, Public Stage: Literary Domesticity in Nineteenth-Century America*. New York: Oxford University Press, 1984.

Kessler-Harris, Alice. *Out to Work: A History of America's Wage-Earning Women*. New York: Oxford University Press, 1982.

Kraditor, Aileen S. *Means and Ends in American Abolitionism*. New York: Pantheon, 1967.

Kring, Walter, and John S. Carey. "Two Discoveries Concerning Herman Melville." *The Endless, Winding Way in Melville*. Ed. Donald Yanella and Hershel Parker. Glasboro, N.J.: The Melville Society, 1981.

Lang, Amy. "Class and the Strategies of Sympathy." *The Culture of Sentiment*. Ed. Shirley Samuels. New York: Oxford University Press, 1992.

———. *Prophetic Woman: Anne Hutchinson and the Problem of Dissent in the Literature of New England*. Berkeley: University of California Press, 1987.

Laurie, Bruce. *Artisans Into Workers: Labor in Nineteenth-Century America*. New York: Noonday, 1989.

Lehmann-Haupt, Hellmut. *The Book in America: A History of the Making and Selling of Books in the United States*. New York: R. R. Bowker, 1951.

Leverenz, David. *Manhood and the American Renaissance*. Ithaca: Cornell University Press, 1989.

Levine, Lawrence. *Highbrow / Lowbrow: The Emergence of Cultural Hierarchy in America*. Cambridge, Mass.: Harvard University Press, 1988.

Levine, Peter. "The Promise of Sport in Antebellum America." *Journal of American Culture* 2 (1979): 623–34.

Lewis, Guy. "The Beginning of Organized Collegiate Sport." *American Quarterly* 22 (1970): 222–29.

Loving, Jerome. *Lost in the Custom-House: Authorship in the American Renaissance*. Iowa City: University of Iowa Press, 1993.

McWilliams, John. *Hawthorne, Melville, and the American Character:*

A Looking-Glass Business. Cambridge, England: Cambridge University Press, 1984.

Martin, Robert K. *Hero, Captain, and Stranger: Male Friendship, Social Critique, and Literary Form in the Sea Novels of Herman Melville*. Chapel Hill: University of North Carolina Press.

Marx, Leo. *The Machine in the Garden: Technology and the Pastoral Ideal in America*. New York: Oxford University Press, 1964.

Matthiesson, F. O. *American Renaissance: Art and Expression in the Age of Emerson and Whitman*. New York: Oxford University Press, 1941.

Mellow, James. *Nathaniel Hawthorne in His Times*. Boston: Houghton Mifflin, 1980.

Michaels, Walter Benn. *The Gold Standard and the Logic of Naturalism: American Literature at the Turn of the Century*. Berkeley: University of California Press, 1987.

Miller, Edwin Havilland. *Salem Is My Dwelling Place: A Life of Nathaniel Hawthorne*. Iowa City: University of Iowa Press, 1991.

Miller, Perry. *The Raven and the Whale*. New York: Harcourt, Brace, & Co., 1956.

Mills, Bruce. "Lydia Maria Child and the Endings to Harriet Jacobs's *Incidents in the Life of a Slave Girl*." *American Literature* 64 (1992): 255–72.

Moss, Sidney P. *Poe's Literary Battles: The Critic in the Context of His Literary Milieu*. Durham, NC: Duke University Press, 1963.

Muller, John P., and William J. Richardson, eds. *The Purloined Poe: Lacan, Derrida, and Psychoanalytic Reading*. Baltimore: Johns Hopkins University Press, 1988.

Nash, Gary. *The Urban Crucible: Social Change, Political Consciousness, and the Origins of the American Revolution*. Cambridge, Mass.: Harvard University Press, 1979.

Neufeldt, Leonard. *The Economist: Henry Thoreau and Enterprise*. New York: Oxford University Press, 1989.

Nissenbaum, Stephen. *Sex, Diet, and Debility in Jacksonian America: Sylvester Graham and Health Reform*. Westport, Conn.: Greenwood Press, 1980.

Patterson, Lyman Ray. *Copyright in Historical Perspective*. Nashville: Vanderbilt University Press, 1968.

Pessen, Edward. *Jacksonian America: Society, Personality, and Politics*. Homewood, Ill.: Dorsey Press, 1969.

Pfister, Joel. *The Production of Personal Life: Class, Gender, and the Psychological in Hawthorne's Fiction*. Stanford: Stanford University Press, 1991.

Pocock, J. G. A. "Virtue and Commerce in the Eighteenth Century." *Journal of Interdisciplinary History* 3 (1972): 119–34.

Porter, Caroline. *Seeing and Being: The Plight of the Participant-Observer in Emerson, James, Adams, and Faulkner.* Middletown, Conn.: Wesleyan University Press, 1981.

Prude, Jonathan. *The Coming of the Industrial Order: Town and Factory Life in Rural Massachusetts, 1840–1860.* Cambridge, England: Cambridge University Press, 1983.

Rachman, Stephen. " '*Es lässt sich nicht schreiben*': Poe, Plagiarism, and the Theater of Absorption in 'The Man of the Crowd'." In *The American Face of Edgar Allan Poe.* Ed. Shawn Rosenheim and Stephen Rachman. Baltimore: Johns Hopkins University Press, 1995.

Renker, Elizabeth. "Herman Melville, Wife-Beating, and the Written Page." *American Literature* 66 (1994): 123–50.

Reynolds, David. *Beneath the American Renaissance: The Subversive Imagination in the Age of Emerson and Melville.* New York: Knopf, 1988.

Reynolds, Quentin. *The Fiction Factory; or, From Pulp Row to Quality Street.* New York: Random House, 1955.

Riess, Steven. *City Games: The Evolution of American Urban Society and the Rise of Sports.* Urbana: University of Illinois Press, 1989.

Robinson, Harriet Hanson. *Loom and Spindle.* New York: Thomas Y. Crowell & Co., 1898.

Rogin, Michael Paul. *Subversive Genealogy: The Politics and Art of Herman Melville.* New York: Knopf, 1979.

Romero, Lora. "Bio-Political Resistance in Domestic Ideology and *Uncle Tom's Cabin.*" *ALH* 1 (1989): 715–34.

Rose, Mark. "The Author as Proprietor: *Donaldson vs. Becket* and the Genealogy of Modern Authorship." *Representations* 23 (1988): 70.

Rosenheim, Shawn. " 'The King of Secret Readers': Edgar Poe, Cryptography, and the Origins of the Detective Story." *ELH* 56 (1989): 375–400.

Ryan, Mary. *Cradle of the Middle Class: The Family in Oneida County, New York, 1790–1865.* Cambridge, England: Cambridge University Press, 1981.

Sale, Maggie. "Critiques from Within: Antebellum Projects of Resistance." *American Literature* 64 (1992): 695–718.

Samuels, Shirley, ed. *The Culture of Sentiment: Race, Gender, and Sentimentality in Nineteenth-Century America.* New York: Oxford University Press, 1992.

Sanchez-Eppler, Karen. "Bodily Bonds: The Intersecting Rhetorics of Feminism and Abolition." *Representations* 24 (1988): 28–59.

Schickel, Richard. *Intimate Strangers: The Culture of Celebrity*. New York: Fromm, 1986.

Schivelbusch, Wolfgang. *The Railway Journey: The Industrialization of Time and Space in the Nineteenth Century*. Berkeley: University of California Press, 1986.

Scott, Joan. *Gender and the Politics of History*. New York: Columbia University Press, 1988.

Sealts, Merton. *Pursuing Melville, 1940-1980*. Madison: University of Wisconsin Press, 1982.

Showalter, Elaine. "American Gynocriticism." *ALH* 5 (1993): 111-28.

Silverman, Kenneth. *Edgar A. Poe: Mournful and Never-Ending Remembrance*. New York: Harper Collins, 1991.

Sklar, Kathryn Kish. *Catharine Beecher: A Study in American Domesticity*. New Haven: Yale University Press, 1973.

Smith, Sidonie. "Resisting the Gaze of Embodiment: Women's Autobiography in the Nineteenth Century." *American Women's Autobiography: A Feast of Words*. Ed. Margo Culley. Madison: University of Wisconsin Press, 1992.

Smith-Rosenberg, Carol. *Disorderly Conduct: Visions of Gender in Victorian America*. New York: Oxford University Press, 1986.

Stansell, Christine. *City of Women: Sex and Class in New York, 1789-1860*. Urbana: University of Illinois Press, 1987.

Stepto, Robert B. *From Behind the Veil*. Urbana: University of Illinois Press, 1979.

Stoller, Leo. "Thoreau's Doctrine of Simplicity." *NEQ* 34 (1961): 147-59.

Tebbel, John. *A History of Book Publishing in America*. Vol. 1 (of 5). New York: R. R. Bowker, 1972-1978.

Thomas, Dwight, and David Jackson. *The Poe Log: A Documentary Life of Edgar Allan Poe*. Boston: G. K. Hall, 1987.

Tompkins, Jane. *Sensational Designs: The Cultural Work of American Fiction*. New York: Oxford University Press, 1985.

———. Afterword to *The Wide, Wide World*. New York: The Feminist Press, 1987.

Wallace, James. "Hawthorne and the Scribbling Women Reconsidered." *American Literature* 62 (1990): 201-222.

Walters, Ronald. *The Antislavery Appeal: American Abolitionism After 1830*. Baltimore: Johns Hopkins University Press, 1976.

Wardley, Lynn. "Relic, Fetish, Femmage: The Aesthetics of Sentiment in the Work of Stowe." *The Culture of Sentiment*. Ed. Shirley Samuels. New York: Oxford University Press, 1992.

Ware, Norman. *The Industrial Worker, 1840-1860.* 1924; rpt. New York: Quadrangle Books, 1964.

Warren, Joyce. *Fanny Fern: An Independent Woman.* New Brunswick: Rutgers University Press, 1992.

Weinstein, Cindy. *The Literature of Labor and the Labors of Literature: Allegory in Nineteenth-Century American Fiction.* Cambridge, England: Cambridge University Press, 1995.

Welter, Barbara. "The Cult of True Womanhood: 1820-1860." *The American Family in Social-Historical Perspective.* 3d ed., 372-92, ed. Michael Gordon. New York: St. Martin's Press, 1983.

Wexler, Laura. "Tender Violence: Literary Eavesdropping, Domestic Fiction, and Educational Reform." *The Culture of Sentiment.* Ed. Shirley Samuels. New York: Oxford University Press, 1992.

Whorton, James. *Crusaders for Fitness: The History of American Health Reformers.* Princeton: Princeton University Press, 1982.

Wiegman, Robyn. "Melville's Geography of Gender." *ALH* 1 (1989): 735-53.

Wilentz, Sean. *Chants Democratic: New York City and the Rise of the American Working Class, 1788-1850.* New York: Oxford University Press, 1984.

Williams, Raymond. *Culture and Society, 1780-1850.* 1958; rpt. New York: Columbia University Press, 1983.

———. *Keywords.* 1976; rpt. New York: Columbia University Press, 1983.

———. *The Sociology of Culture.* New York: Schocken Books, 1982.

Wilson, Forrest. *Crusader in Crinoline: The Life of Harriet Beecher Stowe.* Philadelphia: Lippincot, 1941.

Wilson, R. Jackson. *Figures of Speech: American Writers and the Literary Marketplace.* New York: Knopf, 1989.

Wood, Gordon S. *The Creation of the American Republic, 1776-1787.* New York: W. W. Norton, 1969.

Yellin, Jean Fagan. "Texts and Contexts of Harriet Jacobs' *Incidents in the Life of a Slave Girl.*" *The Slave's Narrative.* Ed. Charles T. Davis and Henry Louis Gates, Jr. New York: Oxford University Press, 1985.

———. *Women and Sisters: The Anti-Slavery Feminists in American Culture.* New Haven: Yale University Press, 1989.

———. "Written by Herself: Harriet Jacobs' Slave Narrative." *American Literature* 53 (1981): 479-86.

Young, Philip. *The Private Melville.* State College: Pennsylvania State University Press, 1993.

Zboray, Ronald. *A Fictive People: Antebellum Economic Development and the American Reading Public.* New York: Oxford University Press, 1993.

Index

In this index an "f" after a number indicates a separate reference on the next page. A continuous discussion over two or more pages is indicated by a span of page numbers, e.g., "57–59." *Passim* is used for a cluster of references in close but not consecutive sequence.

Library of Congress Cataloging-in-Publication Data

Newbury, Michael.
  Figuring authorship in antebellum America / Michael
Newbury.
     p. cm.
  Includes bibliographical references (p.) and index.
  ISBN 0-8047-2858-5 (cloth)
  1. American literature—19th century—History and
criticism.   2. Authorship—Economic aspects—
United States—History—19th century.
  3. Authorship—Social aspects—United States—
History—19th century.   4. Literature and society—
United States—History—19th century.   5. Authors
and publishers—United States—History—19th
century.   6. Authors and readers—United States—
History—19th century.   7. Authors, American—19th
century—Economic conditions.   I. Title.
PS201.N49   1997
810.9'3528—dc21   96-52220
                                                  CIP

  ⊗   This book is printed on acid-free, recycled paper.

Original printing 1997
Last figure below indicates year of this printing:

06 05 04 03 02 01 00 99 98 97